CHINA FOR WOMEN

The Feminist Press Travel Series

Australia for Women
China for Women

Kosima Liu-Weber

Good luck symbol

CHINA FOR WOMEN

TRAVEL AND CULTURE

The Feminist Press
Travel Series

■

The Feminist Press
at The City University of New York
New York

Collection © 1995 by The Feminist Press at The City University of New York
© Copyright on individual pieces remains with the authors and photographers.
All rights reserved
Published 1995 by The Feminist Press at The City University of New York, 311 East 94 Street, New York, New York 10128
Produced in conjunction with Spinifex Press, Australia
Developed from *China der Frauen,* published by Frauenoffensive Verlag, Germany, © 1989

Permission acknowledgments begin on page 355.

99 98 97 96 95 5 4 3 2 1

Library of Congress Cataloging-in-Publication Data

China for women: travel and culture
    p.   cm.
    Includes bibliographical references
    ISBN 1–55861–112–6 : $17.95
    1. China—Description and travel.   2. Women—China
3. Women—Travel—China.
DS712.C48134   1995
950'.082—dc20   94–44578
                                                              CIP

Text and cover design by Tina Malaney
Cover art: Lotus blossom photographed by Kosima Liu-Weber
Typeset by Stanton Publication Services, St. Paul, Minnesota
Printed in the United States by McNaughton & Gunn, Inc.

CONTENTS

PART 4: LANDSCAPES AND CITYSCAPES

Old woman

PUBLISHER'S NOTE

This book, perhaps more than most, would not have been
possible without the assistance and expertise of many
people. We first want to thank Anna Gerstlacher and
Margit Miosga, the editors of the German publication *China der
Frauen*, on which this volume is based and from which many of
the essays (including those by them in Part 4) and the fiction
translated here, as well as the original concept, are taken. Their
book, and hence parts of this one, are the fruits of their many
years of travel to and study of China. *China der Frauen* is part of
the women's travel books series initiated by Gerlinde Kowitzke
and Hilke Schlaeger, publishers of Frauenoffensive Verlag, the
German feminist press that first published *China der Frauen* in
1989. We thank Gerlinde Kowitzke and Hilke Schlaeger not
only for their vision in conceiving of the series but also for their
concrete practical cooperation throughout the process of negoti-
ating for and creating this English-language, updated version of
the book they published.

China for Women is the result of another collaboration as
well, that between The Feminist Press at The City University of
New York and Spinifex Press in North Melbourne, Australia,
our partners in this travel series that began last year with
Australia for Women and will continue after this volume with
books on Greece, Italy, and, we hope, many more parts of the
world. This is very much a joint venture, and would not be possible otherwise. The major editorial and production responsibility alternates volume by volume in the series, but we consult
and work together from the early stages in each case. Publishers
Susan Hawthorne and Renate Klein brilliantly edited *Australia
for Women*, which launched the series on both sides of the

Pacific. For this volume, they were instrumental in providing the most up-to-date information and new essays about women in China, and the suggestions for further reading compiled and annotated by Susan Hawthorne, as well as valuable editorial advice. They gave generously of their time and expertise within the constraints of extremely tight deadlines.

Because we began with a volume in German, *China for Women* also would not have been possible without translators. We were fortunate to find an excellent group that undertook a massive job on short notice and with very tight deadlines. We acknowledge in particular the fine work of Ulrike Bode and Ilze Mueller. Ulrike Bode was also extremely helpful to the volume by locating and consulting with several scholars for answers to important questions, big and small, that she brought to our attention. One of these scholars, Lida Junghans of Harvard University, not only gave advice but also wrote two new pieces that round out Part 4. For assistance to us and to Ulrike Bode, we also thank Ellen Riemschneider.

We are also grateful to Diane Schwartz, who provided knowledge of China and Chinese, commented on parts of the manuscript, and assisted us in contacting people in China essential to putting together this volume. Also invaluable was the consultation provided by Professor Xiaolan Bao of California State University, Long Beach, who alerted us to inaccuracies and pointed us toward numerous essays that add immeasurably to the portrait of Chinese women and their history that we present here. Special thanks are due to Tillie Olsen, who delved into her own library for hard-to-find work by Ding Ling, including the typescript of an address by Ding Ling to the Iowa Writer's Workshop, which has never before been published, and which we are honored to bring to print at last. Tillie was also helpful in our long search for a reproducible photograph of Ding Ling. Finally, our thanks to the publishers and authors of essays reprinted here from other sources for their prompt cooperation and willingness to be part of this project. Despite all the generous assistance from so many, the ultimate responsibility for this volume is, of course, ours.

Romanization

The pinyin system of romanization of Chinese characters was used for all work written or translated originally for this volume. Romanization was not altered in previously published material; hence, there is some variation within this volume.

Currency

Because of the continual fluctuation in exhange rates, currency figures were not converted at each occurrence in the text. As we go to press, the exchange rate is approximately U.S. $1.00 = 8.51 *yuan.*

Florence Howe and Susannah Driver
The Feminist Press at The City University of New York

1
HISTORY AND POLITICS

Eva Siao

On a train

Wang Xiaohiu

Mountains in the mist

A STONE AGE MATRIARCHY:
THE YANGSHAO CULTURE

Eva Sternfeld

Between 1954 and 1957 Chinese archeologists excavated a complete neolithic village in Banpo, seven kilometers (4.3 mi.) from Xi'an, capital of Shaanxi Province. They came upon the remains of forty-five circular houses, a larger building, storage pits, animal shelters, a kiln, a graveyard, and a moat that had surrounded the village. In both the houses and the graves, they found painted clay pottery and implements made of stone or bone. Archeologists estimate that roughly five hundred people lived and worked in Banpo Village approximately six thousand years ago.

In the 1970s a similar, and larger, village was unearthed in Jiangzhai, also in Shaanxi. Here, over ninety houses, among them four large buildings, were arranged in a circular pattern, in addition to a cemetery and a kiln outside the village.

Both sites are classified as Yangshao, named for the place in Henan Province where archeologists in 1921 first excavated tools and clay vessels typical of this culture. Similar finds have since been made throughout the middle Huanghe (Yellow River) area, concentrated around modern Xi'an.

Chinese researchers believe, chiefly on the basis of the burial evidence, that the Yangshao culture was matriarchal. They found no graves of married couples; rather, men and women were always buried separately. The burial offerings indicate, moreover, that in this Stone Age society women had a higher status than men. More objects, and many of great value, were found buried with the mortal remains of women than of men. While the graves of men held a maximum of four objects, women's averaged six. Seventy-nine burial objects were found in the elaborate grave of a young girl from Banpo, perhaps because she was the daughter of a female tribal head. In contrast,

3

other small children were not buried in the graveyard, but in clay urns near the large buildings. Scholars see this feature as indicating that the children were collectively reared by the matriarchal clans.

Researchers theorize that the social life of these Stone Age clans was organized like that of matriarchal families living today in the Yongning Region of Yunnan Province. They believe that the maternal family was designated as the stable social and economic unit for the women of Banpo and Jiangzhai; relationships with men from other families were fleeting. The children remained with their mothers, who provided for and reared them. This arrangement explains the function of the large buildings, which researchers believe served as both the communal space and assembly room of the clan, and as the living quarters of the female head of the kinship group, the older women and men, and the children. Several smaller, usually circular, houses equipped with fire pits were grouped around the common building, with their entrances facing the latter's entrance. It is possible that the young women of Banpo and Jiangzhai received their lovers in these round houses.

Researchers believe that the high social status of women reflected their economic power. Studies of similarly organized Native American societies suggest that the economic basis of the Yangshao culture, hand-hoe agriculture, lay entirely in the hands of women, while men provided supplementary food by hunting and fishing.

In the archeologists' view, the skillfully made ceramics typical of Yangshao culture were created exclusively by women, when little or no field work had to be done. Pots, bowls, plates, and vases that are richly ornamented with geometric figures, stylized fish, human faces, and fishing nets testify to the high technical and artistic level of the culture. Bowls decorated with images of a fish and a human face may have been ritual objects, not meant for daily use. Researchers believe that the fish and the fish-person were worshipped as totems.

The symbols of Yangshao culture still await feminist decoding. What totems do the fish-people represent? Could they be two women conceiving and bearing a child? The scratch marks found on some of the pottery, suggesting that the culture possessed a kind of script, have also to be decoded.

In the literature of the People's Republic of China, Yangshao culture is evaluated positively. According to "The Matriarchal

Commune Seen in Light of the Yangshao Culture Finds in Banpo," written by a collective of the Banpo Museum and published in the archeological magazine *Wenwu* in late 1975, Yangshao culture is seen as the idyllic cradle of Chinese communism.

> The history of the matriarchal communes of ancient society proves that our Chinese people, like many other peoples, passed through a primitive communist phase without private property, social classes, oppression, and exploitation.

The research literature, however, hardly supplies proof for this theory. Despite the extremely rich finds in Banpo and Jiangzhai, little can be said about the matriarchal Yangshao culture with archeological certainty. Most conclusions are based on speculation and, depending on the viewers' particular political stance, the literature fluctuates between high praise for and cursory remarks about the Yangshao matriarchy.

Jiang Qing, Mao Zedong's radical communist spouse, who struggled for power in China in the mid-1970s, for example, was said to have extolled Banpo and Yangshao culture as a vision of the future: "Primitive society was a matriarchy, patriarchy came later, but in the future, under communism, it will be the other way around—men will make room, and women will assume leadership."

At a time when Communist cadres in Yunnan tried to compel the last matriarchal families into patriarchal marriages, the article cited above from the Banpo Museum celebrated the political organization of the lost matriarchal clans of Yangshao culture:

> Every clan had a head. The clan would elect a leader (generally a woman or an old man) who had proved hard-working and just, and thus was held in high esteem. Though the leader had the power to lead and give orders, s/he enjoyed no privileges, was not exempt from labor, and otherwise remained equal to others in the clan. If leaders failed to carry out their duties, they could be recalled by the clan's general assembly. The clan was organized democratically: all important decisions, such as the election or recall of the leader, the planning of production, the distribution of the means of production, [and] the regulation of relationships and conflicts within the clan, had to be made by general assembly in which both women and men took part. Everyone could make suggestions. After the assembly had reached a decision, all members had to comply with it. The general assembly of the clan was its highest authority.

If the above reads like a political platform, in fact, it does resemble the grass-roots approach supported by the left-wing cultural revolutionary faction surrounding Jiang Qing. It seems reasonable to suppose that in speculating about what happened at general assemblies in the communal houses of Banpo and Jiangzhai, the authors were also thinking of contemporary politics in 1975. Thus, the unprovable statement that the matriarchal clans of primitive society not only elected their leaders but could also recall them may have referred to the campaign to overthrow the radical communists' pragmatic opponent, Deng Xiaoping—a plan then under way, which succeeded in 1976.

At the end of 1976, however, the pragmatists won, and Jiang Qing and her group were arrested. In the ensuing campaign against the faction now demonized as the "Gang of Four," Jiang Qing's feminist comments (among others) were vehemently criticized. Thus, in 1977, the article "Jiang Qing Propagandized for the Matriarchy in Order to Usurp Party Leadership" accused her—probably not without cause—of emphasizing the significance of matriarchy only to legitimize her own claim to power.

In the 1980s, under the banner of pragmatic reform politics aimed at sending Chinese women back to hearth and home in the interest of efficiency, radical communist and feminist models were no longer popular, and the communities of Yangshao culture no longer of interest. In more recent publications, the culture's matriarchal character is mentioned only in passing.

Today, the Banpo Museum's exhibits are eclipsed by another Xi'an archeological sensation—this one a gigantic male fantasy over two thousand years old. To assure his eternal fame, Qin Shi Huangdi, unifier of the empire and first central emperor of China (221-210 B.C.), kept seven hundred thousand forced laborers busy during his lifetime building a monumental burial complex that included an army of terracotta male warriors. This monument, in Lintong, thirty kilometers (about 19 mi.) from Xi'an, awes millions of Chinese and foreign tourists every year.

WOMEN IN CHINESE SCRIPT

Barbara Niederer

In terms of both sentence construction and vocabulary, every language is closely connected to the way its speakers conceptualize the world. The characters of Chinese script, thus, also contribute to an understanding of Chinese culture. In this system of writing, which originated from pictograms, each meaningful element of the language is represented by a specific character.

As the society developed, however, maintaining a purely pictorial script would have led to innumerable complicated characters that would soon have become impossible to manage. In addition, even at the beginning, certain abstract meanings could hardly be expressed in pictorial form. For the script to remain viable, it was vital to use other methods of creating characters. Over time, simple characters and parts of characters were combined, with the meaning and the pronunciation of the components serving as the criteria determining the type of combination. Even documents from the earliest period (approximately 1400 B.C.) show a completely developed writing system with a variety of character types. The different types of combinations shared the common use of certain simple elements that assigned a character to a specific category of meanings: wood, water, metal, fish, humans, or women.

Through the centuries, Chinese script has continued to develop toward increasing abstraction and conventionality. Although this was necessary for the developing society, Chinese characters retained a characteristic quality: in contrast to the letters of the alphabet, they are "motivated," that is, they allow associations and analyses, regardless of whether or not they are scientifically sound. This fact may lead the daily users of Chinese characters to break them down into their component parts, either for their own amusement or in order to better commit them to memory. Historians and archeologists also use them as a kind of historical source to gain information about the culture of ancient China.

The first major work on the analysis of characters was written in A.D. 100 by a Chinese scholar named Xu Shen. In his *Shuowen jiezi* (Explanations of Simple Characters and Analyses of Compound Characters), Xu Shen attempts to explain Chinese characters from older forms accessible only to specialists. Although a number of his "graphic etymologies" were influenced by the world view of his time and have since been refuted, his work continues to be an important reference. Xu Shen was the first to organize the characters according to their so-called radicals or "keys." Of the 9,353 characters he lists, 240 are found under the key *woman*. The character for "woman" is 女 (pronounced: nǚ). It could be interpreted as a representation (pictogram) of a kneeling woman with her hands crossed in front of her. The following are some of the earlier stages in the development of the character:

The positions mentioned above may be interpreted as a gesture of humility, a serving posture, or simply a passive attitude typical of women.

Pictograms are characters that cannot be further reduced. Barely 5 percent of the characters used today are believed to derive from a pictographic source, while over 90 percent are composite characters. Here are a few composite characters in which the character for "woman" is placed on the left side:

 (fù): "Woman, married woman." This character is composed of 女 (nǚ), "woman," and 帚 (zhǒu), "broom." An annotated edition of the *Shuowen jiezi* from the nineteenth century comments: 婦 originally meant "to assist, to help." The woman holds a broom and sweeps, for it lies in her nature to assist others. The married woman is a "helper" (婦人 fùrén), who follows the instructions of her husband and submits to others.

如 (rú): "To match, to be the same as, like, in accordance with, to correspond to, in case." Composed of 女 (nǚ), "woman," and 口 (kǒu) "mouth." The meanings of this frequently used character derive from its original meaning "to follow." The *Shuowen jiezi* comments that it is the nature of woman to follow orders (which are given by the mouth).

奴 (nú): "Slave." Composed of 女 (nǚ), "woman," and 又 (yòu), "hand." From the earliest times 奴 has indicated both male and female slaves, originally criminals who were sentenced to slavery as punishment.

好 (hǎo): "Good, beautiful." Composed of 女 (nǚ), "woman," and 子 (zì), "child." The meanings of good and beautiful are closely bound together here. The double meaning of 好 is found in numerous other characters.

姦 (nuán): "To quarrel, to accuse someone: dumb" (this character is no longer in use). Composed of two women 女. The *Shuowen jiezi* comments that two women who live together (that is, with the same man) necessarily find themselves in conflict.

姦 (jián): "To fornicate, bad, egoistic, shameless, perverse, sneaky, unauthorized, disorderly." Composed of three women 女. According to the *Shuowen jiezi,* the original meaning of this character is "private," that is, to come together outside of wedlock. From the Book of Rites we learn that a gentleman has the right to three women, so long as he observes the rituals. Marriage, according to ritual, is arranged by a matchmaker. In an extended sense, 姦 (jiān) indicates any kind of extramarital relationship between men and women, resulting in such meanings as bad, treacherous, et cetera.

女 (wú): Negative imperative: "thou shall not, you are not allowed to" (no longer common). Composed of 女 (nǚ), "woman", and 一 (yī), actually "one," used figuratively as a barrier: A woman should not fornicate. This prohibition of the highest order becomes a prohibition per se, a grammatical word that expresses the negative imperative "thou shall not."

All components contribute to these characters' full meaning. However, the meaning is not the sum of a simple addition of the meanings of the individual components, but evolves within the framework of a specific society.

Another kind of composite character consists of two elements: one, the radical or key, is a specifying element, and the other is phonetic. Whether or not the character for "woman" appears as the key in specific characters is more interesting than the analysis of the characters themselves. The categories of meaning to which a fairly large group of composite characters containing the character for woman can be assigned include the following:

1. Names (first and family names, names of localities) comprise the largest group among the woman-characters. Even the term "family name" is itself written with a woman-character: 姓 (xìng) is composed of 女 (nǚ), "woman," and 生 (shēng), "to give birth." These facts are often taken as evidence for the previous existence of a matriarchal social structure (prior to the Shang dynasty). Since sufficient material proof is lacking, the discussion of this question continues.

   • Forms of address for female family members.
   • Terms for the different ages of women. (The inventory is richer and more detailed than for men.)
   • Medical expressions that refer to women.
   • Women's jobs or professions.
   • Expressions that refer to marriage.

2. The second largest group of woman-characters is constituted around the meanings of "beautiful" and "good." The most varied aspects of female beauty are emphasized: facial color, eyes, body shape, body size, gait, and others. The meaning "good" is, in turn, arranged within complex behavior patterns expected from women. They are to be restrained, respectful, quiet, modest, gentle, obedient, neat, practiced, skillful, dextrous, elegant, smiling, cheerful, et cetera.

3. In contrast to the foregoing, another, smaller group of

characters refer to women who are "neither good nor beautiful." They are ugly, coarse, noisy, disobedient, et cetera.

- Expressions concerning sexuality.
- Numerous negative expressions that can be applied to men or women: quarrelsome, stupid, jealous, arrogant, careless, insulting, unrestrained, disruptive, obstructive, greedy, false, underhanded, unctuous, slanderous, et cetera.

All of the above makes it clear that a wealth of Chinese characters have been shaped by men's perceptions. Through these characters, women are viewed and described from a male point of view.

After 1949, two newly created authorities, the Committee for Character Reform and the editorial board of the new journal *Language(s) in China (Zhongguo yuwen)*, received numerous letters suggesting the "thorough eradication of the phenomenon of inequality between men and women in Chinese script." One such letter, from a female teacher named Cao, together with the editor's answer, was published in *Zhongguo yuwen* in 1952. In her work, she writes, she is frequently asked why this or that character with a negative meaning is combined with the character for "woman." In response, she compiled a list of suggestions for changing sixteen misogynist characters. To replace the old characters, however, she invented complicated constructions that would have been difficult to popularize. In addition, she says she would like to banish offensive characters along with their meanings.

The editor's response decisively rejects Cao's suggestion: "A general disadvantage of all Chinese characters is that looking at their elements produces a meaning. If we were to alter Cao's sixteen characters, we would have to do the same with countless others. . . . The result would be the greatest disorder in our script." I am not aware of more recent suggestions for changing the characters assigned to woman. A member of the Committee for Character Reform commented merely that women "have understood that the question of equality does not lie in the written language, but elsewhere."

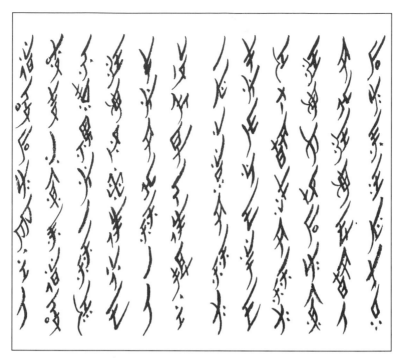

Women's writing from Hunan

Cathy Silber

Two sworn sisters of Jintian village

WOMEN'S WRITING FROM HUNAN

Cathy Silber

One spring day in 1919, thirteen-year-old Yi Nianhua disobeyed her grandfather. Up in the loft, with brush and ink, she drew intricate blossoms across the top border of a white fan. Beneath them, she wrote a letter in verse to a girl she had never met. Sixty years later, Yi could still write from memory the girl's reply. "Every word you wrote makes my heart beautiful," it said in part, "but I have to obey my parents. If it were up to me, I'd be there with my whole heart."

Yi Nianhua and the girl who never came to visit, like generations of women in one small part of southwestern Hunan Province in China, wrote in *nüshu*, the women's script—a writing system used solely by women. In the rice-farming villages of Shangjiangxu Township in Jiangyong County, where women's lives were ruled by the "three obediences" of the same Confucian patriarchy that prevailed throughout China (to one's father, then husband, then son), a thriving women's literary culture was so much a part of everyday life that local people called the standard Chinese script *nanzi* (men's words). With their own script and an exclusively female audience, the women of Shangjiangxu had both the power and the freedom to write the truths of their own lives.

Generally denied access to an education in "men's words," they were spared indoctrination in the textual tradition that subordinated them. Nor did they have to agonize over making their truths palatable to men. Yet because they were not writing in men's words, nothing they wrote would revise the dominant textual tradition in the slightest. But these women maneuvered within social constraints in immediate, daily ways, forming in the process social networks of emotional and sometimes eco-

13

nomic support in which they could voice their objections to the inequities and pain of their lives.

No one knows how *nüshu* began. One local legend says it was invented by an exceptionally talented village girl named Hu Yuxiu, said to have been chosen as an imperial concubine in the late eleventh century. Miserable in the palace, the story goes, she used *nüshu* to communicate her woes to the folks back home. Local historical records attest to her existence, even hail her erudition, but say nothing about concubinage, let alone *nüshu*.

A more plausible scenario would link *nüshu* to some indigenous ethnic group that assimilated the dominant Chinese culture over the course of centuries. Traces of a non-Chinese language remain in the local Chinese dialect that *nüshu* records. Though *nüshu* also shows signs of influence from the standard Chinese script, it is far simpler to use, at least for speakers of the local dialect. Just one *nüshu* character, in principle anyway, represents every spoken word with the same sound. So, for example, one symbol would cover "new," "knew," and "gnu"; context makes meaning plain. That means local men could understand *nüshu* if they heard it read aloud.

However the women's script began, as far as the people of Shangjiangxu are concerned, it was used for nearly a thousand years. In its heyday, women gathered over tasks of needle and thread, upstairs in warm months, or around the kitchen fire in winter, and took turns singing from works in their script. Not every woman could write the script, but many could read *nüshu,* and still more knew several works by heart. Temple fairs and holidays—like the eighth day of the fourth lunar month, known for its women-only potlucks—provided further opportunity for women to exchange *nüshu* texts.

By the time of the 1949 revolution, younger women no longer learned *nüshu.* As the older generation of writers died, *nüshu* died with them. Because women customarily had their favorite writings burned or buried with them at death so as to enjoy them in the afterlife, no texts dating before the late nineteenth century survive. Most of the extant writings—about two hundred—belong to this century. Written in verse on paper, cloth, and fans, they include women's autobiographies, vows of sworn sisterhood, letters of condolence or recrimination, books for brides, accounts of local or national events, prayers, a Confucian instruction manual for girls ("don't show your teeth when you smile"), and renditions of tales popular throughout

Yi Nianhua, one of the last nüshu *writers*

nüshu *written on a fan for a* laotong

China. A good many of these were written by two of *nüshu*'s last writers: Yi Nianhua and one of her sworn sisters, Gao Yinxian. I studied *nüshu* with them over six months from 1988 to 1989. Gao Yinxian died in 1990 at the age of eighty-eight. Yi Nianhua died in 1991 at age eighty-five.

Like most men in Shangjiangxu, Yi Nianhua's grandfather did not object to *nüshu*—it was a proper, even prestigious, activity for girls. He did forbid her to write that letter, though. Yi was writing to ask that girl to be her *laotong* (literally, "old same"; *lao*, meaning "old" as in "old friend," is a Chinese term of familiarity and endearment). "Everybody did it," Yi told me, and described how when a girl was eight or nine years old, a girl from another village would be recommended to her as a "same."

Sames had to be the same age and from families of similar standing. Ideally, one was no prettier than the other, and they had the same-size feet. If both girls agreed, after an exchange of letters on fans, in which they would describe themselves as a "couple," "together always," one would visit for a few days in the home of the other. Over the years, they could become quite close, "sitting together, threading needles, choosing colors, talking in whispers." Yi Nianhua wanted a same, but a few months before, a girl had been raped by her potential same's brother and his friends. Parents all over Shangjiangxu were up in arms; the court case was pending. Yi's grandfather put his foot down, and she never did have a same.

Like marriage, which joined two families of different villages, the *laotong* relationship established another line in women's networks; the letters that formed these girl couples often contained lines addressed to their mothers and other female relatives. Books of marriage congratulations and condolences called *sanzhaoshu* (third-day book)—written by the bride's women friends and relatives and delivered to her in her married home on the third day after the wedding to be shared aloud among the women of her new home—also contained lines addressed to her mother-in-law, pleas for leniency and compassion. The "third-day book" Yi Nianhua received from her younger sister recounts the hardships of their family and apologizes for the inadequacy of her dowry. Yi did not need to be told the hardships of her own family—these lines were meant for her mother-in-law.

By expressing how much the bride's family and friends back home cared for her, *sanzhaoshu* warned the bride's new family and village not to abuse her. *Sanzhaoshu* also gave women a forum to vent their grief and anger over their loss and to rail against a tradition that marries their sisters and friends away. One of them reads, in part:

It shouldn't have been that we came in this life girls,
Red plums on the tree, a useless branch.
If we had been sons, we could be together, not torn apart.
Sister, everyone went by so fast,
But I can't stop crying.
I'm mad I have no one to keep me company upstairs. . . .
Sister, in that other home, be at peace.
In that fine home, be calm of heart, please,
Don't take everything to heart.
Smooth your anxious brow, living in that place,
Take the long view, attend the six relations.
Don't let sobbing sorrow build in your heart,
And give people cause to laugh at us ill-mannered folk.
Daughters are like the swallow,
Feathers barely grown, they fly their separate ways.
Just blame the court for making the wrong rules.
The world presses her to marry, not free, just follow the rules.
Being there is hard to compare with being upstairs,
In everything, just follow the rules. . . .

Marriage for women meant leaving home and loved ones to become the lowliest member in a family of strangers, and any rise in status and security in old age depended upon producing a son for the family line. With virtually no opportunities for economic independence, resistance to marriage was not an option for the women of Shangjiangxu the way it was for women in the silk-producing area around Guangdong (Canton). Yet one local folk song involves a pact that two *laotong* made not to marry or ever to have children—a pact that was broken by one of the women, who subsequently died, lore has it, from having sex too soon after childbirth. Written in *nüshu* by the one who kept the pact to the one who did not, this song was sung by Tang Baozhen, a sworn sister of Yi Nianhua and Gao Yinxian:

On red paper, I write a letter.
I'll have my say.
Today you who know my heart haven't gotten out of bed,
Though the sun shines in the room, over the mountains.

17

I told you to avoid it and you didn't,
Now you're ill and it's too late for regret.
A cold or a headache is easy to cure,
But you did it too soon after childbirth and died. . . .
We spoke true words,
And if you'd kept them, you'd still be worth something.
We went to the street, bought red paper,
We bought red paper and made a contract.
We made a contract, and said those words,
Just like buying a field of rice seedlings.

In her fifties, Yi Nianhua became sworn sisters with Hu Chiju, another prolific writer who died in 1976. Sworn sisterhoods were not exclusive the way *laotong* were and ranged in number of members from two on up, through seven ideally. Yi was the third to join this one. Sisterhoods among adult women were formed with invitation letters and cemented with letters and visits back and forth. One of Yi's letters to Hu ("Elder Sister"), a lamentation over her ill-fated life, tells some of the story in her autobiography:

. . . I just count on Elder Sister to ease my heart.
We'll sit side by side for hours, talking in whispers.
We'll console each other.
I was a girl of scanty fate at home,
At four, I had no father to care for me.
Mother was widowed at twenty-eight,
Little Sister, just one year old, knew nothing. . . .
Joining the Lu household was deathly oppressive.
Old and young, the lot of them, inhuman.
The mother-in-law had her own way,
There was sky all right, just no sun. . . .
When I'd been there nine years going on ten,
I had my precious son—I was so happy.
When my son was two,
His mouth got dry and he went to the underworld.
His death cut like a knife. . . .
I'd get up in the morning and cry till night,
Night and day I cried for my son.
When would I cry myself to death? . . .

While this may not count as great literature—indeed, *nüshu* writings are made almost entirely of set phrases—the point is

18

not to impress but to connect. Meaning lies less in the words on the page than in the shared experiences that give rise to the words. Reading one day an autobiography she had written for an illiterate woman, Yi Nianhua burst into tears at the lines, "When I think of what my boy said, how could I have lost my precious son?" After her own son died, she would answer when she heard a child's voice call, then remember and burst into tears. "It was like a knife in my heart," she said.

Denied a place in the history of men, the women of Shangjiangxu wrote their own history, recorded their own knowledge, made themselves central in a literary tradition passed on from mother to daughter for centuries. At first glance, it seems remarkable, unique in the world, though I have heard that nomadic women in Niger have their own secret script, too. Women everywhere, like the writers of *nüshu*, connect with sisters and sames in our own common codes. For Yi Nianhua and Hu Chiju and Gao Yinxian and Tang Baozhen, for me and my friends, or you and yours: lest we forget, sisterhood is local too.

Three women in the pillory

VIEWS OF THE FEMININE IN EARLY NEO-CONFUCIAN THOUGHT

Bret Hinsch

The rise of the Neo-Confucian movement marks an important transition in the history of Chinese women. Before this mode of thought became widespread, customs regarding divorce, remarriage, and education generally allowed women a relatively high degree of personal freedom. The Neo-Confucian movement changed this by reinterpreting the Confucian classics in ways that sharply limited the range of social options open to women. Most significantly, the Neo-Confucians emphasized the flawed nature of *yin*, the basic feminine element, enshrining this antipathy in their complex metaphysical systems. These philosophic abstractions soon influenced works ranging from history to family management. In this way, the attitudes expressed by Neo-Confucians slowly spread into the popular consciousness. Thus, many of the popular notions held toward women in China today date from the beginnings of Neo-Confucianism.

Modern Chinese society remains filled with unresolved tensions between old and new. While eagerly adopting all that the West has to offer, from computers to Coca-Cola, the Chinese sense of self-identity remains rooted in thousands of years of collective experience. For this reason, when we try to understand the status of women in China today, we must look beneath the thin patina of Marxist and feminist rhetoric to find the deeper native Chinese conception of the feminine. Not surprisingly, many of the ideas now current among ordinary peasants and workers found their most articulate expression in the elite literati culture of the Chinese past. In many cases, the notions first worked out in abstruse philosophic treatises gradually found expression in popular culture. For this reason, we must look to the rarified realms of philosophic discourse to fully appreciate the intellectual context of women's history in China.

Western scholars examining the subservient place of women in pre-modern China have often emphasized direct causes such as the organization of the family. Yet this type of highly focused analysis runs contrary to the world view of the Chinese themselves. A fondness for correlative cosmology led Chinese thinkers to see women both in mundane terms and as an integral part of the cosmos. They spoke of femininity as a philosophical abstraction in their famous intellectual works, while outlining the practical implications of these conceptions in widely circulated guides to practical affairs. Only by examining these two different types of texts in conjunction can we begin to understand the intellectual foundations underlying the treatment of women in the last eight hundred years of Chinese history.

The Song dynasty (960–1279) was a pivotal age in the transformation of women's roles. For example, during certain periods prior to the Song, women could more easily divorce their husbands (Ch'ü 1972, 276–77). Chinese women were not yet subject to the agonizing mutilation of foot-binding. Widows could remarry (pp. 42–43, 277, 295–96). Those who chose not to attach themselves to a second husband even had their extramarital dalliances celebrated in popular literature (Zhang 1965). And partly as a result of central Asian influences, women of the Tang (618–907) wielded an unprecedented degree of influence and political power.

All of these sexual and social freedoms were eroded after the Song. One key to this change in the lives of Chinese women can be found in the complex intellectual developments that we now refer to collectively as the Neo-Confucian revival. Important aspects of this intellectual transformation include the popularization of a more direct literary language, the melding of Confucian ethics with cosmology, and a denigration of Daoism and Buddhism. The antifeminine overtones of this way of thought were clearly demonstrated in the chilling effects the importation of Neo-Confucian doctrines into Korea had on the status of women in that country. Like their Chinese sisters, the women of Korea experienced a retrograde abolition of many of their former rights. The most controversial social doctrines of Neo-Confucianism in Korea concerned marriage. Up to the fifteenth century a Korean bridegroom would customarily move into the household of his wife's family. This gave the wife a firm position within the family. But the new wedding ceremony outlined by the Korean Department of Rites in 1434 strictly followed Neo-Confucian models in mandating that a woman should join the household of her husband's family. Completely isolated within a strange family, the position of wives immediately declined (Deuchler 1977, 15–16). Contemporaneous changes in Korea regarding remarriage, divorce, and education had similar consequences regarding women's status. The wide reach of Neo-Confucianism into the heart of Korean and Japanese intellectual life, as well as that of its homeland, gave the views of these influential thinkers an enormous impact on the history of Asian women.

Of course, it would be too simplistic to assert that Neo-Confucian literati sought to portray woman as completely lacking in redeeming features. Within the family, she was seen as a devoted nurturer of her children as well as a competent manager of household affairs. As for the higher moral realm, woman was capable of humanity and a degree of self-cultivation. Yet, by subordinating her to men while separating her from male affairs, female social status inevitably declined.

The elaborate cosmologies of mature Neo-Confucian discourse were invariably based on the dipartate division of the universe into *yin* and *yang*. This pair of abstractions was analogous to the separation of the human world according to female and male. Neo-Confucian thinkers often extrapolated the statements they made about yin and yang from their practical experiences with gender stereotypes. In turn, these abstractions were applied back to gender relations as a philosophic justification for rigid adherence to stereotypical sexual roles. The cosmological and moral reasoning of Song philosophers was loaded with a priori assumptions concerning both women and yin which in their minds mutually reinforced one another.

The Song use of metaphysics to justify subservience of women was augured in the views of the Han (206 B.C.–220 A.D.) literata Ban Zhao. Her reactionary notions concerning women paradoxically led to her canonization as China's most famous female scholar. Only by having such ideas was she acceptable to the male intellectual establishment which had the power to immortalize her. Like her Neo-Confucian counterparts, Ban Zhao saw yin and yang as central to gender relations, and the *Book of Rites* to be the clearest practical exposition of these principles.

> The Way of husband and wife is intimately connected with yin and yang, and relates the individual to gods and ancestors. Truly it is the great principle of Heaven and Earth, and the great basis of human relationships. Therefore the "Rites" honor union of man and woman. . . . (Swann 1932, 84)

She noted the differences between yin and yang, and used them to account for differences between the sexes.

> As yin and yang are not of the same nature, so man and woman have different characteristics. The distinctive quality of yang is rigidity; the function of yin is yielding. Man is honored for strength; a woman is beautiful on account of her gentleness. (Swann 1932, 85)

These metaphysical abstractions provided a foundation for her detailed explanation of female inferiority and subservience. In reality, however, Han women seem to have exercised much greater freedom and influence than those of later imperial history. Increased Central Asian influences following the fall of the Han led to a lessening of this antifemale metaphysics, until its revival by the Neo-Confucians.

The resurgence of these complex theorizings into the mainstream of Confucian thought during the Song led to a growing emphasis on the negative characteristics of yin, and therefore of women. Yin/yang theory reached a particularly high state of refinement in the writings of Zhang Zai (1020–77), one of the foremost leaders of the Neo-Confucian revival. Most generally Zhang Zai saw yang as the active force responsible for the expanding qualities of the physical world, whereas yin passivity resulted in the contraction of matter. Like the battle for supremacy between the sexes, yin and yang "possess each other, and overcome each other. To try to make them one is impossible" (Kasoff 1982, 92). This idea had found previous expression in Daoist-inspired manuals of sexual technique, some even using terminology and imagery from warfare (Van Gulik 1974, 157). The idea that masculine and feminine could not be reconciled with one another paved the way for an increasing segregation of women and restriction of female social roles. The regulation of women was seen as a necessary outgrowth of their inferior moral nature. "When the yang brightness is supreme, the virtuous nature operates; when the yin turbidity is supreme, material desires occur" (Kasoff 1982, 82). Because of woman's weak yin nature she must be subjugated by man and carefully governed by him. Her inferiority was preordained within the grand cosmic scheme because "the nature of yin is always to follow" (p. 81).

The most radical exposition of Neo-Confucian misogynism is found in the works of Cheng Yi (1033–1107), one of the most influential successors to Zhang Zai. Cheng Yi saw a direct link between his cosmological abstractions and gender relations. "[The working of] yin and yang as a complementary pair is what we call the Dao! The interaction of yin and yang and the mating of man and woman are the constant li of nature" (Ts'ai 1950, 108). But the relative merits of masculinity and femininity are not given equal weight in Cheng Yi's thought. "For a gentleman not to be able to see the Great Way which is strong, masculine, central and correct . . . is similar to the 'firm correctness of a female' and is 'a thing to be ashamed of'" (p. 330). He defines a woman's "firm correctness" as being able to obey men even though she may not understand the reasons for her obedience. His ideal wife is meek and obedient, a suitable foundation for family life dominated by men. Cheng Yi fondly remembered the obedience of his own mother by recalling, "Even in small matters she never made decisions alone but always asked Father before she did anything" (Zhu and Lu 1967, 179).

One of Cheng Yi's most controversial opinions was his stand against the remarriage of widows. On paper, his view of marriage was uncompromising. "When man and woman are joined together in wedlock, [the union] is unchangeable throughout their lives. Hence according to the principle of propriety there shall not be any remarriage" (Ts'ai 1950, 330–331). He did not extend his injunction to men; only female chastity is valuable enough to preserve. The practical problem with this inflexible stance was that widows without grown children often lacked the economic means to support themselves. With virtually all honorable professions closed to women, some widows faced the prospect of starvation. Cheng Yi refused to bend on this point. "To starve to death is a very small matter. To lose one's integrity, however, is a very serious matter" (Zhu and Lu 1967, 177). His extreme stance extended even to condemning any man who would marry a widow. Cheng Yi's justifications were again moral. "Marriage is a match. If one takes someone who has lost her integrity to be his own match, it means he himself has lost his integrity" (p. 177). Yet he contradicted this stern injunction by approving of the marriage of a cousin's widowed daughter, arranged by his own father. Despite this inconsistency between his ideals and personal life, his harsh rhetoric remained.

Cheng Yi found supporters among the intellectual establishment for his conservative views. Ye Cai and Wang Fu, both noted literati, vigorously agreed with his position. But other influential thinkers felt Cheng Yi had taken his concerns with moral purity too far. One Qing dynasty commentator, Zhang Boxing (1651–1725), deleted Cheng Yi's remarks on widows from his standard edition of Neo-Confucian works. And when a disciple brought up these prohibitions of Cheng Yi against remarriage of widows to Zhu Xi, noting the inconsistency between rhetoric and reality, that master softened Cheng Yi's injunctions with the equivocation "Generally speaking, that should be the case. But people cannot follow that absolutely" (Zhu and Lu 1967, 179). Chengh Yi's own behavior proved this point. Whereas his draconian code of ethics might be an ideal, only the most uncompromising moralist could advocate its practice in his own family. Still, Zhu Xi's ideal widow was one who refused to remarry. He mentions exemplary cases such as that of a young widow who committed suicide rather than lose her virtue through remarriage (Zhu and Liu 1863, 4.7B). Another widow he admired cut off her hair, ears, and nose to make herself unmarriageable. Zhu Xi clearly believed it better for widows to avoid remarriage if possible. But unlike the uncompromising Cheng Yi, Zhu Xi did not demand female martyrdom, however admirable he thought it to be.

Chengh Yi's position on the sanctity of marriage could not be compromised in the case of a starving widow, yet he encouraged the divorce of a wife with whom the husband is not satisfied. "If the wife is unworthy what harm does it do to divorce her? . . . Nowadays ordinary people take divorce to be a shameful act and are therefore afraid to do it. It was otherwise with the ancients" (Ts'ai 1950, 331–32). By invoking Bronze Age traditions Cheng Yi took his position so far as to say that a husband could even divorce his wife over a trifling matter. The example he used was the ancient story of the man who divorced his wife for shouting at their dog in front of her mother-in-law. In his interpretations, this man was showing his generosity by not revealing the true reasons which led to the divorce. "The gentleman cannot bear to divorce his wife by exposing her great faults, and so he divorces her on the ground[s] of a small mistake. From this one can see the greatness of his generosity" (Ts'ai 1950, 333). Cheng Yi wanted to see men of his own day given the chance to show their generosity by divorcing their wives over inconsequential matters. Perhaps he thought that by refusing to expose a woman's true faults he would not prevent her possible remarriage. But this rationale contradicts his stand against the remarriage of women.

When asked to explain why a wife divorced under such circumstances should not feel bitter, Cheng Yi returned to philosophic abstractions. "When one does a thing he need only take heed that he does it in full accordance with li, why should he try to make everybody understand? Nevertheless the wise will naturally understand it" (Ts'ai 1950, 333). Presumably the man, being intellectually superior to his wife, would be in a better position to understand the organizational principle or propriety (li) which underlies their marriage. This supposed superiority of male philosophic insight was another justification for the social subjugation of women.

In his grand systemization of Neo-Confucian thought, Zhu Xi included a passage from the works of Cheng Yi which elaborated on the imperative necessity for sexual hierarchy, proof that adherence to "principle" would yield practical benefits in personal life.

> Between man and woman, there is an order of superiority and inferiority, and between husband and wife, there is a principle of who leads and who follows. This is a constant principle. If people are influenced by feelings, give free reign to desires, and act because of pleasure, a man will be driven by desire and lose his character of strength, and a woman will be accustomed to pleasure and forget her duty of obedience. Consequently, there will be misfortune and neither will be benefited. (Zhu and Lu 1967, 272)

Zhu Xi saw the same sensual temptations having different effects on male and female natures. In a man, libertinism merely proved his own lack of self-control. But in a woman it showed her failure to conform to external social norms. Adherance to moderation was a keystone of Zhu Xi's teachings. Men were expected to find the principles of the universe within themselves through self-mastery and introspection. But women were excluded from this philosophic scheme because of their inferior yin nature. Unable to conform to li (principle/propriety) through self-knowledge, they must depend on their fathers, husbands and sons to force them into conformity with the cosmic order. Zhu Xi taught that even a bright and talented woman

27

must be barred from power. And he criticized the famed aggressive independence of the women of Henan (Zhu and Liu 1863, 5.13A–14B). The subtle implications of abstract Neo-Confucian metaphysics justified a revival of ancient restrictions on the most basic female freedoms.

Another outgrowth of this view of women as morally inferior to men was the idea that women are the chief cause of family discord. The philosopher Zhou Dunyi (1017–1073) gave family harmony a central place in his philosophy by drawing an analogy between managing the family and governing the world. He attributed the difficulties encountered in family management to cosmological principles found in the ancient classic of divination, the Yi jing.

> If members of the family are separated, the cause surely lies with women. This is why the hexagram kui [to part] follows the hexagram jiaren [family], for "When two women live together, their wills move in different directions." (Zhu and Lu 1967, 202)

Aside from the inferiority of yin and the inability of women to fully understand li, Zhou Dunyi added another metaphysical explanation for female inferiority. He argued that the general cosmic order revealed in the hexagrams of the Yi jing points to a natural female disregard for harmony, a cardinal Chinese virtue.

Cheng Yi also wrote on the metaphysical necessity of strictly regulating married life. In contrast to the relaxed attitudes of earlier literati such as Ouyang Xiu, Cheng Yi saw increased regulation of family roles as a burning moral necessity with deep roots in the underlying principles of the universe.

> The text of the second lowest, undivided line of the guimei [marriage of a maiden] hexagram says that correctness and tranquility should be maintained. This principle is not out of accord with the normal and correct relationship between husband and wife. People today consider indecent liberties and improper intimacies as normal and therefore consider correctness and tranquility as abnormal, without realizing that these are the normal and lasting ways of the relationship between husband and wife. (Zhu and Lu 1967, 173)

The way to maintaining correctness and tranquility is through the unfailing adherence to hierarchical roles based on gender. Strict obedience of women to men would eliminate contentiousness in the family and maintain the social harmony mandated by the Yi jing cosmology.

"Correctness" of women also increasingly came to be interpreted as including their separation from men. Cloistering women within the confines of the inner household would guarantee sexual propriety and prevent women from developing lives separate from the husbands on whom they depended for guidance in all matters. The renewed popularity of this ancient notion helped kindle a revival of interest among Neo-Confucian literati in the ancient books of ritual and etiquette. The Song saw an explosion of scholarship on those classic works (Balazs and Hervouet 1978, 27–38). Some of this interest was merely philological, having been spurred by the growing sentiments of Neo-Confucian antiquarianism. Yet many classicists were concerned with reconciling these archaic prescriptions of the Zhou and Han dynasties with the radically different social conditions of the Song. In doing so scholars were able to pick and choose among the multitudes of complex traditions and taboos of the ancients. One of the main bodies of social injunctions they revived from these works dealt with the social submission of women and the necessity of their seclusion from men.

Cheng Yi referred to the *Book of Rites (Li ji)* in his description of his mother's perfect behavior. He praised her for following the injunction, "Women do not go out of doors at night. If they do, they carry a lighted candle" (Zhu and Lu 1967, 180). Zhu Xi and his disciple Liu Qingzhi (1130–1195) elaborated on this ideal at great length in their work *Elementary Learning (Xiao xue)*. Presumably intended to be read prior to the *Great Learning (Da xue)*, this small book was completed in 1187 as a guide for teaching the young. Because of its wide use in primary education for many centuries, this compilation of quotations from ancient sources had an enormous influence on developing the perceptions of social norms for generations of scholars. It is also one of the most straightforward expositions of the Neo-Confucian rethinking of popular views toward women. In it we find the end results of the transformations of social norms brought about by the new Song metaphysics. Zhu Xi's philosophic speculations led him to select sections of the *Book of Rites* and other classic works which emphasized the submission and obedience of women as educational material for the young.

He goes on to quote the *Book of Rites* on the proper way for raising boys and girls, an appropriate subject for his young readers. The ancients began differentiation between the sexes at an early age. "When children can speak, boys are to answer promptly, girls are to be quiet" (Zhu and Liu 1863, 1B). This text goes on to mandate different types of clothing for boys and girls. The great separation between the sexes takes place at the age of seven. At that time, "boys and girls cannot use the same mat and cannot eat together. . . . From the age of ten girls cannot go outside. Their governess teaches them geniality and submissiveness of speech and manner" (pp. 1B, 2B). This submissiveness would simply be conformance with their passive yin nature.

Zhu Xi further stresses this obedience by reference to a quotation attributed to Confucius.

> Woman yields to man. For this reason virtue alone should not regulate her—there is also the Way of the Three Obediences. When she is with her family a woman obeys her father. When married she obeys her husband. When her husband dies she obeys her son. She never dares to follow her own inclinations. (Zhu and Liu 1863, 11B)

The *Elementary Learning* goes on to specify the most important types of obedience. First among these is that she never leaves the household compound, a principle which Zhu Xi emphasizes at length (Zhu and Liu 1863, 11A–12B). Only by being removed from all possible temptation could female purity be assured. As this section of the text confidently concludes, "This is the way of rectifying female virtue!" (p. 12A).

These preconceptions concerning women espoused in the writings of influential literati diffused throughout the range of elite and popular culture. Manuals of household management like that of the twelfth-century pragmatist Yuan Cai, entitled *Precepts for Social Life (Shi fan)*, popularized the most practical implications of the Neo-Confucian view of women. Although not himself a Neo-Confucian, Yuan Cai repeated much of what can be found in elite philosophic writings, including the segragation of the sexes. He advises the reader, "Your wives and daughters are often petty, quick-tempered, quarrelsome, obstinate, cruel, oppressive, and ignorant of the ancient and recent moral truths" (Ebrey 1984, 290). The control of female peccadillos was considered more carefully in the practical writings of the stateman and man of letters Sima Guang (1019–1086). His *Precepts for Family Life (Jia fan)* included an explanation of the centrality of ceremonial conduct (*li*) to family management. As for the working definition of this term, "the separation of males and females is the chief element of **li**" (pp. 47–48). In another work, *Family Forms (Sushui jiayi)*, he borrows heavily from the ancient books of ritual in both content and style as he repeats the prohibitions made by Zhu Xi and others against the free association of men and women (Sima 1927, 71.3B). While not part of the Neo-Confucian movement, Sima Guang justified his beliefs concerning the place of women through methods which would later be echoed in the works of Zhu Xi, using both philosophic terminology and reference to classical examples.

Beginning with these ideas expressed in Neo-Confucian and other Song works, attitudes expressed toward women developed a new vocabulary, tone, and mode of reasoning. Although scholars are uncertain as to the precise extent of deterioration of female social status under the Song itself, this new way of thinking about women made possible the later erosion of freedoms best symbolized by foot-binding. Neo-Confucian thinkers melded together various classical ideas about women with metaphysical conceptions in such a way as to provide explicit justification for social subordination of women. Stripped of their elegant literary language and subtle argumentation, the more general attitudes engendered by these theorists gradually worked their way into popular consciousness. In this debased form, they continue to influence the lives of Chinese women down to the present. For example, contemporary popular notions about female pollution, subordination of women as part of the "natural" order, and division of labor based on sex all find support in the teachings of Neo-Confucianism. Feminists in China today may not feel obligated to refute the specific arguments of Neo-Confucian metaphysicians. Nevertheless much of the so-called feudal ideology which they decry became systematized and popularized during the Song. Forms may change, but the ideas continue.

REFERENCES

Balazs, Etienne and Hervouet, Yves, eds. 1978. *A Sung Bibliography [Bibliographie des Sung]*. Chinese University Press, Hong Kong.

Castiglione, Baldesar (Charles S. Singleton, trans.). 1959. *The Book of the Courtier.* Doubleday, Garden City, NY.

Ch'ü T'ung-tsu (Jack L. Dull, ed.). 1972. *Han Social Structure.* University of Washington Press, Seattle.

Deuchler, Martina. 1977. "The tradition: Women during the Yi Dynasty" In Mattielli, Sandra, ed. *Virtues in Conflict, Tradition and the Korean Woman Today* (pp. 1–48). Royal Asiatic Society, Seoul.

Ebrey, Patricia Buckley, trans. 1984. *Family and Property in Sung China, Yuan Ts'ai's Precepts for Social Life.* Princeton University Press, Princeton, NJ.

Kasoff, Ethan. 1982. *An Analysis of the Thought of Chang Tsai (1020–1077)*. Unpublished doctoral dissertation, Princeton University, Princeton, NJ.

Liu, James T. C. 1967. *Ou-yang Hsiu, An Eleventh-Century Neo-Confucianist*. Stanford University Press, Stanford, CA.

Sima Guang. 1927. *Sushui jiayi* [Family forms]. In Zongyi, Tao, ed., *Shuo fu*. Shang Wu, Shanghai.

Swann, Nancy Lee. 1932. *Pan Chao: Foremost Woman Scholar of China*. Century, New York.

Ts'ai Yung-ch'un. 1950. *The Philosophy of Ch'eng I*. Unpublished doctoral dissertation, Columbia University, New York.

Van Gulik, Robert Hans. 1974 reprint. *Sexual Life in Ancient China, A preliminary survey of Chinese sex and society from ca. 1500 B.C. till 1644 A.D.* Brill, Leiden.

Veith, Ilza, trans. 1949. *Huang Ti Nei Ching Su Wen, The Yellow Emperor's Classic of Internal Medicine*. Williams and Wilkins, Baltimore, MD.

Wilhelm, Richard and Baynes, Cary F., trans. 1950. *I Ching [Yi jing]*. Princeton University Press, Princeton, NJ.

[Zhang Wenchang] Chang Wen-cheng (Howard S. Levy, trans.). 1965. *China's First Novelette, The Dwelling of the Playful Goddess*. Dai Nippon Insatsu, Tokyo.

Zhu Xi and Liu Qingzhi, Chen Xuan, annotated. 1863. *Xiao xue jizhu* [Elementary Learning, with collected commentaries]. Siku Biaozhu.

[Zhu Xi] Chu Hsi and [Lu Zuqian] Lu Tsu-ch'ien (Wingtsit Chan, trans.). 1967. *Reflections on Things at Hand, The Neo-Confucian Anthology*. Columbia University Press, New York

CHILDHOOD AND GROWING UP: 1867–1881

Ning Lao, as told to Ida Pruitt

Childhood, 1867–1870

My father called me Little Tiger and I was my mother's youngest child. The name she called me is known to no one now alive. My sister and my brother called me Meimei (Little Sister) and the neighbors called me Hsiao Wutse (Little Five) because I was the fifth child my mother bore. Two died before I was born.

We lived in a courtyard by ourselves when I was born. We lived near the truck garden that had belonged to the family, to my father and my father's uncle. In the garden were cabbages and turnips and onions, garlic, leeks, and chives.

The garden had once been part of the property of the Temple of the Goddess of Mercy, the Kuan Yin T'ang. Ten generations ago, a Taoist priest came down from the hills, from Wei Yeh Shan, near Hsu Chia Chi, thirty li [about 10 mi. or 16 km.] from P'englai, and became the abbot of the temple. He was our ancestor. He was a man with a square face and a strong disposition. My grandfather had the same square face and I have it also. That is why my father called me Little Tiger. Also, he said, I had a strong disposition.

Our family had been well-to-do at one time. We had the land our ancestor left us and my grandfather and his father before him had been among those who worked as overseers on the estates of General Ch'i. When my mother married into the family, we owned the garden and the house in the Chou Wang Temple section of the city and some other small houses besides. The family had servants and plenty to eat.

My father was an only son and was spoiled by his father. His parents died when he was seven or eight. He was brought up by his uncle, his father's younger brother, who made his own four sons work in the garden but sent my father to school. The uncle said that in this way he was faithful to his dead brother. My father studied the classics for about eight years but his studies never amounted to anything. When he was grown, the uncle put him in a shop to learn business.

Money went out, the neighbors said, because my father and his cousins had too good a time, eating and playing. My father hired an actor to teach him to sing opera. This actor-teacher lived with the family and had to be paid well. He also smoked opium. Each year there was less than the year before. When my grandfather died, what was left was divided between my father and his uncle, the younger brother of his father.

My father tried to work in the garden but he had not the strength or the skill and he was ashamed. He sold the garden to one of his mother's aunts, to pay his debts, and went to Chefoo and peddled bread. He knew how to make bread, and carried it around the street in a basket. That was the year I was born. From the time I was conceived, the fortunes of the family went down. The destiny determined for me by Heaven was not a good one.

The neighbors said that my mother was not a good manager, that she could not make the money stretch so as to "get over the years" successfully. At New Year's time great loaves of bread were steamed in the iron cooking basin. If, when the lid of the cooking basin was raised, the loaves shrank, they were thrown into the fire. Sometimes she threw three or four cookings into the fire before the loaves came out round and full. This is what the neighbors said my mother used to do. I never saw it, for we had nothing to throw away when I was growing up.

My mother did not live the life she was brought up to live. A woman in childbed should have at least five hundred eggs to eat. When I was born she had only eight eggs. My mother's father, when he lived, sold oil in the streets, beating a small bronze gong, and supported the family comfortably. My mother had a round face and gentle ways. She was a carefully reared and sheltered person. How could such a person, living behind walls, know how to manage poverty?

If a dog comes to a court it is good luck. If a cat comes it is bad luck. If a wild goose lights in a court the family will have good fortune. If a tame goose flies away, the fortunes of the family will disintegrate. There was a goose in our court and it flew away, following the wild geese.

My father did not see me until I was about a year old. Then he came home for New Year's and lived again with us. We were

34

living in the Tung Nan Ying Tse section of P'englai, in the house we had moved to when he sold the garden. All winter he sold *nien kao,* cakes made of glutenous millet. He could carry two or three hundred catties* weight of cakes but he could not shout the calls to tell people he had cakes to sell, so a neighbor and he were partners. My father mixed and steamed the cakes and the neighbor shouted as they walked the streets, each with his baskets. My father was a good cook and he taught me how to cook.

My father peddled cakes for a year or two and then my uncle got him a place in a general store. Here my father sold behind the counter and he also helped in the truck garden belonging to the Chü family who owned the store. He was buyer for the store and the garden. He helped to place the produce of the garden and to water the garden in the dry season. He was part of the time in the shop and part in the garden.

The Chü family lived in a great house on the north main street and they had another [near] the Chang Hsin Miao, in the district of the temple of the goddess who protects little children. She can control the Dog of Heaven who bites little children and takes them away.

The eldest son, Chü Ta Shaoye, had passed the military examinations and had the rank of *hsiu tsai.* He could use the bow and arrows well. Their family and ours had been friends for many generations.

Chu Ta Shaoye used to say that after five hundred years people saw each other again—came back in similar incarnations.

Though each year our living was less than the year before we had a good life at home. My mother was kind to us. She cooked good things for us to eat and she loved us.

My father was strict but he was good to his family. He taught us manners and what was seemly for a woman to do and what was not seemly.

In the evenings after we had eaten our meal we sat around and talked. Sometimes my father's uncle came to spend the evening with us. In the winter we sat on the *k'ang* and sewed, my mother and my sister and I. The men smoked and talked. In the summer we sat in the courtyard.

---

*A catty is equal to about 1.5 pounds avoirdupois.

Growing Up, 1870–1881

When I was three or four years old we moved to the Chou
Wang Temple neighborhood, to be near the garden. We had the
three northern *chien** in the court, the ones facing south. There
was a two-chien east house in which the neighbors lived. This
was the first time our family had lived in a court with others.
The house had a thatched roof. Before we had always lived in
houses with tile roofs.

The house was convenient to the garden where my father
worked part of the time. It was also convenient for my mother
and my aunt to see the plays on the open stage across the street.
My father was very strict and would not let them out to see the
plays. My mother and my aunt took benches and stood on them
so they could look out the high north windows.

I was a difficult child to manage. I liked to play too much. I
played with my brother and sister and the children of the neighbors. We played on the streets and in the garden next door.

I climbed trees, and hanging by the rope from the windlass I
would let myself down into the well. I would put my toes into
the cracks between the bricks that lined it. My mother did not
know that I did this. She would have been frightened had she
known. There was nothing that I did not dare to do. I was the
baby and my parents favored me.

They did not begin to bind my feet until I was seven because I loved so much to run and play. Then I became very ill
and they had to take the bindings off my feet again. I had the
"heavenly blossoms" and was ill for two years and my face is
very pockmarked. In my childhood everyone had the illness
and few escaped some marking.

When I was nine they started to bind my feet again and they
had to draw the bindings tighter than usual. My feet hurt so
much that for two years I had to crawl on my hands and knees.
Sometimes at night they hurt so much I could not sleep. I stuck
my feet under my mother and she lay on them so they hurt less
and I could sleep. But by the time I was eleven my feet did not

---

* A *chien* is a unit of space with a constant relationship between height, width,
and length—the space between the supporting pillars, floor, and ceiling. In a
large house, therefore, the chien is large and in small house, small. The usual
house in this part of the country was three or five chien. Some of the smaller side
houses might be two chien. The partitions from pillar to pillar, front to back,
could be put in or taken out at will. A room could be from one to five chien. In
poor families such as these, a chien tended to be a room.

hurt and by the time I was thirteen they were finished. The toes were turned under so that I could see them on the inner and under side of the foot. They had come up around. Two fingers could be inserted in the cleft between the front of the foot and the heel. My feet were very small indeed.

A girl's beauty and desirability were counted more by the size of her feet than by the beauty of her face. Matchmakers were not asked "Is she beautiful?" but "How small are her feet?" A plain face is given by heaven but poorly bound feet are a sign of laziness.

My feet were very small indeed. Not like they are now. When I worked so hard and was on my feet all day, I slept with the bandages off because my feet ached, and so they spread.

When I was eleven we moved into a house in the corner of the garden. The wall between the house and the rest of the garden was low. I was a very mischievous child. When I was naughty and my mother wanted to beat me, I would run and jump over the wall and she could not catch me.

One day we wanted to go out to play, a neighbor's little girl and I. My mother said that we could go when I had finished grinding the corn. The neighbor's child said she would help me so that we would finish sooner. We ran round and round the mill, but to grind so much corn takes time. We were impatient, so while she ground I took handfuls of the corn and buried them under the refuse in the mill house, a handful here under some dust and a handful there under some donkey droppings. Then we told my mother that we were through. She came and saw that the hopper was empty. But the chickens did not give us face. They scratched here and a pile of corn showed. They scratched there and another pile showed. My mother scolded us. "You naughty, mischievous children." She started after us to beat me, but we ran and jumped over the wall and climbed into a pear tree in the garden. By this time there were several of us. My mother came to the foot of the tree and called to me but I would not come down.

"If the other children were not there I would shake the tree until you dropped and I would kill you."

I was very daring. I climbed all the trees, and one of our games was to jump over the open mouth of the well. If we had missed we should have fallen in and drowned. We were also very fond of swinging. This was especially popular at New Year's time. I said that I would go out and swing. My mother told me to wait until we had eaten, but I was too impatient.

"Then," said my mother, "I will have to call you and you will forget to come."

But I went and played with the other children. It was my turn to stand on the swing and work it up, while one of the other girls sat in the seat. Some other children thought we had been swinging too long and tried to pull us off. The swing board overturned as we swung up and we fell. I fell on my face and raised a great lump on my forehead. The other girl fell on the back of her head. I went home. My mother said, "Here indeed is a new thing, that you should come home without being called."

I had my hand over my forehead and she did not see the lump. I lay down on the k'ang and went to sleep. They were all there, the whole family, and they ate the *chiaotze** that we had for New Year's. A cousin was visiting us and my father was there. They had finished eating when I awoke. My head ached and I was hungry. I cried and said, "Mother, look at my head." She rubbed it for me, but as she rubbed she said, "Now I see why you came home without being called."

The first time I saw a foreigner I was very small, perhaps six or seven. I was so frightened that I fell to the ground and hid my face in my arms. I crouched and dared not look up until they told me he had gone. He was a big man with a beard and a big voice. His name was Deemster but they called him the Pastor. Foreigners were strange in their appearance, with clothes that looked like nothing under the heavens. But I think what frightened me most were the eyes, so far back and sunken into the face.

The man's wife used to go from house to house calling on the women. If she came to our house and my father heard of it he always became very angry and scolded my mother. My mother was gentle and liked to talk to the foreign woman. The foreign woman had a school for girls and urged my mother to send me to school. But my mother knew there was no use even to think of it. My father became enraged at the very idea and would not listen. If I had been allowed to go to school, how different my life would have been. I might have been somebody in the world.

When I was about eleven, a Li family moved next door into a house where Ho Chü-chü (Ho the Pearl) and another prostitute had lived.

---

*Italian ravioli and Russian *pelmeni* are both similar to and probably derived from the Chinese *chiaotze,* one through Marco Polo and the other through proximity.

The soldiers came, as was their custom, three of them one day, and found Lao Li chopping wood in the court.

"What have you come for?" he asked the soldiers.

"We have come to call," they said, and pushed past him into the house. The man was old and could not hold them. He shouted, warning his family, and the soldiers shouted, demanding women.

Li Fu-tze, the daughter, was fifteen. She jumped over the wall into our court and so escaped. She went to the mission compound. When the missionaries first came to P'englai, people would not sell or lease houses to them, so the city elders gave them the temple compound of Kuan Yin T'ang, where my ancestor was once abbot. Most of the buildings had fallen down and the priests gone away. The missionaries built their houses in the garden that had belonged to our family generations ago, and what were left of the temple buildings were repaired and used as a school for girls and a school for boys. They also built a church. Therefore, the mission compound came to be known as the Kuan Yin T'ang. Li Fu-tze's mother worked as amah for Mrs. Deemster and Li Fu-tze went to the girls' school.

When the students in the boys' school heard the story, they went to the Li house, beat the three soldiers, and dragged them to the Kuan Yin T'ang by their queues. It was the place of the students in the boys' school to defend the pupils in the girls' school. They were school brothers and sisters for they studied under one master; in one society, the church; and the customs governing family relationships are very binding on those who study under one master and belong to one society.

Two of the soldiers got away but one they tied to a tree by his queue. Yuan Shih-k'ai, who was later president of China, was their officer. He was not a very high officer at that time. He came and saw Dr. Deemster and asked for the man the students had captured, for Dr. Deemster was as a father in the family and the responsibility was his. Also, according to custom, Yuan Shih-k'ai wanted Dr. Deemster to be the *shuo-ho-ti*, he-who-talks-harmony, the peacemaker.

Yuan Shih-k'ai's soldiers carried their comrade back to the camp on boards. But the man was so angry that he died of heat in the intestines. Therefore it became a big affair, a matter that had to be taken up by all his fellows.

One or two hundred soldiers went to the chapel on Sunday and surrounded it. But the girl students managed to slip out the side door. The soldiers went hunting for Lao Li but could not find him. They started to search all the houses. It was evening, at twilight. My mother was salting vegetables in the court and had not enough salt. She had gone to the Kao family to borrow some, but I was at home watching the gate and I saw the soldiers. I was only eleven and they did not molest me but I was frightened. I sat in the gateway and watched. The riverbed was full of people. It was autumn and the river was low. The white sand could not be seen for the black of the soldiers' uniforms.

The soldiers found Lao Li at his home and beat him up and took his fur coat. He ran and jumped over the wall into our court. His ear was bleeding. He fled to Lao Yen's house and jumped the wall to Lao Sun's house, and begged for his life to be saved, calling, *Chiu ming, chiu ming!* The soldiers followed him with swords and sticks.

His wife ran around begging for someone to act as peace-maker. The soldiers beat her over the head until she was unconscious. Lao Sun, a gardener who also made straw sandals and made money gambling, a man of ability, tried to make peace. He held out his arms and tried to stop the soldiers, but they beat him also, he who had no part in the quarrel. Then Lao Li ran to Kuan Yin T'ang and Dr. Deemster came forward and made the final peace.

After that the soldiers often came to the church services.

Yuan Shih-k'ai became good friends with my uncle. I saw them often talking together.

The last time I was beaten by my mother was when I was thirteen. And this is the way in which it happened. My sister was to blame that I got the beating. She did not have a good heart and she locked me in so that I could not run away. My uncle, my mother's brother, came to see us and was to take one of us back to visit him. My sister wanted to go and I wanted to go. I said that she could not go without me and she said that she would. I said that if I could not go she should not. I held to her coat and said I would not let her go. My mother told me to behave and tried to whip me but I ran and was jumping across the wall when my sister came with soft words and said that my mother's anger was gone and that I was to go home. I went home and my sister shut the house door after me and hung the chain over the iron loop on the lintel above the house door on the outside. I was caught. I could not run and my mother beat me. She broke a broom over me. She broke a stool beating me. I screamed and said that I would not do it any more. She said, "The more you say you will not, the more I will beat you."

So I said, "I dare to do it again. I dare to do it again."

She asked me why I said that. And I said, "You will beat me if I say I dare and you beat me if I say I do not dare."

It was a great beating, and when she had finished I lay on the k'ang. I was sore all over. When my father came home he asked about it, seeing me lying on the bed. My mother said, "She could not run away. Her sister had latched the door. So I had to beat her."

My mother was sorry that she had to beat me. My mother loved me. And after that I needed no more beating for I knew that my mother loved me and I was beginning to have the reason of a grown person. That was a great beating.

After my sister married I slept in my parents' room, for my father was home at night only every other month. One month he slept in the store where he worked and one month he slept at home. This was because there were so many clerks in the store they could not all sleep there at once.

But when my sister came home we slept together in our old room.

One night we were in our room about to sleep when I heard a stone drop as it was dislodged from the wall. I listened and heard the scrunch, scrunch of the snow as someone walked over it very carefully. Then I said to my sister, "See. There is a round hole in the window."

And she said, "Did you paper the windows freshly today? Are you sure there was no hole?"

And I said, "I papered the windows freshly. I am sure there was no hole. That has been made by someone with a wet finger tip."

"Put your finger through," said my sister. "I am sure you will find nothing but cold air."

My mother heard us talking and said, "Why do you children talk? Why don't you go to sleep?"

And of course by the time my father had got on his clothes and lighted the lantern the thief was long since gone. Cat thieves were common in P'englai. There were no policemen and the streets were not lighted.

When I was thirteen my parents stopped shaving the hair from around the patch of long hair left on my crown. I was no longer a little girl. My hair was allowed to grow and was gathered into a braid at the back of my head. It was braided in a wide loose plait which spread fanlike above and below the knot that held the hair at the nape of the neck. It was a like a great butterfly. Girls do not wear their hair that way now. Part of the hair was separated and braided into a little plait down my back. When the little braid was gathered into the big braid I was a woman and not allowed out of the gate. So we have a saying that the girl with the full head of hair is not as free as the one with a bare head, that is, partly shaved. And at the age of thirteen I was taught to cook and sew.

My father was a very strict man. We were not allowed, my sister and I, on the street after we were thirteen. People in P'englai were that way in those days. When a family wanted to know more about a girl who had been suggested for a daughter-in-law and asked what kind of a girl she was, the neighbors would answer, "We do not know. We have never seen her." And that was praise.

We were not allowed, after we were grown, to raise our voices in talking. When there was a knock at the street door, no matter what we were talking about we had to stop. If a stranger came into the court we had to disappear into the inner room. When my father came home, even if we had been laughing and talking, we were silent the moment we heard the latch fall in the socket as the front gate was opened. We stood with our heads bowed and our hands by our sides until our father was sitting on the k'ang. Then we took off his shoes and lighted his pipe. Even my brother did not dare to say anything to my father.

My father was very strict about the way we dressed, my sister and I. He wanted us to wear plain and dignified clothes only. He would never allow us to wear fashionable clothes. The hats we wore were bands of black satin across our foreheads. There were silver and jade ornaments sewed on them. They were held on by heavy cords passing under the knots in which our hair was combed. Everyone at that time was wearing little silver chains instead of the cords. The ends fell below the left shoulder and little bells on them tinkled as one walked. My sister and I very much wanted to wear such chains. My sister said to me, "Let us put our coppers together and buy a chain. When you are going out you can wear it, and when I am going out I will wear it."

Our father heard us talking and beat us. We were both married then. We never got our chain.

It was also very fashionable to wear little black headache plasters on the temples. One day my sister came home decorated in this way. My father was very angry. He asked her if she was a prostitute to so decorate herself.

My sister was married when she was fifteen, and I was married when I was fifteen. I was eight when my sister was married. My sister's match was considered a very suitable one. Her husband was only three or four years older than she and he had a trade. He was a barber. And the father-in-law was still young enough to work also. But my sister was a child, with the ways of a child and the heart of a child. She had not become used to housework. She did not know how to mix wheat bread or corn bread. She got the batter too thick or too thin, and so her mother-in-law would scold. She had no experience and could not plan meals. At one meal she would cook too much and at the next not enough. This also made her mother-in-law angry and she would scold. Though my sister had not learned to work, she had learned to smoke. This also made her mother-in-law angry. She would say that my sister was not good for work but only for luxury. So there was bitterness.

Her mother-in-law forbade her to smoke. She took her pipe and broke it into many pieces. My sister made herself a pipe from a reed and smoked when there was no one around. One day her mother-in-law came suddenly into the room. My sister hid the pipe under her clothes as she sat on the k'ang. The lighted pipe set the wheat chaff under the bed matting afire, and her mother-in-law beat her. When her husband came home, his mother told him the story and he also beat my sister. There was a great quarrel and her mother-in-law reviled her with many words that were too hard to bear.

She said, "In the path around the mill does one not look for the hairs of the mule?" She meant to call my sister a mule and also to say that there were no signs of a daughter-in-law where such signs should be—there was no work done. She went out of the house to find her husband, saying that she would show my sister when she came back what real anger was like. My sister went crazy.

In P'englai it is the custom for the women to stand in their gateways in the evenings to watch whatever may be passing by. When my sister went to the gate that evening she did not stop and watch as is the custom, but went out of the gate and walked south. She walked until she reached the south gate of the city, and she walked out of the gate. She walked three li [about 1 mi. or 1.6 km.] to the village of the Three Li Bridge. All the people came out to see the crazy woman. The cry went out for all to come and see the crazy woman. We lived near the north gate of the city, but we had an aunt who lived outside the south gate at

43

the village of the Three Li Bridge. She too came out to see the crazy woman, and she said, "Is this not Yintze, the daughter of my sister? Come with me." And she took my sister home with her.

That very evening my brother went to my sister's mother-in-law's home to fetch my sister and bring her back to our home for a visit. When he got there she was gone and no one knew where she was. All that night he searched for her, and her husband and father-in-law searched, but they could not find her. The next day my aunt sent her son to tell us where my sister was, and we went and fetched her home. But her mother-in-law claimed that we had hidden her and that she had left home that night for a bad purpose. So she stayed with us for six months.

And she was not right for all those six months. She had come crying and combing her hair with her fingers, so that her hair was in all directions and we could not comb it out. Then one day we found that her hair was cut, and we never knew who had cut it. Straight off it was cut, between the knot, into which a woman's hair is bound at marriage, and the head. Later we found the hair hanging on a bramble bush in the court of the Chou Wang Temple. It must have been cut off by the demon who was troubling her. All these six months she talked to herself, and at times she was stiff and still. But she got better and the fits became less frequent.

We asked friends to talk for her to her mother-in-law and husband, and at last it was arranged that they should take her back. A separate house was rented for her and her husband so that they did not live with the old people. She got on with her husband and they liked each other, but still at times she had the spells. She would cry and shout, and her arms and legs would become stiff. The demon that troubled her was not a very powerful one. It enabled her to talk but never to foretell the future.

Seeing that my sister had so much trouble with a young husband, my father and mother said that I should be married to an older man who would cherish me. When the matchmaker told of such a one and that he had no mother—she was dead— my parents thought that they had done well for me. I was to have an older husband to cherish me, but not too old, and no mother-in-law to scold and abuse me.

Our neighbor, the man who carted away the night soil, made the match for me. He was a professional matchmaker. He did not care how a marriage turned out. He had used the money. As the old people say, "A matchmaker does not live a lifetime with the people he brings together." The matchmaker hid four years of my husband's age from us, saying the man was only ten years older than I. But he was fourteen years older. I was twelve when the match was made, and I became engaged— a childhood match. I still had my hair in a plait. I did not know anything. I was fifteen when I was married.

They told me that I was to be a bride. I had seen weddings going down the street. I had seen brides sitting on the k'angs on the wedding days when all went in to see them. To be married was to wear pretty clothes and ornaments in the hair.

I sat on the k'ang, bathed and dressed, in my red under-clothes and red stockings. The music sounded and they took me off the k'ang. I sat on the chair and the matrons combed my hair for me into the matron's knot at the nape of my neck. They dressed me in my red embroidered bridal robes and the red embroidered bridal shoes and put the ornaments in my hair. An old man whose parents and wife were still alive carried me out and put me in the wedding chair that was to carry me to my new home. I knew only that I must not touch the sides of the chair as he put me in, and that I was dressed in beautiful clothes. I was a child, only fifteen by our count, and my birthday was small—just before New Year. We count ourselves a year old when we are born and we all add a year at the New Year. I was counted two years old when I was a month old, for I was born near the end of the old year. I was a child. I had not yet passed my thirteenth birthday.

I was frightened. I was homesick.

It was the year of the broom-tailed star. I can still see it distinctly. And there were many rings around the sun that year.

Agnes Smedley in 1939

SILK WORKERS

Agnes Smedley

Just as I arrived in Canton in the hot summer months of
1930, another General was killed by his bodyguard for the
sake of the fifty Chinese dollars offered by a rival General.
Such events had begun to strike me as sardonic. The Kwang-
tung Provincial Government was semi-independent, but in the
hands of generals who took by violence what they considered
their share in the loot of the south. They whirled around the
city in bullet-proof cars with armed bodyguards standing on
the running boards. Such was the spirit of the generals and of
the officials whom they brought to power with them.

I interviewed them all and put no stock in what they said.
They treated me magnificently, for foreign journalists seldom or
never went south in the hot summer months. So I had a
Government launch to myself, with an official guide to show
me factories, paved roads, new waterworks, and the Sun Yat-sen
Memorial Hall. For truth I depended on Chinese university
professors, an occasional newspaper reporter or editor, teachers
and writers, the German Consul in Canton—and on my own
eyes and ears.

The real reason I went south in the hottest part of the year
was to study the lot of the millions of "silk peasants" in a silk
industry which was rapidly losing its American markets to
Japanese magnates. But I did not wish to see the silk regions as
a guest of the powerful Canton Silk Guild, for the Guild, after
all, was like a big laughing Buddha, naked to the waist, his fat
belly hanging over his pajama belt. At last I found a group of
Lingnan Christian University professors who were engaged in
research in the industry. One young expert was leaving for the
Shuntek silk region for a six weeks' inspection tour. I went with
him to the Canton Silk Guild, where he argued with a suspi-

cious Guild official until given permission to travel on Guild river steamers and enter the region in which millions of peasants toiled. There the millionaires of the South Seas had erected many large filatures; the spinners were all young women.

Next day the young expert and I boarded a river steamer. Some twenty or thirty Guild merchants were the only other passengers. The steamers had armor plating and machine-guns to protect the merchants from "bandits." The "bandits," I learned, were peasants who took to the highway for a part of each year in order to earn a living.

I once calculated that, if these "bandits" had attacked and captured our steamer, they would have secured enough food to feed a whole village for months. At meal times the merchants hunched over the tables, eating gargantuan meals and dropping the chicken bones on the floor. They talked of silk, money, markets, and of how much their firms were losing. The silk industry was indeed fighting for its life, but if there were losses, it clearly did not come out of the hides of these men. I pined a little for Jesse James.

My young escort was awed by these men, but when he spoke of the silk peasants or the girl filature workers, hostility and contempt crept into his voice. His particular hatred seemed to be the thousands of women spinners, and only with difficulty could I learn why. He told me that the women were notorious throughout China as Lesbians. They refused to marry, and if their families forced them, they merely bribed their husbands with a part of their wages and induced them to take concubines. The most such a married girl would do was bear one son; then she would return to the factory, refusing to live with her husband any longer. The Government had just issued a decree forbidding women to escape from marriage by bribery, but the women ignored it.

"They're too rich—that's the root of the trouble!" my young escort explained. "They earn as much as eleven dollars a month, and become proud and contemptuous." He added that on this money they also supported parents, brothers and sisters, and grandparents. "They squander their money!" he cried. "I have never gone to a picture theater without seeing groups of them sitting together, holding hands."

Until 1927, when they were forbidden, there had been Communist cells and trade unions in the filatures, he charged, and now these despicable girls evaded the law by forming secret "Sister Societies." They had even dared strike for shorter hours and higher wages. Now and then two or three girls would commit suicide together because their families were forcing them to marry.

For weeks my escort and I went by foot or small boat from village to village, from market town to market town. The fierce sun beat down upon us until our clothing clung to our bodies like a surgeon's glove and the perspiration wilted our hat bands and our shoes. At night we took rooms in village inns or pitched our camp beds under mosquito nets in family temples. All the roads and paths were lined with half-naked peasants bending low under huge baskets of cocoons swung from the ends of bamboo poles. Market towns reeked with the cocoons and hanks of raw silk piled up to the rafters in the warehouses. Every village was a mass of trays on which the silkworms fed, tended night and day by gaunt careworn peasants who went about naked to the waist.

At first curiously, then with interest, my escort began to translate for me as I questioned the peasants on their life and work. Their homes were bare huts with earthen floors, and the bed was a board covered by an old mat and surrounded by a cotton cloth, once white, which served as a mosquito net. There was usually a small clay stove with a cooking utensil or two, a narrow bench, and sometimes an ancient, scarred table. For millions this was home. A few owned several mulberry trees—for wealth was reckoned in trees. But almost all had sold their cocoon crops in advance in order to get money or food. If the crop failed, they were the losers. Wherever we traveled the story was the same: the silk peasants were held in pawn by the merchants and were never free from debt.

Only as we neared big market towns, in which silk filatures belched forth the stench of cocoons, did we come upon better homes and fewer careworn faces. The daughters of such families were spinners. It was then that I began to see what industrialism, bad as it had seemed elsewhere, meant to the working girls. These were the only places in the whole country where the birth of a baby girl was an occasion for joy, for here girls were the main support of their families. Consciousness of their worth was reflected in their dignified independent bearing. I began to understand the charges that they were Lesbians. They could not but compare the dignity of their positions with the low position of married women. Their independence seemed a personal affront to officialdom.

The hatred of my escort for these girls became more marked when we visited the filatures. Long lines of them, clad in glossy black jackets and trousers, sat before boiling vats of cocoons, their parboiled fingers twinkling among the spinning filaments. Sometimes a remark passed along their lines set a whole mill laughing. The face of my escort would grow livid.

"They call me a running dog of the capitalists, and you a foreign devil of an imperialist! They are laughing at your clothing and your hair and eyes!" he explained.

One evening the two of us sat at the entrance of an old family temple in the empty stone halls of which we had pitched our netted camp cots. On the other side of the canal rose the high walls of a filature, which soon began pouring forth black-clad girl workers, each with her tin dinner pail. All wore wooden sandals which were fastened by a single leather strap across the toes and which clattered as they walked. Their glossy black hair was combed back and hung in a heavy braid to the waist. At the nape of the neck the braid was caught in red yarn, making a band two or three inches wide—a lovely splash of color.

As they streamed in long lines over the bridge arching the canal and past the temple entrance, I felt I had never seen more handsome women.

I urged my young escort to interpret for me, but he refused, saying he did not understand their dialect. He was so irritated that he rose and walked toward the town. When he was gone, I went down the steps. A group of girls gathered around me and stared. I offered them some of my malt candy. There was a flash of white teeth and exclamations in a sharp staccato dialect. They took the candy, began chewing, then examined my clothing and stared at my hair and eyes. I did the same with them and soon we were laughing at each other.

Two of them linked their arms in mine and began pulling me down the flagstone street. Others followed, chattering happily. We entered the home of one girl and were welcomed by her father and mother and two big-eyed little brothers. Behind them the small room was already filled with other girls and curious neighbors. A candle burned in the center of a square table surrounded by crowded benches. I was seated in the place of honor and served the conventional cup of tea.

Then a strange conversation began. Even had I known the most perfect Mandarin, I could not have understood these girls, for their speech was different from that spoken in any other part of the country. I had studied Chinese spasmodically—in

Manchuria, in Peking, in Shanghai—but each time, before I had more than begun, I had had to move on to new fields, and all that I had previously learned became almost useless. Shanghai had its own dialect, and what I had learned there aroused laughter in Peking and was utterly useless in the south. Only missionaries and consular officials could afford to spend a year in the Peking Language School. Journalists had to be here, there, and everywhere.

I therefore talked with the filature girls in signs and gestures. Did I have any children, they asked, pointing to the children. No? Not married either? They seemed interested and surprised. In explanation I unclamped my fountain pen, took a notebook from my pocket, tried to make a show of thinking, looked them over critically, and began to write. There was great excitement.

A man standing near the door asked me something in Mandarin and I was able to understand him. I was an American, a reporter, he told the crowded room. Yes, I was an intellectual—but was once a worker. When he interpreted this, they seemed to find it very hard to believe.

Girls crowded the benches and others stood banked behind them. Using my few words of Mandarin and many gestures, I learned that some of them earned eight or nine dollars a month, a few eleven. They worked ten hours a day—not eight, as my escort had said. Once they had worked fourteen.

My language broke down, so I supplemented it with crude pictures in my notebook. How did they win the ten-hour day? I drew a sketch of a filature with a big fat man standing on top laughing, then a second picture of the same with the fat man weeping because a row of girls stood holding hands all around the mill. They chattered over these drawings, then a girl shouted two words and all of them began to demonstrate a strike. They crossed their arms, as though refusing to work, while some rested their elbows on the table and lowered their heads, as though refusing to move. They laughed, began to link hands, and drew me into this circle. We all stood holding hands in an unbroken line, laughing. Yes, that was how they got the ten-hour day!

As we stood there, one girl suddenly began to sing in a high sweet voice. Just as suddenly she halted. The whole room chanted an answer. Again and again she sang a question and they replied, while I stood, excited, made desperate by the fact that I could not understand.

The strange song ended and they began to demand something of me. They wanted a song! The *Marseillaise* came to mind, and I sang it. They shouted for more and I tried the *Internationale*, watching carefully for any reaction. They did not recognize it at all. So, I thought, it isn't true that these girls had Communist cells!

A slight commotion spread through the room, and I saw that a man stood in the doorway holding a flute in his hand. He put it to his lips and it began to murmur softly. Then the sound soared and the high sweet voice of the girl singer followed. She paused. The flute soared higher and a man's voice joined it. He was telling some tale, and when he paused, the girl's voice answered. It was surely some ballad, some ancient song of the people, for it had in it the universal quality of folk-music.

In this way I spent an evening with people whose tongue I could not speak, and when I returned to my temple, many went with me, one lighting our way with a swinging lantern. I passed through the silent stone courtyards to my room and my bed. And throughout the night the village watchman beat his brass gong, crying the hours. His gong sounded first from a distance, passed the temple wall, and receded again, saying to the world that all was well.

I lay thinking of ancient things . . . of the common humanity, the goodness and unity of the common people of all lands

THE WOMEN TAKE A HAND

Agnes Smedley

When I first met old Mother Tsai, she had already emerged as a leader of the women in the valley. She was unusually tall for a "south Yangtze Valley" woman; her skin was brown, and the veins on her old hands stood out like ridges on a hillside. She was thin and hard, and when she spoke, her voice was firm and almost harsh. Her hair, touched with white, was drawn back from a high forehead and rolled in a knot at the nape of her neck. As a peasant woman and the mother of many sons, she had suffered bitterly all her life, but of this she never spoke. Her white cotton jacket was neatly buttoned up close around the neck and her dark cotton trousers always seemed to have just been washed. Though none of these people ever ironed their clothing, hers must somehow have been pressed beneath some weight. She was the embodiment of dignity and staunchness.

It was difficult to believe that she was sixty-eight, for she seemed much younger. She was, she told me, a widow with four children. Of her three sons, the two elder were in the New Fourth Army, and the younger, a boy of fifteen, helped her and her daughters-in-law till the fields.

Before the war, life in the villages had been drab and monotonous. But when the New Fourth Army had marched into the valley the year before, the world had seemed to enter with it. Many girl students had joined the political department of the army; when they went knocking on the doors of the village women, the old world had crumbled. The ladies of the gentry had refused to receive them, sending their menfolk instead, and thus suggesting that the girls were prostitutes. But when the girls knocked on Mother Tsai's door, she looked into their eyes and knew they were not bad. She invited them in, placed bowls of tea before them, and called her daughters-in-law and neighbor women to come and sit with them. And in this way the Women's National Salvation Association was born in the valley. It grew until it had over a hundred members.

Mother Tsai's lean, tall figure could often be seen walking along the paths from village to village, urging women to join literacy classes, and attend discussion groups to learn what the war was about and how they could help. After the day's work was done, women could be seen sitting on their doorsteps, cutting out pieces of cloth and sewing. When I asked them what they were doing, they replied: "Making shoes for the army."

More and more women took over the field work previously done by men. The younger men had joined the army and the older men and boys helped in the fields or carried supplies to the battlefield and brought back the wounded. On every festival day, members of the Women's Association would go to the hospital to "comfort the wounded" with gifts of food, sing songs, and talk with the soldiers. It was always Mother Tsai who delivered the speeches in the wards, telling the wounded that they were all her sons and the sons of the Women's Association. And she never closed a speech without telling them about women's rights, or urging them to induce their womenfolk to join the association. Some men had never heard such talk before and they listened with respect. About such matters Chinese men everywhere seemed much more civilized and tolerant than Occidental men, and only a few ever opposed the new movement.

The women had become particularly confident after army women had conducted classes. One of these classes covered Japanese espionage and sabotage methods in the war zones and it urged women to become the "eyes and ears of the army," to combat defeatism, watch everywhere for spies or traitors, and boycott Japanese goods. One phrase covered all such activities: "Guarding the rear of our army." After that they never just sat and listened while their menfolk dispensed wisdom; they took part in conversations, conducted propaganda about almost everything on earth, went to mass meetings, and questioned every stranger who passed through the valley about his family and his family's family down to the tenth generation.

Now and then a man rose to protest against the "new women." There was, for instance, the merchant Chang, who declared that, when the women got going, they wore out men and exhausted horses. Mother Tsai was the worst of all, he said, and an idea in her head rattled like a pea in an empty gourd. She had become particularly obnoxious to him since she had discovered that he was buying up all the small white beans from the lah tree. The people made candles from these beans, but Chang had begun cornering them and selling them in Wuhu. Now, the city of Wuhu had been occupied by the Japanese, and the women soon wanted to know just why any person traded in it. How was it, they asked, that Merchant Chang could pass through the Japanese lines, month in and month out, without difficulty? And why had the wax beans of the valley suddenly found such a big market? Perhaps the Japanese made oil from them! No one respected Merchant Chang anyway, for everyone knew that he had a hand in the valley's new opium-smoking den, where the village riffraff and even some family men had begun squandering their money.

Mother Tsai one day walked straight into Chang's shop and put the question to him. With withering contempt, the merchant asked her if she wanted to buy his beans. This was not only an insult, but it mocked the poverty of the old lady and of every peasant family in the valley. Merchant Chang soon learned what it meant to despise the will of the people. Not a soul would buy or sell him anything, and when he passed through the streets people looked the other way. Once a little boy threw a stone after him and called out: "Traitor." And one day as he passed a farmhouse, he distinctly heard a dog being set on him.

At last Merchant Chang went in anger to the local government official. The official called in Mother Tsai for a friendly talk. The old lady went, but not alone. The entire membership of the Women's Association escorted her to the official's door, and her son, her daughters-in-law, and several relatives accompanied her right into his home. Other villagers trailed along and it looked as if the whole village was waiting outside the official's residence. The official himself was not a bad fellow. In fact, he was patriotic and liberal-minded. But when he saw the crowd, he became more liberal-minded than ever. He asked Mother Tsai to explain her talk with Chang, and she told him about the traffic with Wuhu and about the opium and gambling den. The opium, she pointed out, came from some corrupt officers in a provincial Chinese army farther to the west. There had never before been an opium-smoking den in the valley, and the Women's Association asked that it be closed down.

The offical admitted the evil of opium and gambling, but

said there was no law against either. A new opium-smoking law was expected soon; until then he urged the women to argue with the men "with love in their hearts." Old Mother Tsai replied: "We women have already argued with love in our hearts. The men will not listen. They tell us to go back to our kitchens and not interfere in men's affairs."

Mother Tsai ended the interview by announcing to the amazed offical: "We women have risen. We will not allow rich men to despise the will of the people."

Nor could the official do anything about Merchant Chang. There was no proof that he traded with the Japanese. True, he replied, men had seen him in the streets of Wuhu. But he might have slipped through the Japanese lines like other men. There was no law against this.

March 8 brought matters to a crisis. This was always cele-brated throughout China as International Women's Day and the valley buzzed with preparation for a mass meeting in the great courtyard of an old ancestral temple. Men leaders had been in-vited to say a few words of greeting, but it was a woman's day. All the front seats in the temple courtyard were reserved for women, while soldiers, officers, and civilian men were invited to sit in the back. The faces and names of the women scientists, writers, and revolutionary leaders of many nations shouted at us from scores of posters. A number of them called on the women to "revive the spirit of Florence Nightingale."

On this morning Mother Tsai led the entire Women's National Salvation Association to the army hospital to present gifts to the wounded. Before going to the wards, they called to present me with ten eggs and a chicken. Mother Tsai sat very straight and asked me to tell Western women how the women of China had struggled to emancipate themselves. "You," she said, "express the high spirit of womanhood by your willing-ness to eat bitterness with us." I was deeply affected by her trib-ute.

I went with the women to the hospital wards and watched them bring in great bamboo baskets filled with eggs, cakes, and half a slaughtered hog. Their husbands proudly carried the gifts down the aisles for the wounded to see and exclaim over. And when this was done, all the women gathered and sang the *Consolation for the Wounded* song, telling the soldiers, "O men of honor," that they had "suffered the wounds of war for mil-lions of women and children."

It was a beautiful and moving scene. After it was finished, I talked with Mother Tsai and her followers. They wished to know what else they could do to help the wounded, and I proposed that they make pillows and pillowcases, embroidering each case with such slogans as "Hero of the Nation" or "Toward the Final Victory." They accepted the idea eagerly and I started the campaign with a donation of money for cloth and silk thread, assuring them that they must not thank me, that this was my fight as well as theirs.

The mass meeting that afternoon was a tremendous success. Mother Tsai had an attack of stage fright, but conquered her fear and went on to speak of women's rights and their part in the war. Before finishing, she announced that her association was going to root out all evils in the valley, including gambling and opium and idleness. In concluding she revealed that news had just reached her that one of her own sons had been wounded at the front. It was an honor to be the mother of a man who had suffered in such a cause, she said, and it made her own duty so much the greater.

She was about to leave the stage, but halted to stare. For all the soldiers and commanders had risen and were holding their rifles high in the air. To the stirring strains of the *Volunteer Marching Song* the old lady moved slowly off the stage.

A few days later one of the army doctors called me out to the outpatient clinic of the hospital, and to my amazement I found old Mother Tsai lying injured on a stretcher. As I bent over her, she began in a weak voice to tell me what had happened. It was all about the opium and gambling den, she said. The Women's Association had argued with the men to close it down, and when they had refused, she and the other women had stalked into the place and peremptorily ordered the men to go home. The ruffians had shouted abuse at them. Finally Mother Tsai had brought a big stick down across the table, scattering all the money and mah-jong cubes around the room. Other women had started to follow suit, the men had fought them, and there had been a great row. Almost every woman had been beaten—Mother Tsai worst of all.

For days the valley was in an uproar. Fathers, husbands, and sons, soldiers and commanders stalked about in a fury. Mother Tsai's bed was surrounded by a crowd of women, every one of them with some sort of bruise, but all of them chattering happily. For the opium den had been closed down and Merchant Chang and every man who had beaten a woman had been jailed. "A great victory—a great victory," the women kept saying.

Old Mother Tsai appealed to me:

"Now, American comrade, write to the American Women's National Salvation Association and tell them about this. Tell about our victory and tell them that without sacrifice there can be no victory."

I think my voice trembled a little as I said I would do that, but I sat thinking of American women—women well clad and well cared for, convinced by a thousand movies that "love" was the solution of all problems. I doubted whether many of them could appreciate the conditions under which Chinese women lived and struggled.

It was a few weeks before Mother Tsai was back on the field of battle. One day I glanced up from my desk and found her standing in the door, a small group of young women behind her—all smiling. I went outside with them and found men, women, and children carrying pillows. Each pillowcase was embroidered with flowers and birds, and across each stretched such a slogan as I had suggested. Later the women went from bed to bed, presenting each man with a pillow. The surprise and pleasure of the patients was payment enough.

There were too few pillows, however, for several wounded men had just come in, including two Japanese prisoners of war. Promising to make others for them, Mother Tsai induced two Chinese soldiers to surrender their pillows to these Japanese. With the presentation, she delivered a speech about the rights of women. The Japanese gazed up at her with amazed and embarrassed smiles.

"It's grand, simply grand," I exclaimed to a doctor. "The old lady has the Japanese on their backs, and they can't do a thing but lie there and listen to her talk about the equality of women. What a dose for them! Just what they deserved!"

SHAN-FEI, COMMUNIST

Agnes Smedley

This is the story of Shan-fei, daughter of a rich landowner of Hunan Province. Once she went to school and wore silk dresses and had a fountain pen. But then she became a Communist and married a peasant leader. In the years that followed she—but I will begin from the beginning—

Her mother is the beginning. A strange woman. She was old-fashioned, had bound feet, and appeared to bow her head to every wish of her husband who held by all that was old and feudal. Yet she must have been rebellious. She watched her sons grow up, go to school, and return with new ideas. Some of these new ideas were about women—women with natural feet, who studied as men did, who married only when and whom they wished.

When her sons talked the mother would sit listening, her eyes on her little daughter, Shan-fei, kicking in her cradle. And long thoughts came to her. What those thoughts were we do not know, but we know that at last she died for the freedom of her daughter.

This battle was waged behind the high stone walls that surrounded her home. The enemy was her husband and his brothers. And the mother's weapons were the ancient weapons of subjected women: tears, entreaties, intrigue, cunning. At first she won but one point: her husband consented to Shan-fei's education, provided the teacher was an old-fashioned man who came to the home and taught only the Chinese characters. But Shan-fei's feet must be bound, and she must be betrothed in marriage according to ancient custom. So the child's feet were bound and she was betrothed to the weakling son of a rich neighbor, a corrupt old man with many concubines.

Until Shan-fei was eleven years old, her father ruled as

tyrants rule. But then he suddenly died. Perhaps it was a natural death, and perhaps Shan-fei's mother wept sincere tears. Yet the funeral was not finished before the bandages were taken off the feet of the little girl, and the earth on the grave was still damp when Shan-fei was put in a school one hundred *li* [33 mi. or 53 km.] away.

But though the bandages were removed, the little feet had already been crippled by five years of binding, and the half-dead, useless toes remained bent under the feet like stones to handicap the girl throughout her life.

Anyway the bandages were gone, and with them the symbol of one form of enslavement. There remained the betrothal to the rich man's son. Such betrothals in China are legally binding, and the parents who break them can be summoned to court and heavily punished, just as if they had committed a dangerous crime. Shan-fei's mother, however, seemed to have tendencies that the feudal-minded ones called criminal. For she was suspected of plotting and intriguing to break the engagement.

Worse still, it was rumored that she did not advise Shan-fei to be obedient as girls should be but encouraged her to be free and rebellious. This rumor spread like fire when the news came that Shan-fei had led a students' strike against the corrupt administration of her school. She was nearing sixteen at the time, the proper age for marriage. Yet she was expelled in disgrace from the school, and returned home with her head high and proud. And her mother, instead of subduing her, whispered with her alone, then merely transferred her to a still more modern school in faraway Wuchang on the Yangtze, where rumor further had it that she was becoming notorious as a leader in the students' movement. Moreover, men and women students studied together in Wuchang.

Things became so bad that at last the rich landlord filed a legal suit against Shan-fei's mother and summoned her to court, charged with plotting to prevent the marriage. But the old lady defended herself most cunningly and even convinced the court that all she desired was a postponement of the marriage for another two years.

She convinced the judge—but not the landlord. And, as was the custom, he called to his aid the armed gentry of the countryside; when Shan-fei returned home from her vacation that year, they made an attempt to capture her by force. They failed and Shan-fei escaped and remained in Wuchang for another year. When she came home again, her capture was again attempted. With the aid of her mother she again escaped, hid in the homes of peasants, and returned by devious ways to Wuchang.

When she reached Wuchang, however, the news of her mother's death had preceded her. Perhaps this death was also natural—perhaps not. Shan-fei says that her mother died from the misery of the long drawn-out struggle and family feud. "She died for my sake," she says, and in her manner is no trace of tearful sentimentality, only a proud inspiration.

Shan-fei's school comrades tried to prevent her from going home for the funeral. But this was more than the death of a mother—it was the death of a pioneer for woman's freedom. And Shan-fei, being young and unafraid and a bit proud that she had escaped the old forces twice, thought she could defeat them again. Lest anything should happen, she laid plans with her school comrades in the students' union that they should look for her and help her escape if she did not return to Wuchang within a certain period.

The body of the old mother had scarcely been laid to rest when Shan-fei's ancestral home was surrounded by armed men and she was violently captured and taken to her father-in-law's home, where she was imprisoned in the bridal suite and left to come to her senses. She did not come to her senses but, instead, starved for one week. Her hunger strike was broken only by another woman rebel within the landlord's family.

This woman was the first wife of the landlord, whom the Chinese call "Mother" to distinguish her from his concubines. The old lady watched and listened to this strange, rebellious rich girl, around whom a battle had been waged for years, and also used the ancient wiles of a woman to gain the girl's freedom. This freedom, granted by the landlord, meant only the right to move about the home and the compound but did not extend beyond the high surrounding walls.

In China, however, few or no secrets can be kept, and news travels on the wind. Perhaps that is how one girl and two men students from Wuchang happened to come to the neighborhood and bribed a servant to carry messages to Shan-fei. Finally, one late evening Shan-fei mounted the wall by some means and disappeared into the dusk on the other side. That night she and her friends rode by starlight toward Wuchang.

This was the late summer of 1926, and China was swept by winds of revolution. Soon, the southern armies laid siege to Wuchang. And Shan-fei gave up her studies and went to the masses. She became a member of the Communist Youth, and in this work she met a peasant leader whom she loved and who was loved by the peasants. She defied the old customs that bound her by law to the rich landlord's son and announced her free marriage to the man she loved. And from that day down to the present moment her life has been as deeply elemental as are the struggles of mother earth. She has lived the life of the poorest peasant workers, dressed as they dress, eaten as they eat, worked as they work, and has faced death with them on many a battlefront. Even while bearing her unborn child within her womb, she threw all her boundless energy into the revolution; and when her child was born she took it on her back and continued her work.

In those days the Kuomintang and the Communist Party still worked together, and, as one of the most active woman revolutionaries, Shan-fei was sent back to her ancestral home as head of the Women's Department of the Kuomintang. There she was made a member of the Revolutionary Tribunal that tried the enemies of the revolution, confiscated the lands of the rich landlords and distributed them among the poor peasants. She helped confiscate all the lands of her own family and of the family of her former fiancé.

When the revolution became a social revolution, the Communists and the Kuomintang split, and the dread White Terror began. The militarists and the feudal landlords returned to power. Shan-fei's family and the family of her fiancé asked the Kuomintang for her arrest. And this order was issued. It meant death for herself and her child. Two women and three men who worked with her were captured, the women's breasts were cut off, and all five were beheaded in the streets. But the workers bored air holes in a coffin, placed Shan-fei and her baby inside, and carried them through the heavily guarded gates of the city out into the graveyard beyond the walls. From there she began her journey to Wuchang. Once she was captured because her short hair betrayed her as a revolutionary; but she pleaded her innocence with her baby in her arms and was released.

She reached the Wuchang cities only to be ordered by the Communist Party to return to the thick of the fight in western Hunan during the harvest struggle, when the peasants armed themselves, refused to pay rent or taxes, and began the confiscation of the lands. Shan-fei was with them during the days; at night she slept in the forests on the hills, about her the restless bodies of those who dared risk no night in their homes. Then troops were sent against them. The peasants were defeated, thousands slain, and the others disarmed.

Again Shan-fei returned to Wuhan. And again she was sent back to the struggle. This time, however, she went, presumably as a Kuomintang member, to a city held by the militarists. Beyond the city walls were peasant armies. Inside, Shan-fei worked openly as the head of the Women's Department of the Kuomintang; secretly, she carried on propaganda amongst the troops and the workers. Then, the chief of the judicial department in Wuhan met her and fell in love with her. He was a rich militarist, but she listened carefully to his love-making and did not forget to ask him about the plans to crush the peasants. He told her—and she sent the news to the peasant army beyond. One of the leaders of this army beyond was her husband.

At last the peasants attacked the city. And so bold had Shan-fei become in her propaganda among the troops that she was arrested and condemned to death. She sent for the official who was in love with her. He listened to her denials, believed them, released her, and enabled her to leave the city. But the peasant army was defeated; among those who emerged alive was her husband, who at last found her in Wuhan.

Shan-fei was next put in charge of the technical work of the party, setting type and printing. She would lay her child on the table by her side and croon to it as she worked. Then one day her home was raided by soldiers. Her husband was away and she had stepped out for a few minutes only. From afar she saw the soldiers guarding her house. Hours later she crept back to find her child. The soldiers had thrown it into a pail of water and left it to die. Not all the tender care of herself and her husband could hold the little thing to life. Shan-fei's husband dried her bitter tears with his face—and Shan-fei turned to her work again.

Some things happen strangely. And one day this happened to Shan-fei; she went to visit the principal of the school where she had once been a student and decided to remain for the night. With the early dawn next morning she was awakened by many shouting voices. She imagined she heard her husband's voice among them. She sat up and listened and heard distinctly the shouts: "We die for the sake of Communism! Long live the Revolution!" Her friend covered her ears with a pillow and exclaimed: "Each day they bring Communists here to shoot or behead them—they are using that open space as an execution ground!"

A series of volleys rang out, and the shouting voices were silenced. Shan-fei arose and blindly made her way to the execution ground. The soldiers were marching away and only a small crowd of onlookers stood staring stupidly at the long row of dead bodies. Shan-fei stumbled down the line and turned over the warm body of her dead husband.

The net of the White Terror closed in on Shan-fei until she was ordered to leave Wuhan. She went from city to city on the Yangtze, working in factories, organizing women and children. Never could she keep a position for long, because her crippled feet made it impossible for her to stand at a machine for twelve or fourteen hours a day.

In the summer of 1929 she was again with the peasants in Hunan. Sent into Changsha one day, she was captured, together with two men Communists, one a peasant leader. She sat in prison for six months and was released then only because some new militarists overthrew the old, and in revenge freed many prisoners. But they did not free the peasant leader. Shan-fei bribed a prison guard and was permitted to see him before she left. About his neck, his ankles, and his wrists were iron bands, and these were connected with iron chains. The life of such prisoners in China is said to be two years. Shan-fei herself had not been chained. But she emerged from prison with a skin disease, with stomach trouble, with an abscess, and her skin was pasty white from anemia. In this condition she returned to the peasantry and took up her fight.

In the spring of 1930 she was sent as a delegate to the All-China Soviet Congress. Friends afterwards put her in a hospital and she was operated on for the abscess. During this period she kept the translation of Marxian studies under her pillow, and she once remarked: "Now I have time to study theory."

There are those who will ask: "Is Shan-fei young and beautiful?"

THOUGHTS ON MARCH 8

Ding Ling

When will it no longer be necessary to attach special weight to the word "woman" and raise it specially? Each year this day comes round. Every year on this day, meetings are held all over the world where women muster their forces. Even though things have not been as lively these last two years in Yan'an as they were in previous years, it appears that at least a few people are busy at work here. And there will certainly be a congress, speeches, circular telegrams, and articles.

Women in Yan'an are happier than women elsewhere in China. So much so that many people ask enviously: "How come the women comrades get so rosy and fat on millet?" It doesn't seem to surprise anyone that women make up a big proportion of the staff in hospitals, sanatoria, and clinics, but they are inevitably the subject of conversation, as a fascinating problem, on every conceivable occasion.

Moreover, all kinds of women comrades are often the target of deserved criticism. In my view these reproaches are serious and justifiable.

People are always interested when women comrades get married, but that is not enough for them. It is virtually impossible for women comrades to get onto friendly terms with a man comrade, and even less likely for them to become friendly with more than one. Cartoonists ridicule them: "A departmental head getting married too?" The poets say, "All the leaders in Yan'an are horsemen, and none of them are artists. In Yan'an it's impossible for an artist to find a pretty sweetheart." But in other situations, they are lectured: "Damn it, you look down on us old cadres and say we're country bumpkins. But if it weren't for us country bumpkins, you wouldn't be coming to Yan'an to eat

Nelly Rau-Häring

Shadow-boxing

millet!" But women invariably want to get married. (It's even more of a sin not to be married, and single women are even more of a target for rumors and slanderous gossip.) So they can't afford to be choosy, anyone will do: whether he rides horses or wears straw sandals, whether he's an artist or a supervisor. They inevitably have children. The fate of such children is various. Some are wrapped in soft baby wool and patterned felt and looked after by governesses. Others are wrapped in soiled cloth and left crying in their parents' beds, while their parents consume much of the child allowance. But for this allowance (twenty-five yuan a month, or just over three pounds of pork), many of them would probably never get a taste of meat. Whoever they marry, the fact is that those women who are compelled to bear children will probably be publicly derided as "Noras who have returned home." Those women comrades in a position to employ governesses can go out once a week to a prim get-together and dance. Behind their backs there will also be the most incredible gossip and whispering campaigns, but as soon as they go somewhere, they cause a great stir and all eyes are glued to them. This has nothing to do with our theories, our doctrines, and the speeches we make at meetings. We all know this to be a fact, a fact that is right before our eyes, but it is never mentioned.

It is the same with divorce. In general there are three conditions to pay attention to when getting married: (1) political purity, (2) both parties should be more or less the same age and comparable in looks, (3) mutual help. Even though everyone is said to fulfill these conditions—as for point 1, there are no open traitors in Yan'an; as for point 3, you can call anything "mutual help," including darning socks, patching shoes, and even feminine comfort—everyone nevertheless makes a great show of giving thoughtful attention to them. And yet the pretext for divorce is invariably the wife's political backwardness. I am the first to admit that it is a shame when a man's wife is not progressive and retards his progress. But let us consider to what degree they are backward. Before marrying, they were inspired by the desire to soar in the heavenly heights and lead a life of bitter struggle. They got married partly because of physiological necessity and partly as a response to sweet talk about "mutual help." Thereupon they are forced to toil away and become "Noras returned home." Afraid of being thought "backward," those who are a bit more daring rush around begging nurseries to take their children. They ask for abortions and risk punishment and even death by secretly swallowing potions to produce abortions. But the answer comes back: "Isn't giving birth to children also work? You're just after an easy life; you want to be in the limelight. After all, what indispensable political work have you performed? Since you are so frightened of having children and are not willing to take responsibility once you have had them, why did you get married in the first place? No one forced you to." Under these conditions, it is impossible for women to escape this destiny of "backwardness." When women capable of working sacrifice their careers for the joys of motherhood, people always sing their praises.[1] But after ten years or so, they have no way of escaping the tragedy of "backwardness."[2] Even from my point of view, as a woman, there is nothing at-

---

1. The more literal rendering of this line is as follows: "When a woman capable of work sacrifices her career and becomes 'a virtuous wife, good mother' (*xianchi liangmu*) everybody sings her praises." This of course was the hated stereotype of domestic femininity that May Fourth radicals attacked so violently.—*Trans.*

2. The "tragedy of backwardness" is, of course, divorce.—*Trans.*

tractive about such "backward" elements. Their skin is beginning to wrinkle, their hair is growing thin, and fatigue is robbing them of their last traces of attractiveness. It should be self-evident that they are in a tragic situation. But whereas in the old society they would probably have been pitied and considered unfortunate, nowadays their tragedy is seen as something self-inflicted, as their just deserts. Is it not so that there is a discussion going on in legal circles as to whether divorces should be granted simply on the petition of one party or on the basis of mutual agreement? In the great majority of cases, it is the husband who petitions for divorce.[3] For the wife to do so, she must be leading an immoral life, and then of course she deserves to be cursed.

I myself am a woman, and I therefore understand the failings of women better than others.[4] But I also have a deeper understanding of what they suffer. Women are incapable of transcending the age they live in, of being perfect, or of being hard as steel. They are incapable of resisting all the temptations of society or all the silent oppression they suffer here in Yan'an. They each have their own past written in blood and tears; they have experienced great emotions—in elation as in depression, whether engaged in the lone battle of life or drawn into the humdrum stream of life. This is even truer of the women comrades who come to Yan'an, and I therefore have much sympathy for those fallen and classified as criminals. What is more, I hope that men, especially those in top positions, as well as women themselves, will consider the mistakes women commit in their social context. It would be better if there were less empty theorizing and more talk about real problems, so that theory and practice would not be divorced, and better if all Communist Party members were more responsible for their own moral conduct.[5] But we must also hope for a little more from our women comrades, especially those in Yan'an. We must urge ourselves on and develop our comradely feeling.

---

3. This was simply not true among peasants. Outside the revolutionary elite, divorce was the daughter-in-law's tool against an abusive mother-in-law and the wife's second greatest threat against her husband. The first was suicide.—*Trans.*

4. The word in the text is, once again, *quedian*. For other uses of this word to describe women's failings see *Shanghai, Spring 1930* and "Yecao."—*Trans.*

5. This passage has been edited to achieve sex neutrality. The version of this translation published earlier read, "if each Communist Party member were more responsible for his own moral conduct." Since Chinese does not give pronouns a gender, my revision is in fact truer to the text.—*Trans.*

People without ability have never been in a position to seize everything. Therefore, if women want equality, they must first strengthen themselves. There is no need to stress this point, since we all understand it. Today there are certain to be people who make fine speeches bragging about the need to acquire political power first. I would simply mention a few things that any frontliner, whether a proletarian, a fighter in the war of resistance, or a woman, should pay attention to in his or her everyday life:

1. Don't allow yourself to fall ill. A wild life can at times appear romantic, poetic, and attractive, but in today's conditions it is inappropriate. You are the best keeper of your life. There is nothing more unfortunate nowadays than to lose your health. It is closest to your heart. The only thing to do is keep a close watch on it, pay careful attention to it, and cherish it.

2. Make sure you are happy. Only when you are happy can you be youthful, active, fulfilled in your life, and steadfast in the face of all difficulties; only then will you see a future ahead of you and know how to enjoy yourself. This sort of happiness is not a life of contentment, but a life of struggle and of advance. Therefore we should all do some meaningful work each day and some reading, so that each of us is in a position to give something to others. Loafing about simply encourages the feeling that life is hollow, feeble, and in decay.

3. Use your brain, and make a habit of doing so. Correct any tendency not to think and ponder, or to swim with the current. Before you say or do anything, think whether what you are saying is right, whether that is the most suitable way of dealing with the problem, whether it goes against your own principles, whether you feel you can take responsibility for it. Then you will have no cause to regret your actions later.[6] This is what is known as acting rationally. It is the best way of avoiding the pitfalls of sweet words and honeyed phrases, of being sidetracked by petty gains, of wasting our emotions and wasting our lives.

4. Resolution in hardship, perseverance to the end. Aware, modern women should identify and cast off all their rosy illusions. Happiness is to take up the struggle in the midst of

---

6. The important term is *houwu*, "regret," a constant theme in the writer's earliest fiction.—*Trans.*

the raging storm and not to pluck the lute in the moonlight or recite poetry among the blossoms. In the absence of the greatest resolution, it is very easy to falter in mid-path. Not to suffer is to become degenerate. The strength to carry on should be nurtured through the quality of "perseverance." People without great aims and ambitions rarely have the firmness of purpose that does not covet petty advantages or seek a comfortable existence. But only those who have aims and ambitions for the benefit, not of the individual, but of humankind as a whole can persevere to the end.

3 August, dawn

Postscript. On rereading this article, it seems to me that there is much room for improvement in the passage on what we should expect from women, but because I have to meet a deadline with the manuscript, I have no time to revise it. But I also feel that there are some things that, if said by a leader before a big audience, would probably evoke satisfaction. But when they are written by a woman, they are more than likely to be demolished. But since I have written it, I offer it as I always intended, for the perusal of those people who have similar views.

Translated by Gregor Bento

DAUGHTER OF THE CHINESE PEOPLE

Ding Ling

I am a Chinese writer, a daughter of the Chinese people. I was raised and educated by the harsh life which the Chinese people have lived. It was possible for me to follow the footsteps of the people in my work and writing. For sixty years, it can be said, I have experienced all kinds of sorrows and have gone through extreme hardship. Now, being seventy-seven years old, I have only one wish left: to continue struggling for the cause of the people. As the Chinese saying goes, "Bend oneself to a task and exert oneself to the utmost; give one's all until one's heart stops beating."

I was born in 1904, at the beginning of the twentieth century and [in] the last years of the Qing dynasty. My family was a wealthy and influential clan, and from generation to generation they were government officials. In this family there were all the characters described in the classical Chinese novel *The Dream of the Red Chamber* and *Ru Lin Wai,* the sarcastic saga lampooning Chinese scholars of the Ming. Actually my family was the epitome of a waning feudal family, full of stories of very stirring contradictions. Little by little, parts of the clan disintegrated and declined. My father was an example. By the time of his death, when I was only four years old, he had exhausted all his fortune. I became a poor orphan and my lonely childhood helped me to understand deeply the tragic fate of the people in this twentieth-century feudal society, and the anxiety of the people. This is the reason why I am so fond of reading classical Chinese novels. I felt that they reflected my time and society, and gave me comfort as well as knowledge. I also enjoyed reading European literature and the nineteenth-century novel. This sowed the seed for what would later be my literary career. But even more fortunate, I had an intelligent mother. Once she be-

Ding Ling in 1979 at The Friendship Hotel in Beijing, where she was lodged following her release from prison.

came a widow, she managed to free herself from the bonds of the feudal family, fought her way into society, and supported herself by teaching. She not only accepted the concept of Western democracy, but also held a vague hope for a socialist revolution. She often told me her impassioned and heroic stories. Because of these early influences, I was able to discard the sadness which was gathering in my young heart. In 1919, the dawn of the May Fourth Movement, I was fourteen years old. My mother and I both participated in the movement, which inspired me greatly. That movement liberated me from the small world I used to live in, and in which I thought that education only would lead to personal success and create for one the possibility of having the upper hand in the society. That movement taught me to care about the world, the condition of the people, and the country and [about] the necessity to liberate China from thousands of years of feudal shackles and hundreds of years of colonialism. So I went to Chong Sha and Shanghai and entered the first common school for girls, where I met and was influenced by the famous revolutionaries of that time. I participated in some of the mass movements. The Chinese Communist Party then was in its early stages, seeking the path to connect Marxism with the Chinese reality. Because of my *petit bourgeois* fantasy I wanted to soar high in an utterly free sky, but in face of the dark reality of the time I was doomed to fail, and sank in an abyss of misery. I felt lonely and frustrated. I wanted to speak up and shout loudly but I had no way to do so except to pick up my pen and write down my anger and rebellion against the old Chinese feudal society. Therefore, it was only natural for me to follow my predecessors, Lu Xun, Qu Chiu-bai, Mao Dun, and like them, I did not write for art's sake or for my own amusement. I wanted to write for the people, the liberation of the nation, the country's independence, democracy, the progress of the society. Many of my contemporaries and many of the younger generation also joined the literary field because of these reasons. I don't mean to imply that there are no people in China who don't believe in art for art's sake.

After the failure of the 1927 revolution the Communists were massacred by the KMT counterrevolutionaries. I couldn't avoid thinking about what the way out for China might be. Naturally, I stood on the side of the people and my thinking moved gradually more and more toward the Left. Even though at that time I had little fame as a writer, still I could use the fame I had to influence some influential people. I could have found myself a job that paid well and gradually have climbed into upper-class society. Some of my friends did this. But it was against my desires. I despised this kind of personal vanity and selfishness and resolutely went my own way.

In the thirties when white territory came more and more under the KMT reactionaries, I joined the Leftist Writers' Association and then, soon after, the Communist Party. I wanted to immerse myself into the people, be with the people to share their sorrows and fate, survive as part of their survival. This was reflected in my writing: From writing about the *petit bourgeois* woman who rebelled against—and denounced—feudal society in the late twenties, I became a spokesperson for the working people. This path I chose was not tolerated by the ruling class. It was a time when criminal charges due to one's writing was a common practice.

Exactly fifty years ago, my husband, Hu Yeping, and five other members of the Leftist Writers' Association (including Ron Shi) and some dozen other revolutionaries were executed by the Shanghai garrison headquarters in Longhua prison. Some friends might be surprised: How could they, without any court preceedings, fire machine guns at the young writers? But merely a book with red covers was reason enough for arrest and execution. The writer shared the fate of all other revolutionary martyrs. This illustrates the major characteristic of the new Chinese literature: Its growth is inseparable from politics. The blossoms of the new literature are stained with the blood of martyrs.

In May of 1933, I also was secretly arrested and thrown into jail. But because of the Chinese Alliance to Safeguard Human Rights rally behind me (Soong Qingling, Cai Yunpai, Lu Xun, Yang Sinfou, and others belonged to it), and also because of the support I received from internationally known persons, I did not die. But my works and books were banned and, at the same time, articles which spread political rumors and personal attacks were allowed in the newspapers. Three years later, because of Lu Xun and the Communist Party, I was able to escape from Nanjung and get to the liberated area Xan Pai revolutionary base. At last I was reunited with the people.

During the Anti-Japanese War I traveled with the army to the front to do propaganda work and in Yanan also did literary work. During the war of liberation I participated in the land reform, a movement to abolish the system of feudal ownership. After the founding of New China I participated in organizing and leading literary courses. Those were the times when I often forgot I was a writer. I drowned myself in work and thought that I could be quite satisfied in serving the people and my talent could be fulfilled by being a propaganda worker or a party secretary in a village. Only when I was transferred from this radical work did I then feel deep in my heart those lovable characters and those thrilling scenes which I could not help but want to put down on paper. So I wrote! I wrote novels, prose-fiction, and essays.

When I am writing I never think about the restriction of the form nor what kind of ideology I should tie myself to, nor do I worry about the kind of reaction I will receive. I believed all this was for others to judge—after I had finished and after publication. I write spontaneously—and freely feel and think. I only ask myself to maintain those feelings which initially moved me and not distort those people I love and admire so much.

Many friends and fellow writers are concerned about what I went through these past decades. There are also those who know about the rough and bumpy life of a Chinese revolutionary and are concerned about the future of China. This is natural; I can understand it. And I want to use this opportunity to thank my friends and colleagues.

Way back in 1955, another comrade and myself were identified as an anti-party clique. We were accused of engaging in counterrevolutionary activities and spreading the bourgeois belief in "one bookism." At the time, there were many people who thought this unfair. My husband, Chen Ming, and I lawfully took this to court. Then came 1957, when Chen Ming and I and many other comrades were branded as rightists in the Anti-Rightist Movement which went off limits. I was openly criticized and accused in all the nationwide newspapers and magazines. But since 1976, especially after the eleventh party congress, our party has exposed the crimes committed by the Gang of Four, sincerely criticized the ultra-left mistakes, putting much effort on restoring the precious tradition of judging according to facts. The correction of this historical mistake that began twenty-two years ago was made possible by the encouragement of the new party leadership: Truth was finally restored, and the falsehood of my not being a Marxist and of the so-called anti-party clique was repudiated.

Today, history has opened a new page: My party membership was restored, my salary was restored, and I can write again. I was also elected to the People's Political Consultative Congress and made vice chairman of the Chinese Writers' Association. Within the Association those who were branded rightists because of me have all been rehabilitated. They are all now working in responsible positions in the Association and have been given the chance to write again. Those who helped bring about this wrongdoing have also learned a lot. They have openly apologized. Now we are all working for the realization of the four modernizations and for the new flowering of literature.

After the Anti-Rightist Movement in 1957 I gathered up my courage and with the passionate devotion and love given me by the party and the people, and put aside the rightist cap and all the inevitable obstacles. Chen Ming and I went to Bai Da Huang to open up a new path in life. I performed manual labor, worked as a teacher, and organized housewives—until the beginning of the Cultural Revolution.

I did not go to Bai Da Huang as a punishment given me by the party. After I was criticized I felt I could not close my door and write in Beijing; I could not bear being so far from the life of the people. I could stand being criticized, punished, not having a job or income, but what I could not stand was being expelled from the party—because that meant being apart from the people! But past experience told me that if I did not submit to the political persecution, that would be an excuse to add to my punishment. I had to swallow this bitter herb. Therefore, I submitted and asked to be sent to the bottom of society—to a place where conditions were the most severe, to be with the working people in order to gain their understanding and forgiveness. I asked, therefore, to be sent to Bai Da Huang. It was not possible to refuse my request.

Going through the eight years of the Anti-Japanese War and the four years of the War of Liberation greatly helped me and made it possible for me to bear this severe new test. After working in the fields for a year, I became the Chinese language teacher for the production team. My work was praised by the people and the leaders of the farm. Several times they even tried to have the rightist label which was keeping me and the revolution apart taken away from me. In these years I learned about life all over again and made many good friends.

Regaining the understanding of the people was a very precious thing. It was the best medicine for me then, curing me of my sadness. I will always remember them. At the time when the party leadership agreed to provide me with the conditions to write, the Cultural Revolution broke out. Our party has by now made a historical and comprehensive analysis of this so-called Cultural Revolution. It was an internal disorder brought on by the mistakes committed by the leadership and it was used by the counterrevolutionary clique. China and the Chinese people suffered greatly because of it. It is not hard to imagine that even though I have been a dead tiger I could not escape the disasters. In this period of tremendous destruction, the party's policy was destroyed, its tradition was abandoned and the cadres and the masses were savagely trampled. I myself also endured all kinds of torture. Even though I was helped and protected by many kindhearted people in those hard times, whom I'll never forget, this could not prevent what was to come. My neighbor once said to me, "Death is better than the life you are living now." In April 1970, using the name of The Military Controlling Committee, the Gang of Four arrested me. When they were putting the handcuffs on me, the first thought that ran through my head was "My saviours have come." It was in this way that I ended my twelve years at Bai Da Huang and started my prison life, which lasted for the next five years.

Life in prison was relatively quiet. One could read the *People's Daily* and *The Red Flag*. The healthy forces within the party began resisting the treacherous designs of the Gang of Four at that time. Even in prison I felt the effect. After the downfall of Ling Biao, the food in prison improved immediately. We also could go outside our cells every day and borrow books to read. It was at that time that I read the works of Marx and Engles and much of Lu Xun. This gave me great comfort. I persisted in doing exercises in prison, practiced tai ji, and jogged. In order to prevent the deterioration of my speech, since I rarely had the chance to talk to anyone, I used to recite poetry and sing quietly. In 1975, when Deng Xiaoping was in charge of the leadership, many people were released from prison, myself and Chen Ming among them.

In 1975, I was finally reunited with Chen Ming. For five years I hadn't known his whereabouts. Seeing each other again was, of course, a joyous moment, and at the same time we also reestablished correspondence with our son and daughter. In early 1979, with the permission of the central committee of the party, we returned to Peking. During the last two years all my banned books were reprinted; in addition, two new books of mine were published.

This is my life, an ordinary one. Now, as I search within me I truly cannot find any resentment. It is true though that I have had some losses myself, but the losses of the party, the people, and the country were greater than mine. When I was confronted with misfortunes, the party and the people were suffering too. Many people who contributed more than I to the revolution suffered greater misfortunes. Being a revolutionary and a revolutionary writer, how can one wish that there would be more setbacks?

Our country is now trying to recover and is taking steps toward a new future. The situation easily makes one think of the patriotic, classical poets who drowned in their sorrows and were melancholy up to their bitter end. I will not mourn over yesterday's suffering. Furthermore, I will never be one of those who, sincere as they are in their analysis of the situation, ignore the complete picture and see only one part of it. By doing this, they actually cannot help in the reconstruction of the country. I firmly believe that the one billion people of China must unite into one under the leadership of the Communist Party. We must work and study hard, liberate our thoughts, sum up our past experiences, and develop a democratic spirit. Only then can our country contribute to the progress of mankind and world peace, and our literature will enrich the world with its unique cultural experiences. Thank you.

10 October, 1981
Iowa City

*Translated by Kathy Yeh and Marcelia Yeh,
Marilyn Chin, and Anna Lillios*

HOW I EXPERIENCED
THE CULTURAL REVOLUTION

Dai Qing

Perhaps without the student movement of 1989, the Cultural Revolution would be a forgotten chapter in Chinese history by now. There are external resemblances between the two events: flags, banners, and protest marches; naive, obstinate, genuinely enthusiastic students; and blood and oppression. But the resemblance is in form only. In 1966 we took to the streets for a god in us, Chairman Mao, the red sun, the star of deliverance. Our children, on the other hand, took to the streets in order to bring down this god in them; they no longer wanted others to think for them, to speak for them, to order them around. They no longer wanted to be tools, but human beings.

Twenty-nine years ago young people thought differently. In March 1966, I had just finished my studies at the College for Military Technology in Harbin, Heilongjiang Province. My field of specialization was systems for the automatic guidance and control of missiles, and specifically research on high speed precision gyroscopes, which are the core pieces of such systems. I worked in a completely insulated, dust-free lab. I didn't worry much, I lived in the belief that I wanted to become a good engineer for the nation that had raised me.

As far back as we could remember, we had been living in a closed society. All the terms in which we thought followed the "teachings" of Mao Zedong. If the people at the top said the Soviet Union was our big brother, then it was our big brother. If they said the Soviets were social imperialists, then they were social imperialists. We did not doubt that Chairman Mao was "the leader of all oppressed peoples in the world" and that the sky was "radiant and blue above the liberated regions." We lived simply and modestly, wore patched clothing, cut our hair short,

Kosima Liu-Weber

Dai Qing at the women's salon

and combed it smooth. We believed our intellectual life was rich and pure. Luxury and pleasure were things we despised. After all, we were revolutionaries, and how else could you imagine a revolutionary?

In early summer of 1966—I had just started my job three months before—articles with such titles as "Down with the Cattle Devils and Snake Spirits" began to appear in the newspapers. Up to that point, I had hardly read newspapers, only pretending to read political journals sometimes, in order not to be considered "backward." I knew nobody in politics and cultural life and had no idea that infamous political motives might be concealed behind theater reviews.

In China, political decisions have always been made in secret and by a few top government executives. Now Mao in person had turned to the public. It is impossible to find the words to describe how moved we were, what solidarity we felt when we read that wall newspaper with the heading "Bomb the Headquarters!" We immediately went into action. If Mao had given the order "Die!" thousands of young people would have joyfully marched off to be slaughtered. Not that we understood what was involved in the power struggles within the leadership, or that we were dissatisfied with our social situation. As a graduate in a technical field, I couldn't have wished for a better job. I felt no hostility toward the government and the officials. I didn't even know that there were thousands of people who, though mute with fear, were full of hatred for a government that had repeatedly oppressed people and liquidated human beings.

We followed Mao's call and went into action, full of naiveté, with no thought for the consequences. Our passion was completely blind, we had no inside information. Day and night we wrote articles full of condemnation, and printed leaflets. We went to the university in order to watch the mass meetings at which the "crimes of the black band" were denounced. We saw sensitive, polite professors being humiliated, and we suppressed all feelings of compassion and cowardice. We waved the Little Red Book when we walked the many miles to such meetings. Commonly held views can weld total strangers into lifelong friends.

We were denied insight into the mystery of why, in a closed and ideologically controlled society, the masses were suddenly supposed to participate in political trials. We felt we were actually the rulers of the country and believed we were responsible for saving our society. Hadn't Mao instructed us, "Take care of

81

the business of the state, lead the Great Proletarian Cultural Revolution to complete victory!'"?

In the old days I had read Andersen, Pushkin, Dickens, Hugo, Goethe, and Mark Twain, but hardly any works by Chinese authors. I had found Chinese writers stiff and depressing. In the fall of 1966 I suddenly discovered "loyalty." All of Chinese history, ancient and modern, and Chinese culture, in all its aspects, became imbued with the spirit of this "loyalty." I was so full of enthusiasm I couldn't sleep. How foolish I had been till then not to understand: loyalty to Chairman Mao, to his ideas, to his political line, to his words, to his smile, and to the frown on his forehead. Without him there could be no new China, no revolution, nothing—we had nothing at all without him. The word "loyalty" epitomized all our convictions, our passion, our entire lives. We were engulfed in the red ocean of loyalty. Half a century had passed since the last emperor had renounced the throne; now the classic model of the right relationship between a ruler and his subjects celebrated its resurrection in "socialist" China.

Not one family was spared during the madness. My stepgrandmother was sent to the countryside as the "wife of a big landowner" because a few silver coins had been found during a search of her suitcases. My stepfather relapsed into a schizophrenic condition to which he had fallen prey in 1942 during the political purges in Yan'an. When my brother went to pick him up in Heilongjiang, he found him kneeling at minus twenty-two degrees Fahrenheit [about minus forty-four degrees Celsius], begging for Chairman Mao's forgiveness. As a "revisionist" and a "renegade," my mother was thrown into prison. Our maid was freed from "exploitation" and thrown out of the house. My younger brothers, between nine and thirteen years old, learned to bake rolls from cornmeal: the money they were given was not enough to buy anything else. The winter of 1966–67 was extremely cold. There was nothing but hostility, practically everyone had to prepare to be deserted by their relatives for political reasons. Thousands committed suicide during this period, some to escape the humiliations, but most because their family members had decided to "side with the revolution."

Gradually we discovered that our struggle was senseless. No matter how sincerely and with what valid arguments we fought or supported something, everything was decided by the balance of power at the top. In 1967, my friends and I began to feel we had been deceived. We withdrew from the movement, stopped being members of any organization, and lived for the moment. We married and had children. But our apparent light-heartedness was only on the surface; in reality the movement had not let go of us. Dejectedly we watched as young people from the cities were banished to rural areas, as armed clashes among the population spread across the entire country, as power struggles were waged in the work units and cities, and as the army finally took command. Politicians appeared on the stage and vanished again. We no longer had any illusions of being revolutionaries; we began soberly to assess our experiences, all that we had enthusiastically supported or struggled against. As yet, no one dared to question the doctrine; Marxism-Leninism was still sacred to us, though hard to understand.

To this day it is not known why Lin Biao, then minister of defense, suddenly gave the order in 1969 to prepare for a world war, the so-called Order Number One. Field marshals were assigned to different provinces and regions. Except for a small number who stayed behind, engineers who were working on missile projects were sent to the rural areas as a "national resource" that had to be protected. Together with other colleagues, I worked on land reclamation projects in army farms, first on the coast of Guangdong Province and later in Hunan. Covered with mud from head to foot and so exhausted that at night we no longer had the strength to turn over in bed, we had no idea that our projects were classic cases of environmental destruction. When my husband and I were sent to the countryside, my daughter was barely a year old. Unfortunately all my Beijing relatives shared our fate, so that no one could look after our daughter, whom we had to leave behind. A worker, who had been a complete stranger to me until then, took her in. When I saw my daughter again, she was three and a half.

I have a strong constitution, so the hard physical labor didn't bother me. Besides, I had learned from the time I was little that physical work was "honorable and sacred." When I set out to do agricultural labor, I actually believed that "the sweat of physical work" would "cleanse my soul." It was only the actual experience of moving along step by step on endless fields as a supervised laborer, and living together daily with other manual laborers, that gradually made it clear to me that physical work is simply another form of work and that its productive value is limited, that a person's best character traits are by no means formed only while planting rice and hauling clay. Then why, why did Mao Zedong constantly make disparaging statements about the value of intellectual work?

During my work on the army farms, I first observed at close range the narrow-minded ignorance, hypocrisy, arrogance, and intrigue that exist within the army. The myth of the glory and purity of the army, of the "flesh-and-blood relationship" between the people and the army, which had been propagated tirelessly since 1968, dissolved into thin air. The army was nothing but an armed political structure that functioned as an extension of the political system. Why had the military theory of the party elevated the army to something sacred, full of goodness and humanity?

It was in this out-of-the-way corner, of all places, after three years of political abstinence and two more years of agricultural work, that I was suddenly accused of being the ringleader of a counterrevolutionary organization, the "May 16 Group." My husband and I decided to flee. We did not want to wait with folded hands until we were arrested. We had barely arrived in Beijing (by a very roundabout route) and embraced our little daughter in tears when a man from the military committee of my unit appeared on the scene and barked at us: "I suppose you want a taste of the dictatorship of the proletariat!" I was sure this meant prison or, worse yet, one of the arrest cells in the unit referred to as a "study group." I waited, but no one came to arrest me. Days passed. Finally, I heard that Lin Biao and his plane had crashed in Mongolia. The "dictatorship of the proletariat" was no longer interested in me. Only then did I find out that the "May 16 Group" had been a figment of the imagination of the Lin Biao group. I came to the sad conclusion that every time there are power struggles at the top in an undemocratic society, a large number of innocent people have to suffer as window dressing or as a sacrificial offering. Don't victorious generals also turn the corpses of fallen soldiers into little stars on their epaulets?

I had long since lost any interest in politics. The star of hope that appeared in the sky one drizzling "memorial day for the dead," on 5 April 1976, came as a complete surprise to me. Disguised as grief for deceased Prime Minister Zhou Enlai, the suppressed anger of the population against the Maoist dictatorship was vented indirectly but persistently. Mao was still alive at the time. On his last legs, the old man who had commanded the party for forty-one years gave orders that the protest was to be quelled. If we disregard his later written directive ("Hold the course!"), this order was probably his last "gift" to the Chinese people. In the sea of white flowers, few people realized that he had set the Cultural Revolution going and only his death could put an end to this catastrophe.

Mao died. His wife and the officials who had served him as instruments for setting the Cultural Revolution in motion were arrested shortly thereafter. People were ecstatic and spoke of the "victories of October." New leaders assumed power and liberated and rehabilitated those who had been "purged" or "liquidated" during the incessant political struggles of the past decades: "Trotskyites," "Hu Feng elements," "rightist deviationists," "rightist opportunists," "supporters of the capitalist line." New policies were adopted: economic reconstruction, reform, openness.

Yet, just as Mao had assumed power with the help of the army twenty-seven years earlier, these people had also not come to power in a democratic way—they too owed their positions to the army. That is why inevitably a shadow still clouded all the jubilation and hope. The catchword "class struggle" was replaced by the "Four Principles." But we were left with the memory of the prophecy of the old man who had died, like a magic incantation: "A cultural revolution every twenty years."

The nightmare was over. My stepfather and my stepgrandmother have since died. After her return from the "cadre school," my mother no longer wanted to be a "revolutionary," only a loving grandmother. My brothers and sisters passed the university admission test while still in the countryside, and subsequently left China to study abroad. Thirteen years after their parents, uncles, and aunts went to Tian'anmen Square, our children went there. The Chinese nation still has a long road, a very long road, to travel to democracy.

Translated by Ilze Mueller

85

THE EDUCATION OF A TEACHER IN THE CULTURAL REVOLUTION

Mavis Yen

When the Cultural Revolution broke out in in 1966, it was virtually a civil war. I was in Beijing, teaching English in a newly established foreign languages institute. All classes were stopped. As in other organizations, our top leadership was overthrown. Probably the stormiest period of all was in 1967 when the British chargé d'affaires' office was burned down by the Red Guards. In the major universities and even in our unprestigious little institute, fighting broke out between the two factions of Red Guards. So chaotic was the situation that People's Liberation Army teams were sent to restore order throughout the country.

Army personnel arrived at our institute early in 1968. They immediately began reconciling the two Red Guard factions and ordered all absentee students to return. Our top administrators had already been overthrown and ultimately a revolutionary committee was formed. But in the meantime, a campaign was launched to ferret out undesirables among the middle- and lower-level administrators and others. Three categories were targeted in our institute: old revolutionaries, teachers, and those with overseas backgrounds. Along with a dozen or so other teachers and vice-presidents, I was placed under house arrest within the institute. We were interrogated and our life histories were examined.

At first our jailers were very strict. Nevertheless, individual students and workers who had access to us showed their friendliness when no one else was around. I made a number of good friends while I was locked up. One of the teachers, also under arrest, was ordered to fetch my meals from the canteen. This was not intended to make life easier but to put pressure on me. She would always get me the best dishes. I almost starved for a week when one of the school doctors shared a room with me. She would only get me a couple of steamed buns, which she hid in a haversack. She admitted to me that she felt a terrible loss of face at having to do a task like that. The water she filled my thermos with was always lukewarm. I was glad when she was moved elsewhere.

One evening during this tense period, a quotation by Chairman Mao was broadcast. He said that all people under house arrest should be released. We arrestees were taken to a meeting at which the students put on a skit about how war criminals were working and remolding themselves under the watchful eyes of their fellow workers in a printing press. From that time on, the attitude toward us arrestees mellowed. Still time dragged on. A few months later, instead of returning to our original groups, each teacher was assigned to a class of students. Three women students came to take me to their dormitory where I was to sleep in the future. From then on, I was attached to their class and took part in their daily activities such as meetings, discussions, and manual work, even their self-criticism sessions—all directed at remolding our world outlook. We were kept busy all the time, morning, afternoon, and evening.

One night we were roused at midnight and told to prepare for war defense. The very next day we started building air-raid shelters. It was then announced that the institute would move to the town of Minggang in Henan Province in central China. This area had been chosen because it had plenty of rice to feed us, as well as electric power for language training. We teachers left the following week. As the institute had two batches of students, the first was sent to work in factories and allocated jobs directly from where they were working. A number from the second batch came with us, while the others went to work in factories temporarily. The rest of the staff also came to Minggang, and a small caretaker group was left behind.

Although Henan's winters are sometimes severe, the southernmost pocket where we were going was mild, like the rice-growing areas in the Yangzi River valley. We arrived after a rail journey of fourteen hours. We found Minggang was indeed a rich food-producing area. Not only was there plenty of rice, but every other day a free market was held of local farm produce. There was no such free market in Beijing. It was forbidden as a form of capitalism. Also, food prices in Minggang were far lower than in Beijing, and this induced family members who were reluctant to leave to join us.

The township was most hospitable. The women teachers and students of the English department were put up in the local veterinary station. Our kitchen was housed in a barn immediately opposite, above the Ming River, which flowed by the town. We ate in the open air. Several weeks later, we women teachers were moved to more spacious quarters in the local federation of supply and marketing cooperatives. It had an enormous courtyard and telephone connections to all parts of China. The supply and marketing co-ops were the lifeline of the rural economy. They marketed all the farm tools, basketware, carts, herbs, eggs, and other items, while supplying the countryside with industrial products.

Minggang lies on the Beijing-Wuhan railway running directly from north to south. This little marketing town, well known for its chickens, was laid out more or less symmetrically, with a main street down the center, two parallel dirt roads along which antiquated buses ran east and west, and a grid of untidy lanes in between. It boasted a cinema where many of our staff lived over the winter, as well as a drafty theater with broken windowpanes. The town authorities entertained us to an evening of Henan opera here. The locals spoke Mandarin with a lilt that we had to get used to, but they welcomed us with open arms. After all the shouting and noise in Beijing, it was a wonderful feeling. Never mind the dust and other primitive conditions.

This new atmosphere was a mixture of the old and the new. A legless man stationed outside the post office earned a living writing and reading letters for the illiterate. A number of small shops were always open. By contrast, the two state-owned general goods shops closed on Sundays and holidays. A rest house outside the train station catered to travelers' needs, and in the evenings entrepreneurs would sell cooked chickens and turtles, local delicacies, from here. After we teachers moved, we had to cross a wide wooden bridge over the Ming River to reach our kitchen. Early in the morning we would come across a cartload of firewood, ready for the market. Underneath, the drivers would still be snug in their quilts, the remains of a fire and cooking pots beside them—the storybook atmosphere once again.

At first we made mud bricks, dug ditches, worked on road construction, and swept the streets. When the weather was bad we had meetings, ferreting out bad elements and bad ideas. I was put in a labor squad led by the English department's former party secretary. She was an old revolutionary who had been top-pled early in the Cultural Revolution. We had already been in-vestigated, the storm had passed over our heads, so a few days after our arrival we decided to try the pork liver noodles offered by the restaurant opposite the railway station. To avoid attract-ing attention, we sat on tree trunks in the restaurant's kitchen. But I made the mistake of recommending the railway restaurant to a fellow teacher who joined us later and asked me about the town. He then seized the opportunity to put up a poster criti-cizing us for neglecting our remolding. Another time, on our Sunday off, we asked a waiter in the only other restaurant on the main street to open a can of pineapple for us as we had no can opener. Two other male teachers pounced on us. Up went another poster. We had been caught in the act of flaunting our bourgeois habits, it read. Posters always exaggerated. From then on, we would meet early at the railway station on Sundays and take the first train to another town. The only power the ex-party secretary had was over our little labor squad, but she really cared for us. In the hot season she would give us frequent ten-minute breaks. Of course, nobody ever returned till half an hour later!

In the spring we moved to the site just outside the town of a brand-new May Seventh cadre school, which was supplied with electric power. These premises had been built by members of a cultural organization in Beijing, but it had earned them severe criticism for putting their comfort before their remolding. So they decided to start again elsewhere and turned their base over to us.

Our new premises consisted of single-story brick rooms opening onto covered walkways. The floors were of dirt and the ceilings high. There was ample space between the walls and eaves for the escape of smoke and carbon monoxide, as well as a flow of air in hot weather. When it rained, as it often did, from my top bunk I would delight in the misty scene laid out before me, of hills and low-lying fields, just as in a Chinese painting.

We were surrounded by a moat, with toilets spaced out along two sides. Intruders sometimes made off with some of the night soil in the early hours of the morning. One of our jobs was to carry the night soil to the fields, where we mixed it with earth and sealed it up for future use. We did try to grow our own vegetables, but the soil was so poor that we turned the land into rice fields. This meant building channels to lead water to the fields, one layer lower than the next. We had to plow the soil first and then go over it with a harrow drawn by a buffalo. Only when we could see ourselves reflected in the water were the fields smooth enough.

By June it was time to harvest the wheat. It was imperative to finish the work before the rains set in. The peasants always began ahead of us. We would wake up to find them already cutting their wheat in the dark. The first three days we had to work till dark to finish the cutting. On our way back to our base, we would see the peasants working by moonlight. We were the stupid ones, slogging our guts out in the heat of day. The peasants worked in the cool of darkness and slept by day. We even tried to make mud bricks wearing galoshes. How ridiculous we were!

The cooks, who were also teachers, gave us party food the first three days to encourage us. After that, we went back to plain food and worked on the threshing ground. Every day we had to dismantle the wheat stacks and lay the wheat out. We dragged a heavy stone mill round and round. At the end of the day we had to re-stack again, day after day, until the job was completed. We went on to pick the cotton and harvest the sorghum and corn. We thinned the turnip beds. The squad leader frequently assigned me to night-watch duty because she knew I liked it. I would watch the shooting stars and wonder when we would return to Beijing.

By now the second batch of students had already been in the institute two years in excess of their courses and were still living on student subsidies. It was decided to graduate them so they could receive full subsidies, while retaining them for further study in Minggang. In order to house them, we started a building program after the wheat harvest, although it was only mud-brick housing. We teachers laid the foundations and put on the roofs, while the students did the rest.

We went on to build more housing. This was the life for me, I was thinking, when I was called aside and told I had been transferred to the teaching section to do the typing. Only young people were assigned to teach. The experienced teachers had to do farm work.

All along in the dominant thought of everyone was when we might return to Beijing. Down in Minggang we could only deduce what was going on in the Cultural Revolution. We scanned the newspapers to see which high official's name had disappeared or reappeared. We analyzed every scrap of information we could glean.

Meanwhile, the ferreting out of bad elements went on. Not

even the students were immune. One Red Guard faction had been charged with taking part in the burning down of the British charge d'affaires' office. They had to go through a trial by innuendo—not a pleasant experience—before they were finally cleared.

During 1971 new developments took place. China began to open up to the outside world. Now we knew we would return to Beijing. To my surprise, I returned with the students before the next wheat harvesting was completed. The rest of the people from the institute followed a few months later, and from then on our lives gradually returned to normal. Teachers became respected once more. After all, traditional values die very hard in China.

Demonstration in April 1989

A LETTER FROM BEIJING,
JUNE 1989

Ya Lu

My dear sister,

It's been a long time since I wrote to you. From morning till night I am busy with household chores, with my daughter, and with preparations for teaching. There's always something to do. I've been meaning to write you for a long time, but I am afraid. Since one of my students happens to be going to America for college, I'll give her this letter for you.

I want to tell you about the evening of 3 June, which I will not forget as long as I live. After work I went to our parents' house at five. Since their anniversary is approaching, I wanted to buy a cake, fish, and vegetables in the Chongwenmen market. During supper we spoke about the little celebration. Father and Mother were not in favor of it, for the situation in Beijing was very tense. The night before, four people had been run over by an army truck in the street, and more and more curious observers kept coming to Tian'anmen Square. While we were talking about this, there was an urgent announcement on television: civilians were not to go into the streets or stand by the roadside. Everyone was to stay at home. We immediately realized that the situation was serious and knew that something unusual was about to happen.

In spite of the announcement, my husband went out on the street—the appeal of the forbidden was stronger than the prohibition. After the dishes had been washed, Father too went outside, and around 8:00 P.M. the three of us (Juanjuan, Mother, and I) also wanted to go for a short walk. Our little daughter immediately found a few playmates by the courtyard gate. I stopped, Mother continued walking. I had a good view of the main street. Many people were biking home. Their faces seemed calm, they showed no particular excitement. Mother came back about an hour later, and the three of us went home.

We bathed and, at about half past nine, we suddenly heard shots. At first, I did not realize what sort of noise it was. Were those shots or fireworks? I went to the window and turned numb. I saw four people carrying away someone who had been injured, followed by another man with a second injured person. They ran to the little clinic in our courtyard.

Somebody had been shooting at people! While I was overwhelmed with immense fear, I also became very sad.

I turned around and saw Mother and my child sitting on the bed. I couldn't tell them about this horrifying sight; I had to keep the truth from them. They could not endure such a cruel truth. So I swallowed my tears and said that probably only a few warning shots had been fired.

After the two of them had fallen asleep, I crept outside to see what had become of the men. They must come home at once! I had to run against the flow of pedestrians, for everyone was rushing past me in the opposite direction. I saw several injured persons being taken in the direction of the Railroad Hospital on three-wheel bikes. Amid the confusion, I saw my husband, and part of my worry left me. Somebody told me that people had seen an old man and a child lying on the ground shot to death, and that nobody could come to their assistance. My heart was beating furiously. I continued running, and I finally found Father. He was listening to someone recounting what had happened. I pulled him away, and we all went home. I had to make him realize how dangerous the situation was, and that every shot could hit somebody.

At one in the morning we were all in bed, but none of us could sleep. Again we went outside. Although we were scared, we had to see what had happened. From the eleventh floor of our building we had a good view of our street. We saw army vehicles driving east toward Tian'anmen Square. When I saw that, all hope left me.

On the army vehicles we read banners with the inscription, "The People's Liberation Army loves the population of the capital." Although the cars were camouflaged, soldiers with their steel helmets and loaded guns were clearly recognizable. Dear sister, such sights cause a person incredible pain. And all the while you could hear shots—nobody knows how many people were killed that night.

When I think about it today, I realize how dangerous the sit-

Tian'anman Square, May 23, 1989

Tian'anman Square, June 3, 1989

uation was for us, for any one of the bullets could have hit us too. But at the time we were so fascinated that this simply did not register. All I could see were the tanks being stopped by civilians. In front of the Military Museum, soldiers suddenly jumped out of a vehicle and beat people savagely with sticks. Rocks were flying. As I found out later, fourteen wounded people had been brought to the little clinic in our yard at around ten. Lines of injured people formed in front of the gate of the Railroad Hospital. They said that by 7 June forty-two persons had died of their injuries in that hospital alone. A few blocks down the street, by the Muxidi, sixteen persons were shot at the entrance or inside their apartments. Even officials who were protesting in the streets were simply gunned down. The next day, a Sunday, will go down in our history as a Black Day. How many people were really murdered? Nobody here knows, and no one here will find out, either. Probably you who are abroad know more than we do.

A few days later I woke up startled from my dreams, my pillow was wet with tears. How are we to live under such circumstances? I don't know. I do know that my will to live is so strong that it allows me to go on functioning in this cruel situation. We've all been dealing with this terrible situation in our own way: Mother's blood-sugar level has gone up again, and Father's blood pressure is too high. When I fell off my bike yesterday I hardly felt the pain of the injury; my heart is still numb with a greater pain. Every morning when I say goodbye to Juanjuan at nursery school, I don't know if it is the last time, if we will ever see each other again. Right now, playing cards are sold-out here in Beijing, and it is also impossible to get hold of mah-jong games. People have become silent and apathetic.

Dear sister, thank you for thinking of us, of our country. When I hear your voice on the phone, I feel as though you are here with us. You won't be able to come home this year. But you know, behind all the sadness, the energy to go on living must assert itself. We here have no more hope left anyway, and so we place our hopes in you. You must go on studying hard and find your way. Don't worry about the way we live. We cannot say when martial law will be revoked again. Basically, nothing is going to change in the near future. And I don't know what things will look like a couple of years from now. Right now, I have only one favor to ask you: Do not be thoughtless enough to return. Find out exactly how things are going here, so that you don't get into trouble.

I've been listening to the radio a lot recently. The more I hear, the more resigned I become. A sick society broadcasts its sick thoughts by radio as well. I really don't know how long this will go on. Don't worry about our parents, I'll take care of them. Look after yourself and use the time you have. I send you a hug from far away.

Your sister

P.S. Juanjuan practices her violin an hour a day and is making a lot of progress. I am convinced I'm being a good mother in teaching her. Give our regards to your husband too. I know it will be a long time before I can write another letter like this.

Translated by Ilze Mueller

The Goddess of Democracy (postcard)

CHINA'S ONE-CHILD POLICY

Melinda Tankard Reist

China enforces an intrusive one-child-per-couple birth control policy (only slightly relaxed in outlying regions) with fertility decisions controlled by the state. A couple is not free to decide when to have children, nor how many to have. This freedom is cherished by women in other parts of the world and upheld as a human right in various conventions. In China, the central government sets birth targets using a stringent system of rewards and punishments. Every Chinese person belongs to a work unit, and every unit has a birth control committee headed by party officials.

China is the most populous country in the world, with a current population of 1.18 billion. It is hoping to limit the size of its population to between 1.5 billion and 1.6 billion by the middle of the next century, although many experts have described such a target as unrealistic.[1] The numbers for 1992 show unprecedented falls in the birth rate, with the total fertility rate at 1.8 to 1.9, which is below the standard replacement of 2.1. If success is measured only by demographic impact, then China's is a successful program. But at what cost?

History of the Program

Chairman Mao originally thought China's large population was an asset, because under socialism it meant unlimited production. He predicted China would soon be a wealthy and prosperous country. Other Chinese spokesmen at that time denounced birth control as reactionary, anti-humanitarian, and a foreign plot "to kill off the Chinese people without shedding blood."[2]

The first PRC (People's Republic of China) census, in 1953, found one hundred million more people than expected, promp-

98

Nelly Rau-Häring

Factory nursery school

ting the first birth control campaign in 1955. It was interrupted by the disastrous Great Leap Forward campaign of 1958. In 1962 another birth control campaign began, which was similarly interrupted in 1966 by the Great Proletarian Cultural Revolution. The third campaign was launched in 1969. The Gang of Four made birth control part of the class struggle and the dictatorship of the proletariat. The right to bear children was considered a "bourgeois right."

The one-child policy was announced in 1979 and put into place two years later. Women pregnant without a permit were "mobilized" to undergo abortions. All provinces were required to adopt family planning regulations modeled on a draft version prepared in Beijing, but when ambitious targets were still not met, a new drive began in 1983. This required IUDs (intrauterine devices) for all women with one child, sterilization for all couples with two or more children, and abortion for all unauthorized pregnancies. Third and later births were "absolutely prohibited."

In 1983 provincial authorities estimated the numbers of eligible couples and planned to sterilize them all within the next three years. In that year alone there were approximately 21 million sterilizations, 18 million IUD insertions, and 14 million abortions. This led to great resentment among the people, and family planning work was now officially called on to be fairer and more reasonable. But implementation lagged and in 1985 there were new demands for population control. Tighter regulations were adopted at the provincial level. In 1987 family planning workers were told to "take action quickly," "resolutely," and "decisively" and to obtain "practical results."[3]

Despite the strict regulations, the urgent exhortations to curb birth rates, and the widespread unequivocal evidence of coercion in the program, China denies it requires or endorses coercion.

Coercion

A young woman in my factory had been unable to conceive a child despite three years of trying—and three successive birth quotas. Her problem had finally been diagnosed as an ovarian tumor. When surgery was performed, not one but both ovaries were discovered to be diseased. The right ovary, which was completely enveloped by a large tumor, was removed. The left ovary, which had a small, benign tumor, was left alone, for the sake of the female hormones the undiseased portion would continue to produce. In two or three years, the surgeon declared, it too would have to be removed. In the meantime it would be quite impossible for her to conceive a child.

Hearing this, I had listed her on the population control registers as a *bu yun*, a "barren" woman, and revoked her birth quota. Several months later, to everyone's utter amazement, she had gotten pregnant. The doctors declared it a miracle. Her fellow workers offered their congratulations. I went to offer my personal best wishes and found her delirious with joy.

The problem was that I had no remaining birth quotas for 1984. Not only that, but I had already announced who was to receive quotas in 1985. . . . Her situation was so unusual that it cried out for a kind and sympathetic response.

The quota was denied and the woman forced to abort.[4]

The pitting of woman against woman is particularly distressing. Chi An, the narrator of this story, was a birth control worker who betrayed her closest friend after learning she was hiding a pregnancy. She was then forcibly aborted and sterilized. The role of the Women's Federation in the enforcement of these policies is significant.

The persecution of women who do not go to have abortions when ordered can be merciless. Cai Zhen Wei, a family planning cadre, wrote an account that appeared in the Hong Kong Chinese magazine *Dong Xian* in July 1992:

> One day, we went to catch a woman, but she escaped. Therefore, we destroyed the roof [of] the house. Then we threatened her family that if she did not come to see us tomorrow, we were going to destroy the house and confiscate their land. This method did work well in poor areas.[5]

Dong Xian published a photograph of a sign nailed to the door of a house that had been boarded up. It read: "Sealed against the couple who escaped from sterilization."

Fines for an illegal pregnancy can be more than a family's total annual income. Penalties for an unauthorized birth can amount to 40 percent of total income and continue up to fourteen years.[6] The children of nonconformists are penalized by being denied household registration, which is necessary to obtain medical care and other essential services.[7]

Female Infanticide

Poet Fu Xuan wrote in the third century B.C., "How sad it is to be a woman! Nothing on earth is held so cheap. No one is glad when a girl is born. By her the family sets no store." The ramifications of the China program are manifested in a particularly brutal way in the rise of female infanticide. The 1990 census found that for every one female, 12.75 male babies were being born in China. In Chinese tradition, women marry into the family of their husbands and are considered to have left the family of their parents. Up until one hundred years ago, daughters born to peasants were often not even given names. Sons are believed to be able to work harder in the fields, carry on the family name and, in a country where there is no social security system, provide for their parents in old age.

In an eyewitness account one woman, about to have her fifth child aborted, is asked why she became pregnant again. She replies: "I wanted to prove myself. . . . I have produced four girls and they are called Zhaodi ('inviting a brother'), Pandi ('expecting a brother'), Siangdi ('thinking of a brother'), and Sidi ('longing for a brother'). But still no brother comes. In the country you are regarded as inferior if you cannot produce sons. I wanted people to respect me, but I'm finished now."[8]

In a New York *Times* article in 1993, Nicholas D. Kristof reported on a village in Xiamen where in one year only one girl was born thanks to ultrasound and abortion for the "wrong" sex.[9] There are more than 1.7 million girls unaccounted for annually. According to the article, in five of China's thirty provinces, the sex ratio is already more than 120 boys for every 100 girls.

The Fate of the Disabled

There are more than fifty million disabled people in China and the government is trying to reduce their numbers with its new eugenics laws. China's Ministry of Public Health has written a bill designed "to avoid new births of inferior quality people and heighten the standards of the whole population."[10] Originally called "Draft Law on Eugenics and Health Protection," it was hastily renamed "Natal and Health Care Law" after expressions of outrage from the West.

The bill proposes to use marriage bans, sterilization, and abortion to "improve" the quality of the Chinese population.[11] It must be said that many abnormalities are caused by poor prenatal health care in many cases and not because of inherited genetic defects.

Population Control in Tibet

Tears of Silence: Tibetan Women and Population Control contains the testimonies of Tibetan women living in exile who underwent abortion or sterilization against their will.[12] According to Tibetan exile groups, recent Han Chinese settlers in Tibet are allowed to have more than one child as an incentive. "Seeing how much importance China attached to controlling population, this exception to the one-child policy rule in Tibet is very significant, suggesting an unspoken government policy to expand the Chinese population in Tibet," says Ngawang Choephel of the Tibetan Bureau in Geneva.[13]

There are six million Tibetans, about 150,000 of whom live in exile in India and Nepal, while there are 7.5 million Chinese in Tibet and the number is growing. "Tibetans are on the verge of extinction because of a population policy that restricts births of Tibetans and brings Chinese families to Tibet," says Nawang Lhamo of the Tibetan Women's Association. "Tibetans as 'minorities' are legally permitted to have two children if they live in larger towns and three children in rural areas. But in practice, Tibetans are allowed only one child, and extremely coercive methods are used to enforce this rule."[14]

China's tightly organized and controlled state-mandated birth limitation policy has caused, and is causing, immeasurable suffering. A traveler in China can easily see one effect of the program: the one-child families. Much more remains invisible. There is a hidden legacy of the program: the silent pain of women whose lives and bodies have been forfeited to the state and whose human rights are violated daily.

Publisher's note: The Chinese government is responding to protests against and abuses of its one-child policy with the passage of a new law making sex-screening of fetuses illegal (New York Times, 15 November 1994). Clearly this is an area that will warrant ongoing scrutiny from U.N. human rights activists.

NOTES
  1. "China's Family Planning Policy to Stay: Minister," AAP, 31 August 1994.
  2. See "China's Coercive Family Planning Program: Deception, Hypocrisy, and Human Rights," paper presented by Dr. John S. Aird, former senior research specialist on China at the U.S. Bureau of Census, at a symposium on population problems on 6 April 1993 at Grinnell College, Iowa.

3. Ibid., pp. 3, 4.
4. *A Mother's Ordeal: One Woman's Fight Against China's One-Child Policy,* Steven Mosher (New York, San Diego, London: Harcourt Brace, 1993), pp. 275–76.
5. "A Confession of a Birth-Control Plan Cadre," Cai Zhen Wei, *Dong Xian* (Hong Kong), July 1992. Translation by Wei Jianxin, Canberra, A.C.T., Australia, October 1992.
6. Aird, p. 5.
7. "Asylum for a Second Child," Melinda Tankard Reist, *The Age Saturday Extra,* 5 December 1992, p 8. See also "Asylum for Abortion: A Chinese Medical Worker Speaks Out," Melinda Tankard Reist, December 1992, unpublished interview.
8. "Brutal Lessons in the Facts of Life," *The Sunday Age,* 22 September 1991, p. 13. This article also appeared as "China's Wanted Children" in *The Independent* (London), 11 September 1991.
9. "Peasants of China Discover New Way to Weed Out Girls," Nicholas D. Kristof, New York *Times,* 21 July 1993.
10. "Birth of a Nation: China Proposes Eugenics Policy," *Far Eastern Economic Review,* 13 January 1994, p. 5.
11. "Ordering Up 'Better' Babies," James Walsh, *Time,* 2 May 1994, p. 56.
12. *Tears of Silence: Tibetan Women and Population Control,* Tibetan Women's Association (Dharamsala, India, undated).
13. "Human Rights: Tibetans Outnumbered at Home, Crowded Out in Cairo," Kunda Dixit, *Terra Viva* (Cairo), 10 September 1994; *Tibet News,* Spring 1994, p. 3.
14. Ibid.

2
CONTEMPORARY LIFE

Jade, Peach Blossom, and Red Soldier: Naming Chinese Women

Lu Danni

From time immemorial there have been clear distinctions between women's and men's personal names, both in pronunciation and in the meaning of the ideograms. Naming customs have varied through history, however, and the changes in women's names over time mirror changes in political reality and in attitudes toward women.

In the works of our ancestors from the Tang and Song dynasties, women were addressed by their own names. Such women writers as Ban Zhao, Cai Yan (also known as Wen Ji), Zuo Fen, Xie Daoyun, and Bao Linghui all became famous in their own right and under their own names. Subsequently, the ideology of women's inferiority became increasingly widespread and finally took over in the Ming and Qing dynasties.

Both the *Lienuezhuan* (Tales of Exemplary Women) and local chronicles no longer referred to women by separate names; instead, women were indicated by adding the designation *shi* (which means "of the family") to the husband's name. This practice continued in the provinces even after the People's Republic of China (PRC) was founded in 1949. In the countryside, many girls were named generically—"girl" or "sister." If there were several daughters, they were called "oldest girl," "second girl," and so forth. When a girl married, her husband's name was inserted before her father's surname, to which *shi* was added. For instance, if the Wang family's oldest daughter was married by a man called Li, her name became Li-Wang-Shi. When women were permitted to throw off their shackles, they were finally addressed by their own family and first names, just like men.

Today the naming of women reflects a continuing emphasis on gender-based traits. A recent study distinguishes types of women's names according to:

107

1. Gender (woman, sister)

2. Flowers/birds (blooming, plum, peach, orchid, swallow)

3. "Feminine" attributes (hair ornament, bracelet, silk, perfume)

4. Precious stones (jade and other jewels)

5. Beauty (pretty, beautiful, lovely)

6. Character trait (faithful, refined, friendly, graceful, distinguished, pure, compassionate)

7. Weather/time. These names are selected according to the time, weather, and location of the girl's birth and are often linked with names of the flower/bird type. Girls born in the first month of the lunar calendar are given such names as First Spring or Clouds of the First Month. In February and March, names mirror the season, as in Spring Green and Spring Wave. In April the swallows return and with them names like Morning Swallow and Flying Swallow. In May the blooming pomegranate, apricot, and peach trees lend themselves to such names as Lovely Peach or Apricot Flower. The Festival of the Unmarried is held in July on the seventh night of the seventh month of the lunar calendar, and names given at this time (Clever Pearl or Elegant Cloud) mirror this tradition. In August, when the scent of the osmanthus flower drifts over the land and the moon is full, people name their daughters Osmanthus Moon or Fragrant Osmanthus. And in the fall, after the golden chrysanthemums have survived the first frost and the snowflake shrubs yearn for spring, girls are named Autumn Chrysanthemum, Chrysanthemum Scent, and Winter Flower.

8. Masculinized names. Selecting men's names or male ideograms to name women serves to undermine perceived gender differences. This phenomenon has existed through the ages, and it proves that women did not simply acquiesce to their low status during feudalism and indeed placed themselves on a par with men. After liberation, the notion that women and men are equal was actively encouraged, and many parents hoped that daughters would be allowed to develop their potential to the same extent as sons. This stance gave rise to such names as Outdo Men, Match Men, and Compete with Men. Moreover, some women changed their names to Self-Strength, Independent Eagle, and so forth.

Naming also mirrors political movements and social upheavals since the founding of the PRC, as if people had been branded with hot irons, as shown by the list below.

1. The founding phase, 1949–50, brought forth such names as Go South, Liberation, Construct China, and China's Will.

2. During the Korean War (1950–53), names exhorted people to Oppose American Aggression, Defend China, Protect the Land, and Help Korea.

3. The years 1954–57 gave rise to names like Constitution, Peace, Build China, or Marvelous China.

4. During the Great Leap Forward (1958–59), Great Leap, Red Flower, Surpass England, Red Flag, etc., were popular names.

5. Names given in 1960–62, three extremely difficult years, reflect such slogans as Own Strength, Work Our Way Up, Guarantee Diligence, and Strive for Strength.

6. The period 1963–65 saw such names as Battle or Learn from Lei Feng.

7. During the Cultural Revolution (1966–76), women were named Love the Military, Revolution, Red Protection, Red Soldier, and Construct the New.

8. From 1977 to 1980, such names as Civilized, High Culture, and Four Modernizations were favored.

On 17 November 1984, the Chinese Script Reform Commission held a conference in Beijing to evaluate the use of ideograms in first and family names. Statistics show that the ideogram for "red" was used increasingly in names since 1949, though almost exclusively for women.

In the wake of China's opening and the economic reforms launched in the 1980s, the naming of women reflects yet other facets typical of the epoch. First, ideograms expressing the beauty of and respect for one's parents (Sister, Cowrie Shell, Crystal, Treasure) are becoming more frequent. Second, after enduring the chaos of the Cultural Revolution, people long for quiet and tenderness, so they select ideograms related to supposedly feminine traits, such as graceful, nimble, silk, quiet, calm, orchid, and jade. Third, first names are being limited to a single ideogram (this also applies to men). Fourth, contacts to the outside world are gradually increasing, leading to such Western names as Anna, Marie, and Annie. This reveals the spirit of openness and the willingness to discard old norms when naming women in the new era.

Translated by Ulrike Bode

DANWEI

Wang Jian

D *anwei* means "work unit." It is a general term used to designate a specific form of social organization to which most Chinese belong. I shall focus mostly on city dwellers, because over the last forty years (since the 1949 revolution) peasant life has undergone frequent organizational changes. In the late 1950s, the peasants were organized into people's communes and production brigades, but this predominantly collective mode of production was gradually dissolved in the wake of the current economic reforms. Now the peasants live in their original villages (which had never fully disappeared) in individual families (which, irrespective of size, always constituted the basic social unit in the country).

Small and Large Family

In using the word "family," especially in the context of peasants, I must emphasize that China is still a largely agrarian nation with a large peasant population. Since the family mode of production, which characterizes contemporary peasant life, has been the basic form of organization throughout China's history, it inevitably provides the model for the current danwei.

All peoples have specific traditions. In spite of several revolutions, China has been unable to supplant its basic social structure. Hence, changes in the danwei mirror the contradictions among Marxist dogma, attempts at modernization, and tradition.

After the establishment of the People's Republic of China (PRC) in 1949, the danwei was developed as a countermodel to the traditional family structure, to facilitate the transition from autonomous small-scale production to large-scale industrial production. Everyone was to be integrated into the work force, establishing a total social division of labor; housewives left their homes to go to work and children were placed in day-care centers. Families were greatly affected by this new form of social organization, which shifted familial functions to schools, cafeterias, and old-age homes. However, none of this resulted in the dissolution of the family. Although the family structure underlying premodern society was almost totally destroyed, Confucianism and its value system survived. A compromise between collectivization and tradition filled the void created by the family's reduced significance.

Large danweis, defined by Mao Zedong as *yida ergong* (large in size and collective in nature), were founded during the 1958–59 campaign known as the "Great Leap Forward." In the cities they took the form of de-privatized enterprises comprising several small companies, and in rural areas the form of people's communes. This result is easy to understand given Mao's background and education, for he never fully challenged the patriarchal kinship system. Today the *da danwei* (large or important work unit) relates not only to the production of goods but also to the integration of politics, economics, and social life. Apart from their primary function on behalf of the state or society, such da danwei as large companies or universities are also wholly responsible for their employees' welfare. They run cafeterias, hospitals, day-care centers, elementary and middle schools, sometimes even colleges, shops, and entire residential neighborhoods. The small family was thus replaced by a large family, if not by a "large modern village." Until the Cultural Revolution, the da danwei evolved into small, wholly independent socioeconomic units.

The danwei has basically maintained this structure to the present. The enlarged and autonomous system inevitably displays the characteristics of a family. First, the hierarchical danwei functions according to patriarchal principles. The members of a danwei assume the roles of father, mother, sons, and daughters. Such statements as "the directors of my danwei care for me like my parents" or "the relations among my co-workers are as good as those among siblings" are common. The leadership of the danwei makes decisions about administrative, legal, and political matters, just like the head of a family. No one can marry or obtain a new apartment without the consent of the "father." Although some of the danwei's procedures may be democratic (e.g., when commissars of a committee represent members' diverse opinions), experience, tradition, and custom generally prevail. No wonder most people do not want to assume responsibility, for, as a Chinese proverb states, "There are too many mothers-in-law." Each danwei represents a link in a large chain, in keeping with Confucian tradition: "When people are brought together, a family is created; when families are brought together, a state is created; and when in the end the states are brought together, the world is created." Chinese society still comprises such small, medium, and large "families"; the only difference is that the modern term for "state," *guojia,* is formed by combining the words "country/state" and "family/home."

The danwei's second important familial feature is that its members relate to each other in both their work and social life, fostering close relationships that make them dependent on one another. The work force is tightly knit, just like a family. It is hard to imagine how difficult it is to change one's danwei, let alone abandon one's "family" with its structure of lifelong solicitude. People develop—and realize—their identity within the danwei, as revealed, for example, by the demand that people "consider their factory to be their actual family." This dependence explains people's odd habit of asking others to which danwei they belong, before inquiring about their names. For the Chinese, the concept underlying the danwei is natural, and they cannot imagine that anyone (including foreigners) might exist outside such an association. Since each individual's value manifests itself only within the collective, it is understandable that many Chinese students abroad view themselves as representatives of their country. In other words, vis-à-vis foreigners they will identify with the PRC, their large danwei. This mirrors the relationship between, say, the Wang family and other families where only the family name counts, and where first names, such as Jian or Yan, are insignificant.

The Individual and the Danwei

If the danwei comprises both the modern division of labor and the autonomous family, i.e., a form of social organization where everyone is required to work, then what happens to those who cannot or do not have work?

Groups such as retirees, people looking for work (those who have not yet entered the work force as opposed to the unemployed, who have lost their jobs), and physically or mentally handicapped people are assigned to the "residents' committee," which becomes their danwei. (During the Cultural Revolution, retirees had to participate in criticism and self-criticism sessions at the behest of residents' committees.) As qualified workers, retirees may now join a factory that belongs to the street committee and earn some additional money. In theory, those who are physically or mentally handicapped may perform as many community services as their abilities allow. Most people looking for work are recent graduates from middle school. However, the economic reforms have also enabled people to quit their jobs, either to become independent (i.e., to go into business for themselves) or to find a better-paying position. Usually, unemployed youngsters are sooner or later assigned to a danwei by the street committee.

The street committee is the lowest administrative level in the district, a locally defined arena of state power. The street committee is responsible not only for people who do not have work, but also for the leisure time and family matters of local residents. Though the danwei assigns apartments, people must register with the street committee, which distributes many types of ration coupons according to household size. The residents' committee comprises mostly older people; it is subordinate to the street committee, but is not an organ of the state. It organizes all people in a residential neighborhood who do not belong to a danwei. Furthermore, it mediates and settles family quarrels. The street committee has extensive legal authority and issues valid and officially sanctioned family documents such as certificates of marriage, divorce (the courts become involved only in case of conflict about children and property), and family planning. For people to obtain these certificates, they must first gain the permission of their danwei, as a sort of reference. By maintaining personal files on each individual, the danwei possesses extensive knowledge of its members' personal histories and moral conduct, and has the right to judge their political and personal reliability. Wherever one goes in China, people demand to see reference letters issued by one's danwei—a national identity card of sorts.

Hence the danwei is omnipresent. This perfect organization guarantees the relatively smooth exchange of information on all levels of society. Most laws, even state regulations, are publicized within the danwei and enforced from the top down via this channel. Many problems are solved without bureaucratic delays and complications because the members of the danwei and its director know one another.

The absence of comprehensive laws, however, invests a danwei's director, usually a man, with vast discretionary powers, enabling him to act like a king within the closed patriarchal "family." For example, an unmarried teacher, thirty-seven years old, shares a room with other single women and will probably never get a room, let alone an apartment, of her own if she does not marry. She is treated this way because the danwei's director has little consideration for unmarried women. Such arbitrary rules are called *tu zhengce* (local policy). In another instance, a woman whose husband had died on a business trip received a lot of sympathy and support. This encouraged her to begin a new life, though it also caused new difficulties; when she later made friends with a male colleague, she was chided by her danwei director for violating her obligation as a widow to remain chaste.

The familial danwei system assures permanent jobs and creates a certain level of solidarity. The ideogram "iron key" expresses it well. Those who have a job are settled for life; their medical care is guaranteed, and both child support and financial supplements for poorer families are paid automatically. No one starves to death. Besides concerning itself with material matters, the danwei also attends to its members' psychological problems and even helps with matchmaking. It will arrange for a partner if a member is still unmarried at the age of thirty, because "an unstable life could disrupt the work."

This deep involvement has its price. Patriarchal arbitrariness, as well as traditional world views and the conscious or subconscious controls exercised by one's peers, can be extremely destructive. As Wu, a seventeen-year-old girl, puts it: "To me, it is as if we were caught in a net that binds us, suppresses our intelligence, and prevents us from living according to our own wishes."

A retired functionary recalls that she once confided to a woman party secretary that she would like to buy a fashionable red jacket, because she had often envied rich girls for such jackets. For this confession she had to engage repeatedly in self-criticism of her bourgeois ideas, until she never again even dared to think of a red jacket.

During the Cultural Revolution, the degree of external control increased to absurd levels. Gu, an artist and composer, who had been criticized in 1958 for belonging to the rightist opposition, was not allowed to compose music. She did not even play her piano for fear of being denounced by her neighbors.

It is the women who suffer most under the moral controls imposed by the danwei. Shi, a saleswoman, "insulted" her boss when she rejected his attempts at arranging a marriage with one of his relatives; he subsequently assigned her to a more difficult job. Xiao, a worker, was dismissed from her danwei because she visited her boyfriend in another town without obtaining prior permission. However, the real reason for her dismissal was her refusal to divulge how she got there and where she stayed. Though in this case there might have been more to it than mere curiosity, the danwei's director nonetheless felt responsible for her morality as well. As Xiao said, "All I need is for them to insist on examining me to see whether I am still a virgin!"

Though there is truth in Wu's assertion that the "net" represses the individual's intelligence, the danwei also protects its members. Being cared for and feeling secure are pleasant conditions sought by many people everywhere, for as a proverb states: "At home you lean on your parents, in the world you lean on your friends."

There are danweis everywhere to lean on. But when do these people grow up? For those who are intelligent and adventurous, the danwei is stultifying as they cannot express their own, original ideas. Reform policies have enabled people to leave their danwei voluntarily, to become independent or to engage in projects with others. (Their personal files are, of course, sent to the street committee.) One hopes that such people will be able to develop their intelligence successfully on this risky path that they have chosen.

Translated by Ulrike Bode

HOLDING UP HALF THE SKY: THE LEGAL POSITION OF WOMEN IN CHINA

Dagmar Borchard

A married daughter is like water spilled on the ground.
—Chinese proverb

The legal position of Chinese women has improved considerably since the fall of the last empire. Traditionally, women did not have the right to inherit, nor to own property, except for their clothes and a few pieces of jewelry; their right to obtain a divorce was extremely restricted. In contrast, men could divorce their wives for being talkative, belligerent, or not deferential enough toward their parents-in-law; jealousy, malignant diseases, adultery, and the failure to bear sons were other reasons. Widows were not supposed to remarry, but instead had to remain chaste and faithful to the memory of their deceased husbands. Girls who had been engaged in childhood and whose prospective bridegrooms died during the engagement became instant (child) widows.

Marriage and Inheritance

The marriage laws of 1950 and 1980 stipulate a woman's right to obtain a divorce and to choose her mate freely. Concubine marriage, bride-price marriage (where the husband pays a considerable amount of money to the girl's family), arranged marriage, and purchase of child brides (where a young girl is sold to and raised in her future husband's family) were outlawed. A widow's right to remarry was explicitly guaranteed. The inheritance laws of 1985 also stipulate a woman's right to inherit.

However, "Regulations for the Protection of the Lawful Rights and Interests of Women and Children," enacted over the last few years in provinces, counties, and cities throughout China, reveal that laws in support of women's rights require much outside support if they are to be fully implemented. These regulations underscore that women enjoy the same in-

117

Bridal couple from the fifties

heritance rights as men, and that a widow who remarries may take her inheritance to her new family. The laws also stipulate that daughters and sons are equally responsible for their aging parents; whichever beneficiary totally or partially neglects the legator might face a reduction in, if not the total loss of, his or her inheritance. Since daughters generally live with their husband's family upon marriage, while their brothers stay at home (with their parents), men often argue, after the parents' death, that their sisters did not take equal care of the parents, often leading to a reduction in the sisters' share of the inheritance. The legal advice columns of popular magazines are full of letters from women wanting to know whether they can inherit from their parents if they have received a dowry. Frequently, when a nephew of the deceased is the next closest male relative, he will make a claim and try to dispute a daughter's right to her inheritance.

The official marriage ages for women (twenty) and for men (twenty-two) are intentionally high because of China's population policy. Under the new marriage law, the couple is free to decide whether to live with the husband's or wife's family. However, this regulation is aimed less at fostering woman's equality and more at shifting the social burden of caring for the elderly (especially one's parents) onto the shoulders of daughters as well as sons in connection with the single-child-family policy. Couples are required to sign what is called a single-child passport, a pledge to have no more than one child. This passport carries with it several advantages, such as priority in the assignment of day-care center and college spots, jobs, free medical care for the child, extended maternity leave for the mother, and a supplement to the parents' social security income once they retire. Conversely, couples who have a second child must anticipate wage reductions and pay for medical care themselves; they will also find that there is no room for their child in a day-care center nor for the family in larger city housing. People still hope that their one permitted child will be a son who will take care of them after their retirement.

In past years, there has been mounting evidence that more Chinese marry before reaching the official marriage age. Moreover, though the 1980 marriage law does not explicitly outlaw the purchase of child brides, recent reports reveal that this custom has not died out. In the village of Luji, in Anhui Province, sixteen girls were sold to families to be married off later to the families' sons.

Divorce

Getting divorced can turn into a prolonged affair, because, as with most family conflicts, divorce and disputes over inheritance are subject to arbitration. Both the court and the arbiters are required to promote reconciliation if one party opposes the divorce. The spouse seeking the divorce must endure innumerable attempts at mediation by family members, relatives, friends, co-workers, neighbors, and even the street committee. China needs stable families for its modernization drive and good workers to achieve progress. The files of one district show that, in six years, the divorces of 140 couples were prevented by arbiters (most of whom are retirees and homemakers, especially women over sixty).

Women apply for divorce in 70 percent of the cases. Some 400,000 to 500,000 marriages are dissolved annually. According to official figures for 1987, only 1 or 2 percent of all Chinese marriages ended in divorce. The All-China Women's Federation links the low divorce rate to the elimination of forced marriages. Yet, more than 60 percent of all divorcé(e)s are under thirty. The official explanation for this statistic is that young people make rash decisions leading to ill-considered marriages; frequently the partners do not know each other well. Though the divorce rate in large cities like Shanghai and Guangzhou is said to have skyrocketed by 50 percent in recent years, the overall rate is still low, especially because a divorced woman's chances of remarrying are extremely small; her reputation is considered destroyed.

A divorce is particularly difficult to obtain when a third party is involved, someone who has "broken into the family" by having an affair with one spouse. When the court learns that an outsider is part of the problem (as in the case of the writer Yu Luojin, for example), the spouse maintaining the extramarital affair is automatically pronounced guilty. Yu described her experience in two novels, *A Chinese Winter's Tale* and *A Chinese Spring's Tale*. While the first novel was debated as a controversial work, Yu was vehemently criticized (during the "campaign against spiritual pollution") for her second novel, which describes her second divorce. To intrude on a marriage is considered a remnant of a corrupt lifestyle from an earlier era or a sign of bourgeois leanings, and both the "intruder" and the "guilty" spouse must be "reeducated."

Suicide was the last resort in feudal days for a woman to escape the bad treatment meted out to her by her husband or her mother-in-law, or to break away from an intolerable arranged marriage. It was a perfect means of revenge for daughters-in-law, because suicides were traditionally subject to thorough judicial inquiries. Women who killed themselves after a rape or who escaped being raped by committing suicide were honored as examples of chastity and loyalty toward their families. However, a forty-three-year-old peasant woman recounted a recent story to show that, even nowadays, unhappy women may prefer suicide to an arranged marriage. In the neighboring village, a man had married a young girl whom his parents disliked. They accused her of having stolen their son and pushed her to commit suicide. The girl's parents demanded a full bride price to place in her casket. The parents-in-law paid, for fear that the dead girl's spirit might haunt their son and his new wife. Today suicide is the most frequent cause of unexpected death, and the most common reasons for suicide are family quarrels and unrequited love.

At Work

In the drive toward modernization, companies are making every attempt to become profitable. This is achieved, for instance, by cutting back allegedly superfluous and less productive workers—women, in particular. According to an investigation by the magazine *Chinese Women,* women account for 70 percent of all dismissals. Employers are increasingly refusing to hire women because the work units do not want to incur the cost of maternity leave and day-care centers. One factory executive stated flatly that he would rather pay ten thousand *yuan* for a robot than hire a woman. In 1984, 30 percent of all work units wanted to accept only men; frequently, even less qualified men are preferred to women. A woman worker reported, for example, that women had to achieve 160 points on the entrance exam administered by her factory, men only 100 points!

A social security and health insurance system is in its infancy. Only those employed in industry, public administration, health, and education enjoy all legally prescribed benefits and protections. In collective enterprises, many of which were established during the 1958–59 "Great Leap Forward" or during the Cultural Revolution, wages, benefits, and compliance with work-place safety rules depend on each collective's capacity. In terms of benefits, many larger and financially sound companies are comparable to the public sector, whereas small neighborhood collectives cannot finance work-place safety or employee benefits. In collectives, one in two employees is a woman, while in the public sector every third employee is a woman.

There are new regulations designed to improve the work-place status of women. The 1982 Constitution expressly stipulates the state's obligation to ensure wage equality, and the slogan "equal wages for equal work" is often cited. (Nonetheless, on the average, women earn about 30 percent less than men.) Paid maternity leave before and after the delivery of a child has been increased from fifty-six to ninety days. In the past few years, women have been able to extend this leave to six months, even to one year. During this time they receive about 70 to 80 percent of their wages. In the event of a miscarriage, a woman is granted a leave of seven days; after a particularly difficult delivery or the birth of twins, maternity leave may be extended by two weeks. The costs of delivery are borne by the work unit. When a married woman has an abortion in the first trimester, she may take a two-week vacation; if the abortion is carried out at a later date, this is extended to one month. It is illegal to dismiss women or to cut their wages in connection with pregnancy, delivery, and breast-feeding.

Women are required to retire at the age of fifty-five, men at the age of sixty; recent proposals suggest lowering the retirement age to forty and forty-five years, respectively. However, many women like Wei Junyi and Jing Feng (both journalists) believe that it is discriminatory to force women to retire five years earlier than men. At this phase of their lives, they argue, their familial responsibilities are greatly reduced since their children are grown, enabling them to concentrate on their work. If women are forced to retire at an earlier age than men, women's chances to advance and pursue more interesting jobs will diminish.

The position of women has undoubtedly improved in the last forty-five years since the establishment of the People's Republic of China. The marriage and inheritance laws, as well as many work-place rules, should foster equality between women and men. And yet, though a married daughter is no longer automatically considered "water spilled on the ground," the chances of Chinese women conquering their half of the sky are still sadly remote.

Translated by Ulrike Bode

ECONOMIC REFORMS AND RURAL WOMEN

Monika Schädler

In December 1978, the third plenary session of the Eleventh Central Committee meeting of the Chinese Communist Party (CCP) ushered in a period of economic and social reorganization that today is generally referred to as the reform phase. It entailed a radical departure from thirty years of a planned economy initially modeled on the Soviet Union. Aimed largely at farmers, who still account for three-quarters of China's population, the changes profoundly affected the lives of hundreds of millions of people. What were the consequences of the new policies for the roughly four hundred million women and girls in rural areas? How have the conditions governing their lives changed since the early 1980s?

Background

The 1949 revolution smashed the feudal structures that had dominated rural life for thousands of years. The land reform law of 1950 expropriated all large-scale landholdings and distributed almost half of all arable land to formerly landless peasants. Agricultural cooperatives owning land and farm implements were established throughout China between 1952 and 1955. The "Great Leap Forward," Mao Zedong's concrete strategy for strengthening the economy primarily based on the agricultural sector, entailed mobilizing additional productive forces, especially the abundant supply of rural labor. Agricultural production was enhanced through traditional labor-intensive cultivation methods, as well as through the promotion of small industries and forced collectivization. In 1958, all cooperatives were brought together to form people's communes. Although they were initially too large and unwieldy, and were later reduced in size to reflect both local conditions and forms of village organization, people's communes dominated rural life for over two decades.

The people's commune fulfilled both political and economic functions. It represented government agencies and enforced state directives and planned production figures, which it transmitted to the lower echelons. It also operated communal enterprises such as coal mines, fertilizer and canning factories, and small engineering workshops. The production brigade oversaw agricultural machine stations and local enterprises, such as brickyards, spinning mills, and wicker- and basketwork shops. Finally, the production group controlled all cultivation of arable land and functioned as the basic accounting unit. It posted all income from the collective organizations' activities and paid the farmers. Since it was also in charge of its members' welfare, the production group was the pivotal economic unit for individual farmers, even more important than the family.

Collectivization had shifted the ownership of land from families to the collectives. However, farmers continued to own their houses, small agricultural implements, and other simple means of production. In addition, they independently cultivated small subsistence plots.

Just as in the cities, all women in the people's communes were required to contribute to the socialist project; most were engaged in agriculture, and some worked in small factories and services. Everyone was paid according to, first, a point system, and second, individual strength, ability, and qualifications. A maximum of ten points could be accumulated in a workday. The wages were computed on the basis of points assigned, hours worked, and the production groups' income at year's end. Most women were ranked below men. While men with average health and performance levels were usually granted ten points, married women had to content themselves with eight points, at the most, and unmarried women with only six points. To justify the difference, it was alleged that women had inferior capability and strength.

Various services operated by the people's communes facilitated women's work outside the home. Although communal kitchens established during the Great Leap Forward were not popular, day-care and sewing centers significantly reduced the burden on women. In the 1960s, many rural Chinese women

were still performing tasks that had been taken over by industry much earlier in Europe, such as the production of clothes, fabric, shoes, and extensive meals. Attitudes toward day-care centers were divided at first. Many people were uneasy about leaving their children in the care of childless women without the requisite experience. Yet children had to be cared for if mothers were to participate in public life on an equal footing, and not every family had a healthy grandmother who could attend to the young.

The Reform Phase

Between 1978 and 1982, the responsibility for production was gradually shifted from the production groups back to families. Since then, farmers have been directly accountable for both profits and losses. They sign contracts for land cultivation with the villages as representatives of the owners' collectives. At a minimum, these contracts specify the plots, the share or fixed amount of profits to be given to the village, duties and taxes, as well as the contract duration. Often they also stipulate the type and amount of crops to be cultivated and the amount of fertilizer, pesticides, implements, et cetera, provided to the farmer. In the reforms' early phase, households were treated as economic units whose size determined the amount of land assigned to them according to locally specified ratios. In some areas, each family received a certain parcel for subsistence farming, while the rest of the land was leased to the highest bidder.

The elimination of people's communes in the first half of the 1980s caused a sensation, both in China and abroad. The communes' combined political and economic functions had, in many instances, created situations in which economic criteria were not necessarily paramount. For example, many political cadres brought high-status heavy industries into their home regions without considering whether or not these were suited to local conditions. Such enterprises had little autonomy but gave the cadres additional power. Purely political organizations were also established: people's communes were replaced by municipal governments, and production brigades gave way to village committees. On the commercial level, most enterprises were granted greater autonomy, mainly with regard to employment, wages, product sales, and the like. Although they were also made accountable for profits and losses (just as the farmers were), in fact, the enterprise's collective owner (i.e., the municipal or village government) began to assume all losses.

The introduction of a private economy in 1982, which expanded the free markets and liberalized the circulation of goods, resulted in significant changes for family businesses. It spawned about fifteen million licensed commercial enterprises, mostly family-run, and it is estimated that an equal number of farmers operate unlicensed small businesses in addition to cultivating the land. Many people now engage in a variety of activities: working in skilled trades; operating repair shops; and selling everything from farm produce to local specialties, handicrafts, and household utensils.

Employment

Productivity in the agricultural sector (i.e., output per farm worker) has risen substantially since the reforms were launched. Given the limits on the availability of arable land (after Japan and Bangladesh, China's huge mountain and desert regions give it the smallest amount of arable land per person), the need for agricultural labor has been greatly reduced. Though the policies allowing private enterprise have fostered industrial and service sectors which, in turn, have created new jobs, there is surplus labor in most rural areas. As in other developing countries, there is little or no outright unemployment; instead, the majority of those who want to be gainfully employed share available work within the family.

In the people's communes, each gainfully employed person had to work for the production group; there was almost no other way of earning money. The dissolution of communes and the assignment of land to families under the new reforms shifted decisions about the allocation of work to the latter. In wealthy areas, where small industrial enterprises developed in the reforms' early stages, the following division of labor ensued: Educated and strong young men work chiefly in the industrial and service sectors, while women, the elderly, and children are left with the less lucrative task of cultivating the land. Traditional ideology still holds sway. Moreover, since greater autonomy granted to companies now gives them the right to hire their employees freely, more men are hired over women. Women's absences for pregnancy and child care are used by rural enterprises (just like those in the cities) to justify the preference accorded to men.

The dramatically reduced need for agricultural labor unleashed rural-to-urban migration, a new phenomenon in the history of the PRC. Previously, strict regulations had deterred large migratory movements with such measures as residency controls, ration coupons for grain and cooking oil, et cetera. Since the relaxation of these policies in the eighties, about 150 million peasants (a figure roughly equal to one half of the U.S. population) work outside of their home villages or are on the move in search of work. Many of them have converged on twenty-three large metropolitan areas that have reached the limit of their capacity to absorb migrants, who are mostly men from rural regions with highly disguised unemployment. They work as day laborers for peasants in richer areas (who themselves take up more lucrative activities) or, if these migrant workers have the required skills, they take jobs as construction workers, craftsmen, and small traders in the cities. Young unmarried girls frequently go to the large cities to work as domestics. Here, too, young men enjoy greater advantages in terms of income-generating opportunities, because most women must stay with their families in the countryside. Even though a maid's income is far below that of a young construction worker, and city life might be harder on young women, the opportunity to gain experience and money to take back to their villages and use to improve their social status in the long term may well offset the disadvantages.

Education

Money-making opportunities and the dream of striking it rich are threatening girls' education to an alarming degree. As of the late 1980s, only about 45 percent of all girls were enrolled in school. Girls accounted for 83 percent of the more than 2.7 million children aged seven to eleven who did not attend school in 1987. In China's northwestern Gansu Province, 80 percent of the girls were forced to leave school after the fourth grade. In Guangdong Province, all 500 child workers in 49 of 200 factories surveyed were girls! Since girls leave the family after marriage, they are lost to their parents as a source of income, and many believe that educating girls is a waste of time—as long as they are around, they should work to increase the family's income. Moreover, many private entrepreneurs prefer the skilled hands of young girls (as was the case in silk-spinning mills controlled by foreigners in the colonized regions of eastern China). Though a law was enacted in April 1986 making nine years of education compulsory for all, it may be difficult to enforce in light of these material and ideological obstacles.

Marriage

Because it is once again acceptable to be rich, material aspects now carry greater weight in the selection of a mate than they did before the economic reforms. This increases the pressure on families to make extravagant bride gifts or to provide generous dowries. In addition, lavish marriage celebrations, which enhance a family's status, are costing more and more. Girls are forced to earn money early so that the family can pay for their expected dowry—a color television, a refrigerator, or a washing machine. There are also increasing reports about girls being sold as child brides; they move to their future groom's family at a young age to work there, just as in feudal times. Sending such girls to school is, of course, out of the question.

Discrimination against Daughters

The reforms have heightened the traditional preference for male progeny. Men are considered physically stronger than women and thus better able to take advantage of new job opportunities that benefit their families. The reforms have also bolstered traditional family ties. Studies have shown that both households comprising several generations and extended families with various working members have comparatively higher incomes than nuclear families (father, mother, child). And, the dissolution of the collective structures largely eliminated the previously assured care of the old and sick, shifting these responsibilities back to the families. The desire for sons is intensified by adherence to the tradition that dictates that sons remain with their parents after marrying. Thus they contribute to the family's income longer. Furthermore, in the reforms' early phase, a household's size determined the amount of land assigned to it. It is assumed that only a son could ensure the family's claim over the previously assigned land. Finally, it is believed that only sons can continue the family line and ancestor worship—a matter of special significance in rural areas.

The resurrection of this ideology significantly hampers the enforcement of family planning measures in the country. In spite of harsh penalties—an unapproved child is not considered in the assignment of land, and the family must pay stiff fines— rural families have resisted efforts to control the birth rate. On the other hand, if a prenatal exam shows that the fetus is female, many women are more likely to consent to the recommended abortion, especially in the case of second and subsequent children. The high ratio of male to female births is striking. And girls' infant mortality rate is alarming. [See the essay by Reist in Part 1.]

The reawakening of traditional customs and ideologies in China, and its consequent effect of holding women in low regard, is indeed disheartening. Nevertheless, in recent decades some Chinese women were able to enhance both their social status and their self-esteem; a few who have advanced to middle positions in the economic and political realms provide useful examples to others. Cases of extravagant bride gifts, child brides, and female infanticide are known and are continuously denounced, as is the tradition of preventing girls from attending school. Women's challenge now is to take advantage of the new opportunities and to resist the resurrection of misogynist ideologies.

Translated by Ulrike Bode

THE LAND OF WOMEN

Eva Sternfeld

Dashima, of the Yongning Region in Ninglang District, had three sons from her affairs with Zewu and Geruo. Later, Age was her lover for ten years and she had four more sons by him. When she was forty, she suddenly said to Age: "I am too old, I can't sleep with anyone any more, find yourself someone else." From that day, Age no longer visited her. After a while, Dashima entered into a relationship with Lacha, after all. She bore two more sons and, finally, when she was forty-five years old, a daughter whom she named Jiaama. One day, Age saw her with the little girl and said: "I thought you said you couldn't sleep with anyone any more. Did your daughter fall from the sky or did she grow out of the earth?" Dashima answered with a laugh: "I slept with you for ten years and bore only sons, now I have a daughter by someone else, is that nothing?" Age saw her point.

As the only girl, little Jiaama was the center of family attention. Her mother and brothers took care of her and spoiled her. They waited expectantly for the day when Jiaama would be grown up, receive lovers, and have children. When Dashima died in 1957 at the age of sixty-seven, her soul could go calmly on its journey, for her daughter had already borne three children, and two were girls.

This extended family so concerned about its female descendents lives on an isolated plateau surrounded by snow-covered mountains four thousand feet high, not far from the raging currents of the Jinsha River, the upper branch of the Yangzi. The approximately six thousand inhabitants of the plateau, on the border between Yunnan and Sichuan Provinces, are settled around Lake Lugu. They farm, raise animals, fish, and hunt.

More women live in the Yongning Region than men, which

is unusual in rural China. The language spoken in Yongning betrays the high regard for women there. Positive and superior objects are given female attributes. A large basket is called a "mother basket"; a small tree, on the other hand, would be described as a "man's tree." Lake Lugu, around which plateau life is concentrated, is called Xienami (mother lake) in their language; on the north shore of the lake rises a sandstone range, which the natives call Ganmu (woman mountain). The mountain is the inhabitant's holiest shrine; they worship it as their goddess Ganmu turned to stone.

The inhabitants of the Yongning plateau, who call themselves Mosuo, belong to the Naxi minority. Approximately three hundred thousand Naxi live in northern Yunnan, mostly in the autonomous Naxi district, Lijiang. While the Lijiang Naxi have accepted such features of the Chinese patriarchal system as arranged marriages and the sale of brides by their parents at least since 1723, when they subordinated themselves to a Chinese magistrate, in Yongning a matriarchal system based on free love continues to be practiced today.

The inaccessibility of the region probably protected the inhabitants from being taken over by Han Chinese patriarchal culture, in contrast to their tribal counterparts in Lijiang. To reach the region in 1963, a Chinese research team had to travel ten days on foot from Lijiang. In the last twenty years transportation in the region has been better developed, and although the restructuring and reeducation measures of the People's Republic extended to the Yongning Region, the Yongning Naxi have retained their matriarchal customs to the present.

Matriarchal Extended Family

Until the beginning of this millennium, the inhabitants of Yongning lived among six matriarchal clans, which called themselves Xi, Hu, Ya, E, Bu, and Cuo. A tribal princedom replaced the clans during the Yuan dynasty (1279–1368). The once-equal clan members have since lived in a three-class society composed of nobles, peasants, and serfs. While the tribal princes who ruled Yongning until the land reform of 1956 passed their power patrilinearly from father to son, for a long time their subjects did not even have a term for father.

The population lived—and still do—in matriarchal extended families of ten to thirty persons, consisting of a grandmother, great aunts and great uncles, mother, aunts and uncles, sisters and brothers, daughters and sons, nieces and nephews. The *dabu,* or head of the family, is usually the oldest or most capable woman. No family member is married. The young women's lovers come in the evening to spend the night with them and go back to their maternal family the next morning. In the same way, the brothers and younger uncles leave the house in the evening to visit their lovers from other clans. The Naxi call these relationships *a xiao. A xiao* relationships can be short affairs or long-term fixed ties. Long-term lovers are usually introduced to the other members of the family and, from then on, enjoy the privilege of drinking tea and talking with the head of the family in the common room. Short affairs, in contrast, remain a matter for the lovers alone.

A xiao acquaintanceships are begun and ended without complications. Favorite opportunities for getting to know new partners are during baths in the hot springs of the region where men and women bathe together casually, and feast days like 25 July when the goddess Ganmu is paid homage with a picnic and a night spent in the open air. Love relationships begin secretly at first and are made public only if the family agrees to them.

Separation also takes place very simply. If a woman wants to end a relationship, she tells her lover: "You don't need to come again tomorrow." She can also place his things in front of the door. The man has no choice but to disappear. Relationships can be ended for the following reasons: (1) the two are not in emotional agreement; (2) they live too far apart; (3) one of the two begins a new relationship; (4) the family has objections; (5) sexual problems; (6) one of the two is sick; or (7) the man did not bring enough presents.

In general, women and men are not hurt or saddened by separations. When an old relationship is ended, a new one is begun. Most people have at least ten, and in some cases as many as one hundred, such a xiao relationships in a lifetime.

A xiao relationships are always purely sexual ties, even if lasting ten or twenty years. For both partners, the maternal family remains the unit of production and consumption. The man has no rights to his children. Many children do not even know who their father is, since fathers only come to visit at night. Even when they know their father, they do not honor him, because the maternal family is solely responsible for their education. It is therefore not surprising that the Naxi language originally had no word for father. Men did not have their own words for son or daughter; nieces and nephews were the most important children for them.

For a long time, the Naxi regarded bearing children as a matter for women and did not connect it to sexual intercourse. If a woman did not become pregnant, they believed that her reproductive organ was blocked. They begged the goddess Ganmu for help in opening the birth canal.

Children are raised in common by the extended family. When sixty-year-old family leader Gachami was asked in 1963 how many children she had, she answered: "Ten." The translator explained to the Chinese research team: "According to our beliefs, a woman's children are those she has given birth to herself, and also the children of her sisters. Actually, she has only one child, nine children belong to her sisters."

House, cattle, farming tools, and other means of production are the collective property of the family. Individual family members have no private property beyond some clothing and a few objects for daily use. Women can keep gifts they receive from their lovers and men can also keep part of the wages they receive for work performed outside of the family, such as herding horses, to spend themselves.

The position of dabu (family head or administrator) is generally given to the oldest or most capable woman in the clan. The dabu's responsibilities consist of organizing farm work, overseeing the household, calculating expenses, receiving guests, dividing up food, and carrying out religious ceremonies. In a few families in which no woman can or wants to take over the office of dabu, the task can also be assigned to an older uncle. However, certain tasks within the family, such as administering the food stocks, family finances, and the household; the performance of religious ceremonies such as inaugurating a new house and blessing the fireplace; or the puberty ceremony of putting on a skirt, cannot be carried out by an uncle. They remain the women's privilege. Women can also manage all the external affairs of the family independently. They can lend money, get a mortgage, rent out meadowland, and enter into business agreements.

Despite the dabu's authority, family organization is democratic. The dabu cannot make important family decisions alone, but must call a family council and discuss the matter with the old mothers, aunts and uncles, and brothers and sisters. The dabu enjoys no visible privileges over the other family members. She participates in the same work as the others. Although women are responsible for farming, plowing is exclusively men's work. Women enjoy a high position, and in none of the families are women struck or cursed. Relationships are very harmonious in most families.

Yongning Naxi family compounds are built to fit the needs of the matriarchal group. They generally consist of a main house, two wings with two stories, and a barn. The main house contains a 160-square-meter (192 sq. yd.) common room, a grain storage area, and four side rooms. The common room is the center of family activity; the family meets here for meals, discussions, religious ceremonies, and to receive guests. The seating arrangement in the common room is strictly organized; women sit on the right, men on the left of the fireplace. This room is also the sleeping room for the family head, the other older women, and the children. A side room of the main house serves as the sleeping room for the older men who no longer spend the night with girlfriends. The other rooms in the main house are used for food storage. The lower level of the two-story wings serves as shelter for the livestock. In the upper level there are many small rooms, each with its own fireplace and bed. These are the so-called guest rooms, in which the young women receive their lovers. A family has as many guest rooms as there are women in the family. The women also keep their clothing and private belongings in these rooms. When they become older and no longer receive lovers, they leave the guest room and move into the common room with the other older women and the children. The guest room is then either passed along to a young woman or used for storage. The young men of the family have no room of their own; if they do not spend the night with a girlfriend, they sleep either in the old men's room or in the barn.

Other family forms exist in increasing numbers alongside the purely matriarchal family. It is common for a woman's lover to stay with her family in the daytime, frequently because he lives too far away. Sometimes the woman moves into the matriarchal family of the man. Legal marriages and nuclear families have become more common since the 1950s, under the influence of the People's Republic's marriage propaganda. It is often the men who make an offer of marriage, but the women refuse especially when they enjoy important positions within their own matriarchal family. This is apparent in the following interview that Jiaama, daughter of Dashima, mentioned at the beginning of this article, gave to the Chinese research team in 1963 when she was twenty-seven.

Jiaama's Story

When I was thirteen, the ceremony of putting on a skirt was celebrated for me. Mama said to me: "From today on you will no longer be together with the other children, but will do as the adults do. I have cleaned a nice guest room for you, that's where you will now live!" I moved into the guest room as Mama told me.

A few of the girls teased me: "Jiaama, aren't you afraid all alone in the room?" "A little," I said. Then they said: "You don't need to be afraid, a lover will come and keep you company." Back then I thought, who would sleep with a little girl like me?

A year later Dongbao Xibi, from the east bank of the lake, came to our village. We knew one another from before; he is older than I am, but before I was still a little child. This time I was a young girl and he accompanied me constantly. Once he asked me: "Can I come home with you to get something to drink?" I was so excited, I did not know what to say, but just nodded my head.

That night, Dongbao Xibi came to my room. Mama was already asleep and my brothers were all at their girlfriends' homes. The next morning he left when the first cock crowed. After that he came almost every evening and left me again at dawn. Mama noticed it very quickly. She said to me: "Child, *a xiao* is a respectable thing. He can visit you without inhibition, you don't have to do it in secret." After Mama had said this, I became braver. The next day I let Dongbao Xibi eat dinner with us. Mama was very effusive; she baked flatbread and fried extra bacon just for him, and my brothers greeted him warmly.

After we had slept together for more than ten days, I gave him a linen belt. He later gave me a pair of leather shoes. One day he said to me: "I would like to marry you and make you my wife, do you agree?" I said: "It is much better, if you stay my lover. If you announce that you want to marry me, Mama and my brothers will chase you out of the house." He regretted it and never visited me again.

My second friend was Acai Dezhi from Zhipo Village. I remember that I met him in my fifteenth year on 25 July, the holiday of the goddess Ganmu. We strolled together for a while, when he asked me: "Shall we sleep together?" I wanted to. I invited him to come to my house the next evening and we agreed that he would throw little stones on my roof and I would let him in.

A few months later—it was almost winter—I kept vomiting and could not get any food down. I thought I was sick. Whenever I had been sick before, the whole family had always gotten terribly upset, but this time everyone stayed calm. Mama's whole face beamed when she explained to me: "You aren't sick, you will soon have a child. That is very lucky for our courtyard!" And she also said that the whole family welcomed Acai Dezhi. When I told Acai Dezhi this, he was very happy. Once he came with a basket of eggs, and he often gave my mother salt and tea. Each time we ate meat, Mama saved a piece especially for him.

My belly grew larger every day, I could hardly move. Mama was afraid that I would do something wrong. Therefore I was to live with her now, so that she could take care of me day and night. When Acai Dezhi came, he was very surprised that I was now living in the common room. I explained to him: "Wait until the child is born, then we can both move back into the guest room." He muttered something and left. After that he never visited me again.

Soon after that I had a baby boy, whom I named Dashi. I was afraid that Mama would not be happy about it and asked her: "Are you angry that the first child is only a boy?" But Mama said, completely unconcerned: "Why should I be angry, everything has two sides, boys and girls are the supports of our family." Little Dashi was a healthy little fellow and was raised by my mother.

Two or three months after Dashi's birth, Ama Yishi, Chuba Bima, and Jiawa Ewo, all young lads from our village, courted me.

Around this time, Liangzhi Bubu from Sichuan was introduced to me by relatives of my mother's. He told my mother that he wanted to be my lover. He brought her tea and salt and gave me a skirt, a blouse, and a pair of shoes. Mama agreed and said to me: "Liangzhi Bubu is an honest man, better than Ama Yishi." That same evening, he ate with us. When I saw that he was well-built and still young, I was quite satisfied. That night I slept with him.

After I had been together with Liangzhi Bubu for two years, I had the first girl, Yizuoma. People said that the child looked very much like Liangzhi Bubu. Then Liangzhi Bubu became haughty and announced presumptuously that he wanted to become a son-in-law in our family. I said to him: "I have seven brothers, and you want to be a son-in-law. We only slept together, you don't need to get any big ideas afterward." After that, he gradually stopped coming to us.

I was just eighteen then and thought: "Liangzhi Bubu is gone, but there are other men." The news that I had separated from him spread like wildfire. My most important lovers then were Ama Yishi and Jiawa Ewo. Sometimes they both even came to me together. Since they had grown up together and knew one another well, they were very considerate most of the time, and the one who came later let the first one go ahead.

One day it happened that the two had to go to Lijiang, the district center. According to our custom, the girlfriend has to give her lover chicken, bacon, flatbread, and other food when he leaves for a journey; this gesture is considered a "send off." I gave food to both of them. Ama Yishi was so clever that he said to Jiawa Ewo: "Jiaama gave both of us gifts because she wants to have a present in return. We won't have anything more to do with her when we return." Jiawa Ewo believed him and when he came back from Lijiang, he paid no attention to me. Ama Yishi, however, came to visit every night and brought Mama and me presents. Jiawa Ewo noticed this. He told me of the conversation that he had had along the way with Ama Yishi, and my brothers heard about it, too. I was furious and extremely unfriendly to Ama Yishi: "You don't need to come any more, give your gifts to others, we don't appreciate them!" That is how I broke off the relationship with Ama Yishi. Jiawa Ewo's honesty, however, won the sympathy of my family. I was together with him for a long time and had the second girl, Dezhima.

When Dezhima was exactly two years old, the most terrible misfortune came to my family: Mama died. Shortly before her death, my mother had given me her keys. That meant that I was to become dabu, head of the family. That was very difficult for me; I already had enough to do organizing the farm work, doing the housework, and taking care of three children. How was I supposed to be dabu, too? I did it for a few days and it seemed to me as if a weight of a thousand pounds lay on my shoulders. I could hardly stand the pressure. If I took care of one thing, I forgot another. So I consulted my brothers and let my fifth brother take over the duties of dabu. At first he did not want to, but we finally convinced him and he agreed.

During this most difficult time for me, Jiawa Ewo behaved

like a wild goose. When he noticed that it had gotten colder, he went south. To be honest, I did not have any interest in sleeping with anybody at that time. Later, I began a relationship with Dashi Picha. He lives in Wenquan. He frequently comes to our village to trade grain for fish. That is how we met and talked to one another. Every time he comes, he stays in my guest room. That has been for three years now. During this time I gave birth to another girl, little Jiaama."

Matriarchy in the People's Republic

In February 1952 the People's Liberation Army under the leadership of the Chinese Communist Party "liberated" the Yongning Region. The Chinese Communists confronted the Yongning Naxi with mixed feelings. They found in Yongning's variety of coexisting family forms an opportunity to investigate the development of the family. Here they could examine the theses of Friedrich Engels's *Origin of the Family* against living examples. While the Communists were able to find some positive aspects in the matriarchal families of Yongning, the liberal sexuality of the Yongning Naxi could not be reconciled with communist morality. The Chinese apparently did everything they could to speed up the process of transition to patriarchy, which they saw taking place in Yongning.

In 1956, the tribal princes of the Yongning Naxi were removed and land reform was carried out. In 1958 the Yongning Region was declared a people's commune and the villages transformed into brigades, decisively weakening the power of the matriarchal families as economic units, for now all important production decisions were made by the brigades.

Judging from photographs taken in the 1970s, socialist progress had reached Yongning. Roads were built and the first truck arrived. Plowing, the only field work that had been done exclusively by men in the matriarchal families, was now—at least for the photographer—done with the use of tractors instead of a team of oxen. The times when one oriented oneself according to the position of the sun and the moon in Yongning were over. Thanks to a small hydroelectric plant, electric bulbs now glowed in Yongning farmhouses. A photograph shows Naxi women at the controls of the power plant. Every village had its own health station, and several grade schools and a middle school were set up.

Despite these massive inputs, social change in Naxi society

did not occur as quickly as the Chinese development aid workers had intended. Most Naxi took reluctant leave of the matriarchal extended family as their economic base. Life in the patriarchal nuclear family was attractive to very few. In response, at the end of the 1950s, the People's government began a program to lead the Naxi to modern marriage. The first measure recommended as a foundation for future strategies was a thorough study of the historical development and current state of marriage and family relationships of the Naxi. This recommendation was carried out by a Chinese research team that spent the year 1963 living in Yongning and conducting a sociological investigation of family customs there.

As a next step, health stations were to carry out campaigns against the wide incidence of sexually transmitted diseases. According to a 1958 study, 24 percent of the population of Yongning suffered from sexually transmitted diseases. The campaign, however, served not only to treat the sick, but also to teach the population about the causes of disease and, above all, that changing sexual partners frequently encouraged the spread of sexually transmitted diseases. The propaganda did not stop with tips on sexual hygiene. It went on to say that the *a xiao* system of nonbinding free love harmed the revolution, production, and the life of society. It endangered the health of the population and damaged the education of children, especially the generation of young people who were to be raised on the values of communist morality. The reactionary family system of the Yongning Naxi had to be reformed in the interest of the coming generations. Therefore, the propagation of the marriage law of the People's Republic of China was announced. The Naxi were to be taught the advantages of legalized marriage through positive images of model families whom they were to be encouraged to emulate.

Many marriages that were entered into under the pressure of political propaganda did not last long. Matriarchal ideas were still too deeply anchored in the families. And the Naxi often made use of the right to divorce guaranteed them by Chinese marriage law.

A photograph from the 1970s shows the model Naxi one-child family, as the Chinese government envisioned it. Father, mother, and son sit respectably around a table. The child, wearing a Mao cap and the red scarf of a Young Pioneer, is reading aloud to his parents. On the table are a radio receiver, two tea cups, and the thermos bottle which is everywhere in socialist

China. The goddess Ganmu no longer floats over the family, replaced by Chairman Mao, who looks down with a fatherly gaze from a poster on the wall.

A statistic from 1976 suggests that this idyll had, in fact, become reality for many Naxi families. It was determined that in the People's Commune of Yongning, one-third of the persons of marriageable age were married. This moderate "success" surely was achieved only through strong external pressure. During the Cultural Revolution, divorce was made more difficult, loose sexual relationships were strictly forbidden, and marriages were forced by the government's refusal to distribute grain to the unmarried.

Since national minorities policy became more liberal in the 1980s, many of these forced marriages have been dissolved again. At the same time, economic reforms and the de-collectivization of people's communes at the beginning of the 1980s returned a degree of economic autonomy to the families and, thus, created more favorable conditions for the continued existence of Yongning's matriarchal families.

Beijing

LOVE, MARRIAGE, AND VIOLENCE: SEXUALITY IN CHINA

Ina Simson

A re Chinese women prudes? Some Western travelers consider it a sign of prudishness that the Chinese do not display feelings in public—you do not see couples walking arm in arm, or kissing. This behavior runs counter to many travelers' expectations: Didn't the Chinese produce famous erotic tracts? Wasn't sexuality an aspect of Chinese culture that was always nurtured? All this is true. Yet sexuality was freely expressed only by artists and intellectuals; it was reserved for a small elite and used in the philosophical and medical quest for immortality, playing an important role in the development of medicine.

It may be disappointing to some that none of this is visible in contemporary China, but that does not mean that the "classical" ideas of sexuality are buried. Are Chinese women prudes? No. It is Chinese morality that is prudish—a morality cloaked in various guises that has repressed sexuality for centuries and was imposed through the ages by the ruling elite, mostly men, though there were always a few upper-class women who helped stabilize norms of conduct by actively encouraging them. In China, the dictates of morality mainly prevent women from freely developing their sexuality.

Sexual mores were tightened about five hundred years ago, under the Ming dynasty (1368–1644). Earlier, especially during the Tang dynasty (618–907), life was characterized by a relatively diverse set of behavioral norms and a relaxed attitude toward the body. Although the binding of women's feet—aimed primarily at confining upper-class women to their homes and at reducing them to sexual objects—had been introduced in the Song dynasty (960–1279), neo-Confucianism did not take hold until later when it eventually narrowed governing norms to a few static forms of expression and modes of conduct, and hardened sexual morality to a point where sexuality came to be regarded as dirty.

This development started thousands of years ago with the establishment of a patriarchal society in the Zhou dynasty (1122–221 B.C.). As recent archeological discoveries and analyses of ancient texts appear to confirm, however, it was preceded by a matriarchal order. At the time, no one knew that procreation depended on impregnating the female ovum, and only the women could tell with certainty which children were their own. Men were considered unimportant in the birth of children. The attempt to master this uncertainty was one reason for men to overturn the prevailing social order, for they could only establish that their wives' children belonged to them if they controlled women by dictating that they had to be virgins before and monogamous during marriage. Initially these restrictions applied only to the upper classes. A bride's virginity was pivotal for another aspect of the dominant patriarchal order: ancestor worship. The legitimation for men's rule and power was based on their descent, in part magically derived, from powerful male ancestors. Men could ascertain the paternity of their sons only if women were never "touched" by another man.

Mandatory procreation was the corollary of these ideas, as the line of ancestors could not be interrupted. Men took one or more concubines as soon as they could afford it; it enhanced their prestige and increased the certainty of male progeny. If a man's wife could not bear children or had borne "only" daughters, it was acceptable for him to purchase the services of a surrogate mother from the time of impregnation through pregnancy and birth. Sexuality was reduced to compulsory procreation—in the interest of perpetuating patrilineal ancestor worship and producing one or more male heirs. The sons were solely responsible for assuring a family's economic stability, while the daughters left their homes when they married, to serve another family. This also explains the attitude that daughters are a burden, because they have to be fed and clothed only to later benefit others. Female infanticide was widespread. The policy of restricting families to a single child further motivates such acts, for the birth of a daughter automatically buries the dream of having a son. Hence many prefer to commit an illegal act (discreetly, of course)—traditional ideas endure.

The repression of female sexuality started with the postulate of virginity; later, women were required to be chaste at all times. Apart from the Confucian paradigm that women were to be excluded from the public—i.e., male—realm, they had to submit to the "Three Rules of Obedience": As a daughter, a woman had to obey her father, as a wife her husband, and as a widow her son.

Confucianism was paramount in the organization of Chinese society, while Daoism was significant in the sexual sphere. The two ideologies developed roughly at the same time, about 500 B.C., and since then both social models have been irreconcilably opposed. Their precepts could not be more dissimilar. Originally, Daoism posited that women and men are equal within the dualist concept of *yin* and *yang* that encompass humankind and nature alike. The goal is to fuse the two poles, and to create harmony. This concept led to the notion that the sexual union serves the same purpose, i.e., that the fusion of the yang essence (male semen) with the yin essence (fluid emitted by women during orgasm) improves one's quality of life. Concretely, this means that the man must ensure that his female partner experiences orgasm so that he can obtain her yin essence. Since the Daoists also believe that the yang essence is finite (in contrast to the yin essence), the man should hold back his orgasm so as to lose as little as possible of his precious semen. Conversely, women can improve their quality of life by obtaining the yang essence. It is at this juncture that the purported threat of women to men enters into the equation, leading to the idea of women as monsters who drain men of their life essence.

These Daoist ideas were subsumed by Confucianism when men were required to trigger as many orgasms as possible in their women, for only fresh (not stale) yin essence was believed to ensure healthy male descendants. Though women's pleasure was underscored, it served a purpose, and the original notion that women possess sexual knowledge was negated. Forcing men to control sexuality and largely denying women any knowledge of sexual matters served to defeat women's power.

Thus, the history of prudish morality in China is the story of men's fear of women's power: the fear of women's childbearing ability and uncontrollable fertility, and the fear that women's sexuality is innately wicked, capable of leading innocent men to their doom. Various rules aimed at curbing this power served both to channel female sexuality and to devalue it. This is most obvious in the context of menstruation. Menstrual blood was considered polluted, and numerous injunctions forced women to behave in ways that ignored their desires and drastically restricted their freedom of movement. This and many other examples show how women's power was subverted to control them.

The Communist government willingly adopted these prudish morals for its own purposes; at least that is what official reactions to demands for less restricted sexuality convey. For the young generation, the slogan "sexual freedom" means respect for their personal needs and less top-down regimentation of the private sphere. It does not refer to the notions of sexual experimentation that surfaced in the West in the 1960s and 1970s. What is common to both, however, is the battle against conventional mores.

The demand for "sexual freedom" evolved from the battles for equality spearheaded by women's movements after the fall of the last dynasty in 1911. Women devised the slogan "free love, free marriage, free divorce" to frame their preconditions for the equality of women and men, the unrestricted development of individual feelings, and individuals' personal responsibility. In their view, liberated sexuality was the only reasonable basis for a marriage, but their opponents accused them of propagating promiscuity. The commune of Jiangxi, created in the 1930s, was supposed to become the first "field of experimentation" for achieving sexual freedom. Mao Zedong was the commune's chairman, and he encouraged the peasants to choose their mates freely without resorting to traditional matchmakers, rites, and expenditures. For many men, until then unable to afford a marriage, this must have come close to salvation on earth. Pent-up frustrations and deprivation erupted, but women, who had expected to be liberated from past restrictions as well, found that instead they were treated like fair game. Since cohabitation was permitted at first, many men simply "took" women, temporarily or to live with them. Of course, some women defended themselves against such appropriation, and frequently violent confrontations ensued. Though Mao had to retreat from the idea of sexual freedom (henceforth marriages had to be officially registered), he emphasized that the ability to choose a mate for life was intended to emancipate women and could not be exploited to repress them yet again.

The problem was much more complex, however, for the party had lost control and considered it more important to re-

Family planning poster

gain its authority than to learn, together with its rank and file, to exercise unfamiliar freedoms in appropriate ways. The issue of sexual freedom was never again included in the political program of the Chinese Communist Party (CCP).

Today officials use the terms "sexual freedom" or "sexual emancipation" mainly as a deterrent. Sexual freedom is what the people in capitalist countries in the West have; it leads to chaos, anarchy, and immorality, recently also to AIDS, for the latter comes from foreign countries and is the virus of sexual liberation.

In a 1986 poll, 66.4 percent of the women and 59.4 percent of the men advocated a "pure" wedding. However, most men who favor sexual relations before marriage mean that only for themselves, not for women. Men prefer to marry virgins, and women who are sexually active before marriage are considered almost as bad as are prostitutes. On the other hand, most women will sleep only with the man they want to marry and, in fact, only if they can be (fairly) sure of their plans.

The centuries-old moral crutch that turns sexuality into something dirty and immoral is still omnipresent. It is contrasted with the purity of spiritual love—love for the nation and the construction of socialism, and love between two people that should express itself chiefly in mutual understanding and encouragement to work and study. Sexual attraction and

147

satisfaction are mere obstacles to the pure feelings of "true" love. It makes sense for officials to promote late marriages, not only as part of the single-child-family policy. Policymakers assume that people's availability for national development decreases as soon as they indulge their sexuality, i.e., when they marry.

And yet marriage is considered obligatory. It would not be normal for women or men to decide not to marry, or once they do, not to have a child. What might contribute to reducing the birth rate contradicts public morality. While some unmarried couples live together, they are few and far between. Normally, girls and boys live with their parents until they marry, perhaps long after that, often in as little as one or two rooms. Privacy is almost nonexistent, and mutual scrutiny in the *danwei* (work unit) does its part to make innocent meetings among young people as good as unthinkable. So they acquire sexual experience in absolute secrecy.

Although contraceptives are officially distributed only to married women, nowadays it is easier for others to obtain them, if necessary via a married woman friend. Most people do not appear to harbor moral reservations about abortions, though unmarried women must deal with the stigma of having acted immorally. Incidentally, the single-child policy, combined with this attitude toward abortion, resulted in much suffering when it was introduced. Overzealous cadres (among them, women on the neighborhood committees), intent on attaining perfect birth rates in their districts, forced some women to undergo abortions as late as the seventh month.

Better sexual education would give younger women more security and would help young men to deal differently with conflicts, which they still try to solve by violent means. Friends remain the most common, albeit equally ignorant, source of sexual information, though there are attempts to introduce sex education in schools and to establish public counseling offices. Pamphlets, increasingly popular over the past ten years, convey mostly biological facts and do not encourage young people to handle their sexuality in a responsible and assured manner. Questions about pleasure—especially women's—are in most cases simply ignored. Girls and boys learn that women do not have sexual needs before they marry. Once married, however, their sexual arousal is a precondition for intercourse (= procreation), but the pamphlets do not address women's ability to experience orgasm, for procreation does not depend on it.

Masturbation and homosexuality, both considered "youthful sins" and sick acts, are presented as predominantly male variants of sexual activity. The rare girl that might be "led astray" is vividly cautioned about such consequences as infertility, blindness, and menstrual pains. Since female homosexuality is not discussed in these brochures, we may assume that most people cannot imagine it.

Some Western women who have traveled in China believe that lesbian love, though concealed, is relatively widespread. In my view, however, one may not automatically assume this to be true, for the moral barriers and the negation of women's sex drive are powerful deterrents. And yet, among themselves, women frequently express a startling informality about physical matters. I have found myself in situations that I cannot imagine happening to me in Europe. In the ladies' room of the Beijing Hotel, for example, three Chinese women once excitedly showed each other toilet paper soiled with their menstrual blood; apparently they had all gotten their periods at the same time. My presence did not inhibit them in the least. On another occasion, when I was changing a tampon in one of the public toilets, which consists merely of a drain across the floor, other women present did not restrain their curiosity, but assembled around me to comment on the event. Such impressions of physical ease are contradicted, however, by the modesty of young girls who must change in front of one another at swimming pools. Perhaps nudity belongs to a realm more restricted than menstruation.

As foreigners, we must be cautious in our interpretations, for too many aspects of Chinese life are unknown to us. Often we cannot understand why social problems are addressed in such seemingly strange ways. The dramatic increase in sex crimes over the past few years—rape, commercial prostitution, sexual relations with minors, and the sale of underage girls—is met, for instance, with the demand for better sex education, though many different social conditions and problems are the cause.

The economic reforms, introduced in the early 1980s to raise the standard of living and to stimulate the economy, have many ugly facets. Increasing unemployment is one of them. It strikes mainly young people, making them feel superfluous. Those who are unemployed for a long time frequently resort to aggression to compensate for their weakness. Rape is one of the most direct (violent) acts used by men to reassure themselves of their power. Though rape is considered a capital crime, punishments have so far been unable to stem the tide. In contrast to the West, where some blame for the rape might be shifted to the woman, in China the rapist is the focus of the legal system. However, this says nothing about the ability of a woman who has been raped to find a man who will marry her. That could be a big problem, given Chinese men's "virginity" mania.

Unscrupulous profiteering is another, no less ugly outcome of recent economic developments, translating sexuality into prostitution and the sale of women under twenty, the official marriage age. Though prostitution is outlawed, it has a long tradition both as a social institution and as a business with foreigners. Literary descriptions of famous courtesans and so-called flower girls testify that bordellos were an integral part of daily public life before the revolution. At the beginning of the twentieth century, China's colonial masters (both Western and Japanese) expanded this trade, spawning an early form of sex tourism. The Communists stopped these practices by sending prostitutes into factories. Additionally, they instituted reeducation campaigns both to develop women's socialist consciousness and to reintegrate them into "normal" life. These attempts were successful, since prostitution has not been prominent until recently.

Unfortunately, China is catching up with other Asian countries, and Western men's magazines now advertise the qualities of Chinese women. Pimps (some of whom are married couples) have reappeared; they train the women and send them to the right places, mostly hotels frequented by foreigners, mostly businessmen. Men students from the West are offered "sisters" and "girlfriends" to serve as their companions during their stay in China—unofficially, of course, and for good money. All too often, the women hope to marry and be taken abroad by one of these men because they may leave China only if they have sufficient financial resources or connections abroad. An economic emergency may be another motive.

Prostitution is also encouraged by Chinese men. The notion of personal responsibility propagated by the economic reforms has led, among other things, to a significant increase in the importance of domestic production, which is carried out primarily by women, children, and the elderly. Suddenly a daughter may seem important, for she can be sold, so to speak, to the highest-bidding family when she is old enough to marry. Parents' meddling in the marriage affairs of their daughters, especially to increase bride prices considerably, is but one of the consequences. For many men it is much easier to pay a one-time (and lower) fee for their contacts with women; indeed, for poor men this is perhaps the only way of "getting a woman." That, too, has a tradition and explains why the conditions at the Jiangxi commune escalated to such a degree.

In the view of many pimps, it is more profitable and less costly to kidnap and sell predominantly underage girls. Such practices recently came to light when a young woman student from Shanghai was lured to a village under a ruse and sold to a man for roughly 2,500 yuan. After the fake marriage, he raped her and held her prisoner for several weeks. She was finally found, and the case was brought to court; the man was sentenced to five years in prison for the rape. Although trading in human beings is punishable by jail terms of five or more years, so far the dealers have not been deterred. On the contrary, the business is so lucrative that one dealer sold twenty-eight women in a single year for 30,000 yuan. In most cases, they are not reported to the authorities for a reason. Since discussing a bride price is sanctioned by tradition, the dealers are considered an extension of matchmakers, not criminals. Moreover, their "offer" is often much better (i.e., lower) than the price of a regular marriage. In the words of a man party functionary: "Marriages of young people cost about four to five thousand yuan these days. But it costs only 2,500 yuan to buy a wife. So many people in the villages do it, and nobody asks any questions."

China's rulers are reacting to the changes in the realm of sexual politics with insecurity and helplessness. For a long time they could be certain that entrenched morality would function without fail. Fear appears to be the stumbling block. To grant sexual freedom might entail yielding control, and in a patriarchal system that would mean that the mechanisms used to exploit women sexually would have to be dismantled.

Another aspect is that the renunciation of sexual desire leads to the creation of culture, in the widest sense of the term. When morals are strict, sexual needs must be harnessed, preferably in ways benefiting production. Consequently, young people are exhorted to turn their attention to love as late as possible. Once married they are told that intercourse once or twice a week is normal, but that more will diminish their performance at work. Please, if you must succumb to your lust, at least do so in orderly fashion!

Translated by Ulrike Bode

BAOMU: DOMESTIC WORKERS

Jutta Lietsch

Travelers arriving at train stations in Beijing or other Chinese cities immediately notice large groups of families, women, and men huddling in waiting rooms, talking, playing cards, and trying to sleep. Most of them are not waiting for trains—they have nowhere else to go.

In the past few years, the number of people leaving their homes in search of work elsewhere in China has skyrocketed. According to official statistics, in 1989 alone the "wandering population" amounted to about fifty million people. Among them are many young women who migrate to cities from rural areas. They set out for numerous reasons, such as to escape unemployment, poverty, and arranged marriages; to save sufficient capital for a small business, further education, or a dowry; or to acquire new skills—all of which will give them a better start in life once they return to their villages. Some move to the cities simply for the adventure. Many of these women work as domestics.

Housework—No Longer Invisible

Maids in China? Were they not a despised relic of feudal and bourgeois lifestyles eliminated by the Cultural Revolution? In fact, even during China's radical periods, families of high party officials retained domestic workers.

The economic reforms launched at the end of the 1970s intensified women's triple burden: jobs, housework, and caring for both children and the elderly, leading to a modification of the official stance toward domestic work for pay. "Whenever we ask women about problems stemming from the economic reforms, the first thing we hear are complaints about the excruciating burden of housework," noted *Zhongguo Funü (Chinese Women)*, the publication of the All-China Women's Federation (ACWF). How were women going to keep up with men, now that companies had won the right to participate in decisions about their work force and competition for jobs was beginning to make itself felt? "Women who want to satisfy the new requirements must continually improve their qualifications. They must focus entirely on their work. They must strengthen their self-esteem and not allow themselves to be squeezed out, allegedly for being weaker and inferior," women's representatives pointed out.

In 1983, before the establishment of the first job placement agencies, the city of Beijing and the Beijing Economic Institute conducted the first survey of *baomu* (domestic workers) in seven Beijing districts. It concluded that the number of domestics had grown by almost 130 percent each year since 1980 and that there were about 30,000 maids in Beijing. Most of them were employed in Xicheng and Haidian, where the residential neighborhoods of government and university personnel are concentrated. The study distinguished between two categories of baomu: 10,613 domestics were Beijing housewives and retirees, while 18,000 were rural women from all over China; of these, about 11,300 came from the provinces of Anhui and Jiangsu.

Only 258 of the 904 families surveyed were working class, most of them young couples. The lack of adequate nurseries and day-care centers was one of the main reasons for hiring a baomu, though the care of elderly or sick family members was equally important. The renowned sociologist Fei Xiaotong called for the creation of employment agencies for maids to free intellectuals for the demands of their professions.

However, the problem of women's triple burden was not restricted to intellectuals. A study of urban households in Heilongjiang Province revealed that, on the average, women and men (intellectuals, as well as skilled and unskilled workers) together spent almost twice as much time on housework as their counterparts in the United States, France, and even in the Soviet Union. The women spent almost five hours a day on housework, one and a half hours more than the men. Most households were not equipped with such time-saving appliances as washing machines and refrigerators. It was estimated in 1981 that only 5 to 6 percent of all urban families had a washing machine. Many people had to spend hours standing in line each day to buy groceries and consumer goods; in addition, paltry salaries forced people to make and clean most of their clothes themselves. All these factors combined to increase the pressure on the working population.

ACWF Responses

The ACWF put forward proposals for mechanizing, socializing, and professionalizing housework to solve some of these problems. Mechanizing housework depended on an expanded light industry capable of producing efficient household appliances. Socializing housework required the creation of a service sector capable of supplying laundry services, child care, inexpensive meals, and other services. Finally, it advocated professionalizing housework or elevating this work done in the home to the level of a paid job. The ACWF emphasized, in light of increasingly visible unemployment, that its recommendations would help to create jobs, especially for women. Chinese officials had begun to acknowledge at the end of the 1970s that the annually growing number of female high-school graduates forced to "wait for work" (as the situation was euphemistically described) was a problem: in many cities girls accounted for about 70 percent of unemployed youth. Worse yet, these urban millions waiting for the state to assign them jobs were joined by large numbers of women and men returning to the cities after having been sent to the countryside in the 1960s and 1970s. The state-run employment agencies charged with allocating jobs finally had to admit that they were overwhelmed by the huge task and encouraged the unemployed to look for work themselves, "temporarily."

In the early 1980s, a growing chorus of voices advocated another "solution" (all-too-familiar in other countries) to the unemployment problem: women's return to hearth and home. The official women's representatives rejected this idea, quickly and decisively. They had no doubt that pushing women out of the job market would destroy any progress achieved so far in women's liberation, force them back into economic dependency on their husbands and families, and close any avenues for their political emancipation. But the debate persisted. Not only men wanted women to "go home": polls and letters to editors revealed that many younger women seemed to believe that the life of a housewife and mother would be desirable for a few years, if they had small children and if the family had the requisite financial resources. In fact, companies started paying women small allowances to vacate their jobs.

In response, the ACWF printed numerous articles in its magazine examining housework from a theoretical angle. The central argument was that housework as unpaid, private work is a trap for women. However, if a significant number of the largely invisible household tasks performed mainly by women— cleaning, sewing and washing clothes, preserving food, etc.— can be accomplished and paid for in exactly the same way as other products and services, overall productivity will increase by enabling women to save time, which they can then utilize for both leisure and continuing education.

Modernization, increased productivity, and socialization of housework were seen as mutually dependent and as benefiting individual women and society as a whole. This analysis targeted both the undervaluation of housework and the accusation that women take away men's jobs; it also asserted the importance of domestic work within the context of socialism.

Official Job Placement Agencies

A Beijing newspaper announced early in 1984 that the "March Eighth Placement Agency" was looking for women all over China to work as domestics. Interested applicants should have good character, be at least seventeen years old, healthy, and (of course) unemployed. They should submit written permission from their home authorities and a health certificate. Their monthly salary would be at least twenty-five yuan, plus room and board. Organized by the ACWF, the March Eighth Placement Agency was the first employment agency for domestics. Before long, numerous official establishments of this type had been set up not only in Beijing, Shanghai, and Tianjin, but also in smaller cities.

To erase any doubts that the "new" domestics occupied a position contrasting sharply with that of servants under feudalism who had no rights and were severely exploited, the traditional terms *ayi* (aunt, and by extension, any older woman) or baomu (nanny) were to be replaced by *jiawu fuwuyuan* (service personnel for housework). But this designation was too cumbersome, even for those who had invented it, and people soon reverted to baomu and ayi.

Placement agencies for domestics assumed numerous functions related to legalization of residency, access to social services, and legal representation of both the baomu and their employers. As the *danwei* (work unit) in charge of the women, they organized the required physical exams, obtained temporary *hukou* (residence permit), drafted standard employment contracts, and mediated in conflicts. There were also plans to survey the baomu's working conditions each year to protect them. In some cases, the agencies even offered introductory courses about city life to familiarize rural women, in particular, with modern household appliances, hygiene practices, and other information.

Open Baomu Markets

The officially placed *baomu* represent only a small portion of the rapidly growing number of domestics, which was estimated in 1987 to have reached fifty thousand in Beijing alone. Open baomu markets sprang up rapidly. Many of the peasant girls and women, who had arrived without permission from their home authorities, had to circumvent formalities and find employers on their own. This also enabled them to avoid a placement fee (five yuan for the agencies run by the ACWF) and to negotiate higher wages. In 1988, the minimum wage set by the ACWF for a domestic in Beijing was thirty-seven yuan, whereas on the open market women could demand fifty yuan and more, plus room and board.

There are several meeting places of this type (described as "free baomu markets" or "illegal markets") in Beijing, Shanghai, and other metropolitan areas. Both newly arrived women and those wishing to change employers come to these markets daily to wait for and contract with prospective employers. Urban women often try in vain to find a domestic through official channels. "The supply of baomu is tight in Shanghai," wrote a Shanghai paper, "and that is good for the baomu, for it will increase their social status."

The 1983 survey of domestics in Beijing had shown that, on the average, the rural women were twenty-eight years old, while those mainly from Beijing were forty-eight years old. The survey also pointed out that "young domestics are becoming increasingly popular because they are considered more able than the middle-aged or older women who traditionally occupied this role." It went on to say that "girls, most of them between fifteen and nineteen, their heads full of dreams, are arriving in

Beijing from all over China, but mainly from the provinces of Anhui and Henan."

A 1987 report stated that in contrast to the time before the Cultural Revolution, contemporary baomu were younger, better educated, and more self-confident. A survey of one thousand Beijing domestics showed that, on the average, they had completed five years of grade school, and one-half of them had attended lower middle school (fifth to seventh grade) or even upper middle school.

Where Do the Women Come From?

What had started as an individual solution for women from all over China was soon taken up by various provincial ACWF offices. In November 1987, *China Daily* reported that:

> Gansu, one of the poorest regions in China's Northwest, has been successful in finding useful employment for surplus women workers. In the past two years, more than ten thousand girls were trained by the Gansu All-China Women's Federation and sent to large cities (among others, Beijing, Guangzhou, and Xi'an) as domestics. The majority of the women came from twenty-six very poor districts; they had become superfluous after the introduction of the household contract system in 1979.* There are plans to send an additional ten thousand girls to other provinces next year.

Though most of the young women arrive in the cities on their own, their move is often condoned or even encouraged by their home districts, some of which have become famous as baomu suppliers. This includes Wuwei in Anhui Province, which has been providing baomu to urban areas for the past fifty years. Many domestics unite in informal associations determined by regional background (frequently referred to as the Anhui or Jiangsu Gangs). These more or less tight groupings provide information to new arrivals, as well as the advice and support of experienced baomu. In many residential areas, such "protective associations" evolve around certain baomu who represent the others and ensure that only women from their region are employed, if possible; competition from other regions is unwelcome. Families looking for domestics often turn to these agents who, in turn, send for women from their villages.

---

* See the essay by Monika Schädler in this volume.

"A girl who has arrived with the help of such a go-between becomes the latter's protégée. She will give up her first month's wages and present her with gifts on holidays," explained *Xin Guancha* (magazine) in the spring of 1987. These go-betweens occupy a crucial position, for they both protect and control the baomu; if the latter misbehave, people at home will learn of it. Hence, it is vital for the protégées and their good reputations back home to remain on a good footing with the go-between.

Living and Working Conditions

In the cities, where scarce housing forces most families to live in extremely close quarters, housing the baomu is a problem. (This is less true in the suburbs, where private housing construction has recently provided some relief for certain populations.) Since most families make do with one or two rooms, often the baomus share the children's beds or sleep in the hallway. To alleviate this problem, the ACWF has begun advocating so-called big baomu: maids who live with one family but work for several families on an hourly basis.

The difference in expectations between the families and the baomu with regard to wages and working conditions causes frequent and widely known conflicts. Due to the low-wage scale overall, the additional expenses for a baomu can become a burden for some families. And there are complaints about the domestics' high demands: "Because we don't have a washing machine and a refrigerator, no woman wants to work in our house." Or: "We went through four baomu within a very short time. Some of them disappeared after a few days when they had found something better." For many women, the job of a domestic is only a stepping stone to private restaurants or trading companies, where they can earn many times what they are paid as a maid. However, there the working conditions are often characterized by "feudal relations of dependency": twelve- to fourteen-hour working days, no time off, and sexual abuse.

But there are also reports of baomu who are cheated out of their wages by their employers and experience sexual harassment and assault. The ACWF is concerned about the lack of protection for rural women who are not officially placed, many of whom do not know their rights. Another concern is that quite a few maids end up as prostitutes, a trade that has skyrocketed in recent years and cannot be controlled by police raids. The train stations and baomu markets are magnets for pimps, the ACWF reports.

According to official interpretations, these negative manifestations of the social changes wrought by economic reforms are inevitable phenomena that call for new strategies in the transition to modernization. They are the dark side of the positive developments repeatedly invoked in connection with baomu, which include the "modernizing effect" these women will have on rural areas. They can return to their villages with knowledge of new production techniques. A young woman who worked for a private chicken breeder in a suburb, for example, returned to her village with seven hundred chicks. Within a short time, she became a successful chicken farmer and is now one of the wealthiest people in the region.

Domestics in China? "Yes!" say the official representatives for women's policies, but they qualify their emphatic response by adding that this strategy should remain a transitional one—for the individual women, who work in these positions for a few years, and for society at large, because as soon as mechanization and socialization of housework have been achieved with the help of a highly developed service sector, baomu will once again be superfluous.

Translated by Ulrike Bode

"A Successful Woman Is Not Normal": Conversations with Women in Chinese Academe

Susanne Günthner

I n 1983, the first time I plunged into the crowds of people thronging a Chinese city, I was stunned by what I saw: husbands bicycling home with bags of groceries, a piece of meat, or a jerking fish dangling from a string. Fathers with little children on their arms, and grandfathers pushing strollers. "Yes, our husbands help around the house," the woman guide officially assigned to me proudly explained. And then there were women bus drivers, conductors, construction workers, you name it! For me, they were as much part of the "exoticism" as were the women I met at the college where I was to be a visiting professor. To my total surprise, these women were not secretaries, cafeteria attendants, or language instructors. Instead, I was introduced to a woman who taught electrical engineering, the woman dean of the faculty for mechanical engineering welcomed me to the college, and among my women students there were computer scientists, atomic physicists, and professors for cryogenics. "Yes, in socialism women and men are equal," commented my guide, again not without pride.

All of them appeared to be doing their jobs with a matter-of-factness of which European women can only dream. Had it been possible, indeed, for gender equality to sweep away the former patriarchal and Confucian social order with its culturally specific forms of female repression—crippled feet, concubines, and millions of desperate women driven to suicide? Does the ideal of a "socialism with a human face" exist here in China? Did the 1949 revolution truly encompass women? These were some of the thoughts during my first weeks in Shanghai that accompanied my contradictory images of Chinese women based on classic Chinese literature, articles about women in the post-Mao era, and Julia Kristeva's *About Chinese Women,* which I had read with great enthusiasm.

I spent several years in the People's Republic of China (PRC) as a foreign language instructor, and over time my initial fascination with the awesome achievements of Chinese emancipation began to fade. Although I continued to encounter the comment, "In our country women and men are absolutely equal. We do not need a women's movement like you [have] in the West, because our women already have equal rights," gradually familiar complaints about the realities of women's lives began to seep through. "Breaking with the feudal past and thousands of years of male domination just doesn't happen overnight," said some. Others chimed in: "It is true that we are still battling the benchmarks of the old feudal order." Many conversations with women friends, colleagues, and acquaintances, as well as with representatives of the All-China Women's Federation (ACWF) and both women faculty and students at various colleges and universities, conveyed images of women's daily lives that slowly but surely put a damper on my initial naive euphoria.

The Double Burden

Even though a few men "help" around the house, women still do the work. A poll conducted by *Zhongguo Funü (Chinese Women,* the ACWF's publication) in 1986 showed that 50 percent of all working women also had to care for their parents. In 15 percent of all households in which both spouses work in academia, the wife did all the housework. Though 84.8 percent of the women academics believed that their husbands were "helping with household chores," in most cases this was limited to grocery shopping. Given the permanent double burden, the majority of women sacrifice their academic careers for the sake of their families.

The Difficulty of Finding a Mate

When asked why they frequently decide not to pursue advanced degrees though many of them are better qualified than the men, women students told me how difficult it was for highly educated women to find a husband. One Shanghai scientist said: "Most Chinese men do not want a woman who is more intelligent or better educated than they are. Moreover, the men fear that such women will spend too much time on their careers and less time with their husbands and family."

The Higher the Academic Position, the Fewer the Women

A closer look at the academic sector reveals that the highest positions at universities (institute directors, deans, rectors, etc.) are reserved for men. The standard explanation for this phenomenon is that raising children, organizing family life, and taking care of elderly parents is "women's work." Since they must spend more time on housework and family, they have less time and energy for their academic work. Furthermore, it is argued that if more women were housewives and vacated their jobs for men, several social problems such as rising unemployment and the burden of housework on working women could be solved in one fell swoop. However, the ACWF decisively rejects both the view that women ought to be housewives, exclusively, and its consequence: women's renewed financial dependence on their husbands.

The Problem of Finding a Good Job

Yet another obstacle for women academics is that the human resource departments of many work units (colleges, companies, and state institutions) request mostly male applicants from the universities, which remain responsible for placing their graduates. The reason: men are less burdened by household and family, and thus are capable of putting more energy into their work. As explained by *Beijing Weekly*, no. 49 (1986): "Young women need many benefits before, during, and after the birth of a child. Due to their frequent absence from work, their wages are a fairly large burden on financially independent work units. The willingness of women around thirty to work has increased, as have concerns about family matters. When children get sick, the units must grant leaves of absence to female employees so that they can take care of them."

A problem frequently addressed by Chinese women, which can be hard for Western women to comprehend, is the impossibility of living alone, i.e., remaining unmarried. Representatives of the ACWF, with whom I discussed the enormous difficulties of single women, told me: "Of course we help these unmarried women. We find husbands for them." I was equally shocked when men academics told me with absolute certainty, without batting an eye, that women are less intelligent than men by nature and therefore cannot have the same opportunities for advancement as men!

Academic Women Speak

The following are excerpts from conversations held between 1983 and 1988. The discussions were recorded on tape with the participants' consent; the women's names were changed at their request, as was the information about their academic fields, though the basic division into technical fields and the liberal arts was maintained. Given their high educational status, these women belong to a very small minority. They are professors and instructors at colleges and universities, where many of them have had years of contact with foreigners because they often serve as interpreters or guides for "guests."

Mao Zedong said that women "hold up half the sky"; the excerpts below reveal that challenges remain for women who attempt to conquer their half within the academic realm.

Pan

Pan is a professor of comparative literature. She is thirty-two years old, unmarried, and lives in a dormitory for women professors at her college, where she shares a room with three other unmarried colleagues.

You know, dealing with Western literature and people is not always easy for me. For example, I discovered the Western concept of people as individuals only two years ago, and since then I've thought a lot about it. Before that I was completely closed to such notions as the "individual," the "self," and "self realization." The Chinese do not make individual decisions the way Westerners do. Every decision depends on the family, the work unit, and so forth. We, especially women, are socialized to be dependent—on the community, superiors, colleagues, the work unit, and one's family.

If you do not comply with this norm and make an individual decision for yourself, without consulting others, the pressure brought to bear on you is terrible and incomprehensible to Westerners. Since the others think that you are strange and conspicuous, you immediately try to reintegrate. Such Western concepts as autonomy and heteronomy do not exist in Chinese thinking. Here, the governing outlook on life is that it is hard, harsh, and arduous. Fate is cruel, and you have to learn to be strong and accept it. Life in China is an eternal waiting game: we are always waiting for others, for the decisions of others. . . . Yes, life is an eternal wait . . . for what, no one really seems to know. For sudden happiness, a surprising opportunity, perhaps? People also do not make individual plans. It would be absurd, since we are totally governed by the world outside—that is, by politicians, the work unit, the street committee, the family.

I acquired the notion of rationality from Western literature as well. And I try to use reason, and common sense, but it is almost impossible in China; everything is dictated by feelings. Please, don't misunderstand: I have nothing against emotions, but I do not believe that people's actions should be governed by them to the point of excluding everything else. For example, if the director of my faculty does not like me, he will write a negative evaluation about my work as a teacher. However, if you always smile at him, then he will be nice to you. Here, each director expects us to smile when we see him, and even to bow before him. What they want are subordinates! If you do not bow and do not smile, life will be difficult. So, we all continue to smile, out of fear. Conferences and meetings have been terrible experiences. In light of my exposure to people from the West in connection with my training, I have tried to engage Chinese academics in discussions about teaching and science. But it has been useless. "Pan simply wants to advance her career and generate competition" is their immediate reaction, and they stop talking to me. That's why I no longer make suggestions. What's the point, if my colleagues will think: "Ah, I did not suggest anything, and now this Pan is suggesting something. So, to avoid looking bad for doing nothing, I better be nasty and mean to her." This is the sort of thing I meant when I said earlier that people are led by their emotions. These negative feelings condition our daily lives. The Chinese emphasize emotion, not reason.

The language reveals it too. For example, people don't say "I think that" or "I must consider that"; instead they say "I feel that" or "it is occurring to me that." Since we are neither raised to be individuals nor socialized to be rational, we place the heart above everything else. That is why everything is so arbitrary. Chinese women learn to sense and feel what is happening around them. It probably makes us more sensitive to these things than Europeans. Conversely, we do not learn to analyze a situation and think it through. We perceive a situation emotionally instead of rationally. Of course, it is very nice sometimes to feel the warmth of others, their closeness, the community—you never feel alone.

What also struck me, in fact, really surprised me about foreigners is their level of activity. The Europeans in China appear to be doing something all the time. Here, passivity is cultivated. No, "passive" is perhaps the wrong word, "quiet" is better. You are supposed to be quiet, remain quiet, and resign yourself to whatever happens. Women who try to be active get into a lot of trouble. I will give you an example about a recent incident on the bus. It was full, as usual. A woman with a baby got on. She had great difficulty holding on to something to stand securely with her baby. A young man was seated right next to where she stood. I said to him: "Why don't you offer your seat to the woman?" He started abusing me: "That's none of your business! You pig!" Nobody else on the bus intervened, not even the woman with the baby. I was terribly ashamed when everybody turned to stare at me.

You must have a lot of courage and strength to change things in China. And over time you just give up. This attitude of nonintervention, of drifting, this passivity is, of course, deeply rooted in Chinese philosophy, in Daoism. I know that Daoism is very fashionable with some people in the West. I hold this philosophy in high regard too, and I am always in search of inner peace. But I also see its negative effects. Since you are supposed to bear everything, you simply try to avoid problems and confrontations so that there are no bad feelings and, hence, a possibility for inner peace to develop. I do not know whether there is really more inner peace here than in the West. However, when we are faced with a bad experience or a desire that cannot be fulfilled, we repress it. We forget the Cultural Revolution by neither talking nor thinking about it. We do the same with daily life. Anything that could trigger bad feelings is swept under the rug. Perhaps that is why so many of us suffer from ulcers and headaches. There are two types of people in China. Those who try to change things, to make things happen; and, of course, those who are afraid and have given up all hope. The former have a hard time because they endure much criticism; they are very unhappy and try to go abroad.

Please don't misunderstand; not everything Western is good

or smart. On the contrary, I often think that the individualism and the extremes of life in the West are very unhealthy. Our society is still deeply molded by the philosophy of *yin* and *yang*. The union of opposites, the harmony of the two principles also means that one should consider both sides and avoid the extremes. Sometimes, I fear that China will lose its good values if it imports too much from the West. And I am not sure whether we are importing the right things; I would hope that it is not only technology but also rationality, ability to critique, and individual freedom.

Du

Du is an English professor. She is thirty-six years old, married, and has one child. She lives with her husband in a one-and-a-half room apartment made available by the work unit.

You asked me what it's like to be a woman in China. Well, at first I always thought that women and men are equal. Since all women have jobs and are economically independent, we think that gender equality has been achieved in China, in contrast to the West. But our conversations made me question the issue, and I think that life is even more difficult for women than it is for men.

Take the notions about morality, for example. If a man rapes a woman, the man will be censured, perhaps even punished, but afterwards he can resume a normal life with a girlfriend. But the raped woman's life? It is finished. She will never again be respected, no one wants to become her boyfriend or husband. Though people pity her, everyone thinks that she is dirty and worthless as a woman. No one wants that kind of a woman. Frequently, husbands beat their wives if they've been raped and reject them because they're no longer "pure." The party tries, of course, to write articles against such attitudes, and the street committee or the unit try to talk to the husband, but to no avail in most cases. The woman's reputation, her value as a woman, is gone forever. There is a double standard. Women are supposed to be pure. A woman can have only one man. But the same does not apply to men. Worse yet, there is no solidarity among women. They accept all this as preordained. So they genuflect, and then they repress others in turn.

No one talks about sexuality in China. It is impossible for a woman who was raped to discuss her terrible experience, even with women friends or her mother. It is simply unthinkable. In general, sexuality is viewed differently here than in the West. Sex is considered bad, by women and men. Classic Chinese philosophy or ethics holds that sexuality causes sin; hence it must be restricted. Women should dress as unattractively as possible, and men should control themselves as much as possible. That's why women regard their bodies as negative, as a source of evil.

You ask me if that jibes with contemporary street scenes, where young girls run around in miniskirts and high heels, wear make-up, and starve themselves to lose weight? No. But it's a reaction to the injunctions of the Cultural Revolution. And yet even today there are certain things you can and cannot wear. Short skirts are okay, but short tops with spaghetti straps or no bra? Unthinkable, because that's connected to sex! The way foreign women dress in China is considered sloppy and sexy, but for us sexy has a negative connotation, it's considered dirty. Women's pleasure is dirty too. The ideal woman is not supposed to show sexual desire, while it's okay for men. Many Chinese think that since it's unfortunately impossible to avoid sex, it should be limited to marriage, though it should be restrained even then. Our aversion to sex is even promoted by Chinese medical theory, which holds that you lose energy when you sleep with someone. So you're supposed to try to repress it, as much as possible. In general the Chinese think that women can do without sex, but men cannot.

As far as marriage is concerned, that's mandatory. Society demands that you have a place. And then you must also bear one child. The Chinese notion of happiness includes having a family. People who live alone are to be pitied. But then most marriages aren't that happy, yet no one talks about it. It's considered shameful for a woman to admit that her marriage or sex with her husband aren't satisfying. For her to go to a marriage counselor and talk about intimate details of her marriage, the way people in the West do? Impossible! The most she can do is to tell her parents that she's having marital problems. The biggest marital problem in China is that though most women have jobs they also do the housework and care for their husbands and children. They even think that's how it should be! That's why most women forego careers—a profession is not considered as important for a woman as for a man. Though they're happy to be earning their own money, young women don't think that they should be carrying the double burden all by themselves. Many no longer accept it. For example, we really emphasize love in China. Most city people marry for love, especially women academics, while people in the countryside use matchmakers, like my parents' generation. Though young women are demanding that their husbands take part in the housework, unfortunately, most of it is help, not real sharing. One of the differences between my mother and myself is that I could freely choose my husband, yes, even have different boyfriends; I can also participate in family decisions about the children, the household, et cetera. And yet even today, there are women who sacrifice themselves for love and place their careers on the back burner to focus on their families. For me the problems of organizing career and family loom very large. I love my profession and do not want to give it up. Indeed, I want to advance professionally and have a career. Yet it was very difficult for me to find a man who would accept that. Just take *The Ark*, a novella by Zhang Jie, in it all career women are divorced. A recent poll asked male students what they expect from women. Obedience, tenderness, and housework topped the list. That really depressed me. Men are still very feudal in their thinking. Women are very progressive. All they want is equality. They're not demanding that men be obedient, or that they do all the housework. The only thing that women want is that the work be divided equally.

Most men still want a traditional wife, one who takes care of both the housework and them. Of course, she's supposed to be educated, too. Who would want an illiterate woman? She should also have the same interests as her husband, and be forbearing to boot. But intellectually she should be a notch inferior, so that the man can uplift her. They must be kidding!

Jiang

Jiang is a professor of French. She is twenty-nine years old and married. She lives with her husband in a studio-apartment.

Here, most people associate the term *funü yundong* (women's movement) with one of two things. Either with the Chinese women who participated in the war of liberation before 1949 and fought against the "four powers"—feudal political authority, religious oppression, the traditional family structure, and the power of men. Or with the women's movement in the West where women apparently must still fight for equality. The notion that there could be a women's movement in China makes us laugh! We believe that our women were emancipated long ago. Women were officially liberated by the founding of the PRC in 1949. They have the same rights and obligations as men, they have jobs and professions, they are financially independent (of men), and they earn the same amount of money. As far as other differences are concerned, most Chinese men and women believe that it is natural for women to be physically weaker and intellectually inferior. Even today the majority of Chinese—including educated people—perpetuate the notion that women are not as intelligent as men. In turn, women accept their inferiority as emblematic of female nature.

Do we women have the same opportunities as men? I'd have to think about that. Girls are at a disadvantage in terms of educational opportunities. To be allowed to go to college, they must achieve higher scores than the boys in many subjects on the college placement exams. You ask why? Officially, it's necessary to maintain a certain ratio of male to female students, but actually it's simply a method to keep out the women, since the girls generally do better than the boys! Men are also said to be more creative and better capable of developing—although their exam scores are lower than those of women. That's why men are preferred, especially in the so-called hard sciences. They even prefer less able men to good women for the foreign language institutes! The reason? Same thing: the ratio of men to women must not tip in favor of women. Now, you're going to ask why Chinese women would accept something like that. Probably because they think that's the way things are. It wouldn't even occur to them to question it.

But the problems don't stop there. Women who complete their college education must contend with additional difficulties. As you know, the university assigns all college graduates to work units. The problem is that the good and desirable work units don't want to hire women. Women are considered *fudan* (a burden). People believe that a woman can perform only half of what a man can do. Women marry, they have a child (which means that they take maternity leave), and, in addition, they do most of the housework. Since all these things are considered bad for the work units, most of them request only male college graduates. But there has been a change insofar as work units will be assigned men only if they are willing to hire a certain number of women as well. It's like buying cigarettes: Until a few years ago, when you wanted to buy a pack of cigarettes, you also had to buy a nonseller (say, a bag of sweets) to get your cigarettes. There isn't much that can be done about it. Of course, the work units don't say openly that they "don't want women." That would be stupid. They say: "This is hard work, that is why we need men." They act as if they're showing consideration for women, as if all of this were designed to protect them.

As far as promotions are concerned, women are considered "flying pigeons." That means that women often leave their work unit because they marry and move to their husband's city or work unit. Since it's uncertain whether an unmarried woman will remain with her work unit, it's not expedient for the latter to hire "flying pigeons." As far as the opportunity to do graduate or postgraduate work abroad is concerned, the ratio is 1:9, i.e., one woman to nine men. People believe that women are "not suited" to leading positions. If a woman wants a career, she must first achieve twice as much. She must prove that she is not a "normal" woman, because traditionally women are the symbols of "weakness and beauty." Hence a successful woman is not a normal woman; she is considered a "strong" woman. Newspaper headlines refer occasionally to "strong woman so-and-so," simply because she is a good manager.

Liang

Liang is an English teacher, thirty-one years old, married, with one child.

It is often not easy for women academics to find a husband. But to remain unmarried is almost inconceivable for us. No one wants that. Chinese magazines frequently write about well-educated women not being able to find suitable mates. The better educated the woman, the more difficult it is for her to find a husband. Does that mean that smart women are not as gentle? Of course not. A male acquaintance once explained to me that a woman with a degree cannot marry a man without one. The women don't want men who are less educated than they are. Conversely, men don't want women who are better educated than they are, because that would threaten their position and their image within the family. A woman is not supposed to have more abilities and knowledge than a man.

It is said that "a career woman does not know much about practical matters." Her career will require a great investment in terms of time and energy. This means simply that a woman who is getting a doctorate will not get a man. What's more, in a society that considers marriage an absolute norm, she is also making herself an outsider! So, a woman who wants to avoid this problem—that is, if she wants to have a career but not be an outsider, or wants to be married without having to renounce her career because of social forces—must catch a man early on. As soon as she has him, she can go on to get her doctorate!

Fan

Fan is twenty-eight years old and works as an administrator at a college in southern China.

In China the family is very important. I think that's very good. No one is alone. I've read that in the West a lot of people are very lonely, and that old people must live and die alone. That's really sad. We take care of our relatives, as one should. Of course, there are problems in relationships, especially here in Shanghai where people live three or four to a room. The advantage is that you are never lonely. When a woman has a child, her parents baby-sit while she goes to work. That's wonderful for them. It's also why parents always want their children to have children as well. It is simply inconceivable to us that old people in the West are lonely. We also frequently read that Germans don't like children, that they prefer dogs. Here, people think that the larger the family, the happier it is. Because then there are people who will take care of you when you're old. That's the obligation of each generation: One generation takes care of the next. When a Chinese woman says that she doesn't want a child, we think that she's not normal. That's how it is here.

Translated by Ulrike Bode

CREATING A SPACE FOR WOMEN
WOMEN'S STUDIES IN CHINA

Li Xiaojiang and Zhang Xiaodan

In Chinese modern history, the 1980s are a crucial period during which many important economic and political events and changes occurred. The major cause of these events and changes was the economic reform ushered in during the late 1970s, after Mao's death and at the end of the Cultural Revolution. The economic reform was a new policy issued by the Chinese government for the purpose of revitalizing the economy. The main idea of the reform has been both to adjust the structure of economy mainly by introducing market mechanisms into the planned economy and to change the method of management by giving more power and responsibility to local bureaus and firms. In the rural areas, land was distributed to each household while the collective communes were disbanded. It is not an exaggeration to conclude that the economic reform greatly influenced the lives of Chinese people. In addition, along with economic reform, the doors of the country have been reopened to the Western world. Meanwhile, criticism of Mao and the conservative ideological control, although sporadic, has gradually become possible. Under these special political and socioeconomic circumstances, without getting much attention at the very beginning, women's studies as a new academic discipline is quickly sprouting and blossoming.

The questions are, Why did women's studies come into existence in the 1980s but not earlier? What does women's studies involve and what developments have been made? What are its characteristics compared with those of previous Chinese women's liberation movements and those of Western women's movements? In order to answer such questions, let us first present a brief historical retrospection.

The first tide of the women's liberation movement in China emerged more than one hundred years ago. In 1840 after the Opium War—Britain's invasion of China—both the Chinese government and people were forced to face a serious national crisis. Some male politicians started a movement called Constitutional Reform and Modernization, and, for the first time, the topic of women's liberation was raised by participants within the movement. These reformers mainly considered women's problems to be a negative result of the feudal system; they advocated women's education and monogamy and were opposed to foot-binding. Relatively few women other than the wives, concubines, daughters, sisters, and other female relatives of these male reformers followed their example and worked toward improving women's conditions. But the discussion of women's issues and other activities for women's liberation receded after the Constitutional Reform and Modernization movement failed (Lü and Zhen 1990).

With the May Fourth movement of 1919, women's issues were again openly discussed, including women's autonomy in choosing marriage partners, women's virginity before marriage and celibacy after the death of their husbands, women's right of inheritance, women's education and work, prostitution, and foot-binding. Various women's groups were established and many women's magazines were published. In spite of an increasing number of female participants, however, male intellectuals played the main roles as the leaders of the movement. These men were the first to raise women's issues, but they continued to treat women's difficulties as just another part of the general social problems caused by the feudal system. In these discussions, women were only the object for studying; the importance of inspiring women's self-consciousness of their own valuable identity was not recognized. Furthermore, although many women's problems were being discussed and some theoretical issues were touched on, the movement was ultimately more political than academic. In other words, these male radicals and their female followers struggled for basic human rights for women; they had not yet pushed themselves to question more deeply patriarchal social structures and ideologies. At that time, no one seemed to consider the possibility that women's studies could be an independent discipline within the academic world.

Although Chinese women legally gained equal rights in 1950 after the Communist Party's rise to power, women's studies still did not appear as an independent academic discipline. In socialist China, Chinese women's equality was guaranteed for the first time by the Constitution of 1950. Further, the Marriage Law of the same year gave both women and men the right to choose their own marriage partners and demand divorces. Through the party's protection and advocacy, more women participated in the work force under the policy of equal pay for equal work. In addition, women's paid employment outside of the home gained political approval through the Communist Party, which believed that women's participation in social labor was a prepable for their emancipation. Compared with that of their older foot-bound sisters, the position of Chinese women in society had improved significantly both economically and ideologically during the 1950s. Thus, many people of that era commonly believed that Chinese women had achieved complete liberation and, therefore, had no problems at all.

Economic reform knocked down this common belief not only by making some potential problems more visible but also by creating new problems. Generally, we can divide these problems into two groups: the first includes female infanticide impelled by the birth control policies, the abduction of women by illegal traders, commercial marriage by which women are sold to their husbands' family, prostitution, and the lack of educational opportunities for girls and young women in rural areas. These problems, which seemed to disappear for a period of time after the Marriage Law in 1950, reemerged under the pressures of the new economic reforms. Clearly, the existence of such problems reinforces how common male superiority still is in China, even after women allegedly have been liberated for more than forty years. The second group of problems can be said to occur on a subtler level. Such issues include women employees who lose their positions for discriminatory reasons or otherwise, female college graduates who find it difficult to get employment, and women who are shut out of political leadership opportunities. This other set of obstacles for women seems to have emerged during the reform. These new problems even more directly challenge the equality that Chinese women have obtained, because it has been commonly thought that the success of Chinese women's liberation is reflected in the equal rights that Chinese women have achieved with regard to education, employment, and political administration. Both sets of problems, in fact, raise doubts about the state of women's liberation itself.

The visibility of these problems greatly shocked, confused, and annoyed those who thought that Chinese women had already been liberated. Women's issues then became hot topics in newspapers and magazines as well as in casual conversation. With further discussion, some scholars, especially some women researchers, realized that certain relations, for instance, between women's liberation and women's employment, were not as simple as people had believed; previous theories about women's liberation failed to explain these new problems. Therefore, these scholars felt an urgency not only to study these problems in order to solve them, but also to develop theories to address the broader confusions—including their own—surrounding women's liberation itself. Ultimately, these scholars are seeking to explore what women's liberation really means and where the movement should go. Thus, we can safely say that, unlike the development of women's studies in the West, the rise of women's studies in the 1980s in China was not the result of a distinct feminist movement; on the contrary, women's studies grew out of an attempt by a few liberal women leaders in governmental women's organizations as well as some intellectuals, both male and female, to reobserve, rethink, and redefine the liberation of Chinese women. In other words, rather than theoretically claiming or appealing for equality between men and women, the discipline of women's studies in contemporary China was initially designed to meditate upon the equality that Chinese women had supposedly achieved according to law established by the socialist revolution of 1949.

Women's studies today has been gradually shaped by two parallel forces. One force is the Women's Federation. The Women's Federation once was—and among certain people is still—thought of as the only legitimate women's organization in China. Similar to two other organizations—the Trade Union and the Youth League—the Women's Federation is a government agency, which itself contains a system of hierarchical bureaucracy. The highest level is the National Women's Federation; under its leadership, each province, city, county, town, village, firm, and institute has local branches attached to the National Women's Federation. The main role of the Women's Federation at each level is to be the bridge between the party and Chinese women in general. Unlike the Trade Union and the Youth League, however, the Women's Federation does not have an open membership system. Only women leaders and representatives, selected from those who are considered to perform well in various circumstances by the higher party superiors, can represent the government and its ideas; as party representatives, these women work to protect women's benefits as well as to motivate women to follow governmental policy. For instance, the leaders of the National Women's Federation and its branches in the provinces usually go to local gatherings, especially in rural areas, to explain new policies affecting women; in addition, some women leaders have worked as social workers or consultants to help solve conflicts between women and local supervisors, between women and their husbands, and between mothers-in-law and daughters-in-law. At the beginning of the economic reform, women leaders in the federation had difficulty, since previously held principles and methods did not adequately address those women's particular problems. For this reason, many began to question the necessity of the organization itself. It was under this pressure that the Women's Federation for the first time realized the importance of a theoretical study of "the woman question."

In response, the National Women's Federation founded the first Institute of Women's Studies in 1983. Thereafter, women's institutions and research bodies have been established by local branches of the Women's Federation in many Chinese cities and provinces. These institutions and research bodies have different focuses, although some of their tasks overlap. The institutions work mainly on training women who work for the federation at various levels, while the research bodies seek ways to deal with women's problems and study measures for protecting women's benefits in order to provide reference to the policymakers in the federation. Both have held a series of special seminars on such topics as the abduction of women, women's employment, and funds for childbirth and child care. In 1984 and 1986, the Institute of Women Studies in the National Women's Federation held two national conferences on women's studies. The main topic of both conferences was the relation between economic reform and women's liberation. According to statistics from the Women's Federation, from 1985 to 1990 there were forty-five conferences on general theories of women's liberation, eight conferences on special women's issues, and three conferences for exchanging information, which were held in twenty cities, districts, and provinces (Beijing Women's Federation and Beijing Women's Studies Institute 1992, 576). These institutions and research bodies have also organized investigations, collected data on women in different fields, and published the information in women's magazines and newspapers, which have increased in number to more than forty since 1985.

The second force that has shaped women's studies is the academy itself. Before 1985, most academic investigations into women's issues were initiated locally and voluntarily by individual women intellectuals. This term is used in China to describe women of higher education who work as professionals—professors, doctors, researchers, writers, artists, and so forth. In 1985 the first nongovernmental[1] institute of women's studies was set up by Li Xiaojiang, a young teacher in the Chinese literature and language department at Zhengzhou University in Henan Province.[2] In 1987, this institute developed into a formal women's studies center in Zhengzhou University and became the first research organization of women's studies in any Chinese college or university. In the past few years, the center's tasks have been varied and numerous: to find and attract academic interest in women's studies from all over the country, to give public lectures on women's issues, to arrange elective and required courses in women's studies for undergraduate and graduate students at Zhengzhou University, to compile a women's studies book series, and to organize and hold conferences on women's studies. The center is a model for bringing together women scholars from different academic fields and building women's studies as an independent discipline. For most women scholars, the center's success indicates another way to work on women's issues beyond the Women's Federation.

Since the establishment of this first center, more nongovernmental women's studies centers and groups have been founded at universities and institutes. Many of these formal study centers or less formal study groups, such as at Beijing University, Beijing Foreign Studies University, and Fudan University, have created specific courses or lectures on women's studies. For example, in 1989–90, members of the women's

---

1. The term *nongovernmental* is used to describe any institute or organization not set within the official network according to the will of party authorities. This kind of organization was allowed to exist legally only after the late 1970s.

2. One might expect that the first women's studies center would originate at a university in a major city such as Beijing. In fact, however, the lack of proximity to the central government probably allowed the discipline of women's studies to flourish with fewer ideological restrictions imposed by the Chinese Communist Party.

studies center at Beijing University offered two elective courses in the history department and the Institute of Comparative Literature: "The History of Chinese Women" and "Feminist Literary Criticism." Other groups have also tried to connect their coursework and research to women's problems in daily life. The women's study group at Beijing Foreign Studies University has organized graduate students to study women in various communities in Chinese society; one such project involves an educational fund in rural areas to guarantee a certain amount of money to educate girls as well as boys. Another example, the women's study group at Shanghai Social Science Academy, working with the Shanghai Television Station, televised a series of special forums in 1988 titled "Women's Image in Public Media." Topics included the authenticity of women's images in movies and television, how these images influence social life, how the public views women's images on magazine covers, and what images of women the media should create.

There are significant differences in emphasis and purpose between the government-sponsored research bodies and nongovernmental women's studies centers and groups. The research agencies officially and financially attached to the Women's Federation insist that women's studies be based on Marxist women's liberation theory, while academic women's studies groups try to broaden their theoretical scope to reevaluate the women's movement of the early twentieth century and women's liberation since 1949. In addition, rather than formulating policies for women as the research bodies have done, the scholars in the nongovernmental groups have been more concerned with how to establish women's studies as an independent academic discipline.

Women leaders of the Women's Federation and academy-based activists did not always work well together. Formerly, the Women's Federation often did not include these professional women in its network of services. This is not because the women leaders in the federation intentionally ignored professional women, but because they always considered themselves women's helpers and protectors and thus thought only rural and working-class women needed their assistance. There were also communication barriers, stemming from the federation's own structure: universities, institutes, and other professional firms housed no active branches of the Women's Federation. In some places, in fact, the only reminder that the Women's Federation even existed were the free movie tickets distributed each year on International Women's Day. On their part, professional women were not satisfied with the ideas and attitudes of the Women's Federation, which they thought were not representative of their own interests.

Despite their initially awkward relationship, these two forces in the women's studies movement began to help each other in the 1980s and have continued to improve one another. The establishment of these research bodies within the Women's Federation is one of the ways that the organization has tried to shatter its own closed structure; through the research bodies, therefore, the federation started to connect itself with women scholars and other intellectual women. The researchers in these federation-sponsored research bodies have actively introduced academic members and their research results to the public through conferences, lectures, and publications. (In China the major newspapers, magazines, and publishing houses are usually controlled by the government and its organizations, such as the Women's Federation, which controls the major women's magazines and newspapers.) In turn, these scholars' opinions are becoming important sources for policymakers. Women academics also readily consult federation surveys and data, since the funding and organizational authority needed for these kinds of nationwide studies are often unavailable to university-based scholars. Both groups of women strive very hard to avoid working too narrowly in their own fields of expertise. Thus, the enterprise of women's studies represents a kind of sisterhood that is entirely new in China.

Many female scholars began research in their respective fields and then moved to women's issues. In the development of women's studies as a separate discipline, the study of women's history has played an important role, with particular progress in the collection of data on the women's liberation movement. Scholars are now able to analyze more clearly the historical progress of the Chinese women's movement under the leadership of the Communist Party. Some scholars also try to fill in the blanks existing in the traditional study of history; special subjects concerning women include the history of Chinese women's education and the historical change in the value of women in Confucian ideology. The most influential publications in this field include *The History of the Chinese Women's Movement*, by the National Women's Federation (1989); *Chinese Women's Movement, 1840–1921*, by Lü Meiyi and Zhen Yongfu (1990);

Evolvement of Women's Value in Ideology, by Du Fangqin (1989); and *Chinese Women's Past and Present,* by Tao Chunfang (1985). The study of women's literature is becoming one of the most active forces in women's studies. In the middle of the 1980s, there was a common debate about the definition of women's literature, revolving around three differing opinions. One opinion defined women's literature as works about women and written by women authors. Another school of thought proposed that all literary works written by women can be called women's literature, whether they are about women or not. The third opinion was that all literature written about women written by male or female authors should be considered women's literature. The first opinion now is widely accepted as the idea of women's literature (Beijing Women's Federation and Beijing Women's Studies Institute 1992, 128). Some scholars in this field have borrowed methods and ideas from Western feminist literary critics. For example, Meng Yue and Dai Jinhua in their *Emerging from the Horizon of History* have tried to analyze how literary works can conceal a patriarchal system and what cultural value can be gained when women are treated as the subject of novels, short stories, and poems (Meng and Dai 1989). Other significant books published in this field include *Ballad, Poetry and Amorousness,* by Kang Zhengguo (1989); *On Contemporary Women Writers,* by Li Ziyun (1985); *Delayed Tide—Contemporary Women's Literature,* by Yue Shuo (1989); and *Women's Literature,* by Sun Shaoxian (1987).

Another active field in women's studies is sociology. In recent years, sociologists have presented many papers on women's employment, population mobility, social welfare, and prostitution.[3] The study of marriage and family is especially booming. According to data collected in *The Index of National Newspapers and Magazines,* from 1979 to 1987 there were 350 papers published on marriage and family—13.7 percent of all sociology papers published in those years. Admittedly, some papers are still at the level of collecting data or presenting preliminary reports, but others cover more specific issues, such as women's role in transforming family structures and the impact of women's employment on marriage and family.

The development of demography as another specialty

---

3. On the possible change in the structure of employment for women, see Zhu 1988; and Xing 1989. For discussions of the trend of peasant women moving to cities and urban centers under economic reform, see Gao 1990; and Jing 1990.

within women's studies is also significant. For instance, some scholars have studied the relation between the birthrate and women's employment. Other scholars have examined such variables as childbirth, death, education level, and employment. *The Population of Chinese Women,* edited by Zhu Chuzhu (1991), is the first book published in this field. There are also many important papers on the female population, such as "The Analysis of the Average Age of Women's Childbirth" (Li 1988), "The Quality of Female Population and Social Development" (Zheng 1987), and "The Study of Chinese Elder Women Population" (Yang and Wang 1989).

In the field of law, many scholars have begun to concentrate on studies about the principle of equality between men and women, legal protection of women's employment and suffrage, the rationalization of marriage law, women's legal rights in divorce cases, women's equal rights of property within the family, and the legal aspect of artificial insemination.

In the area of political science, women's suffrage became a hot topic, especially in the mid-1980s. Some scholars are studying the decreasing number of female leaders in the government at various levels. Some also study the decline of women's participation in politics. These studies not only continue to explore the general significance of women's suffrage and women's political consciousness but also discuss concrete ways for women to join the political leadership.

The discovery of a "women's script" by women scholars has been a driving force to connect women's studies with philology. Examples of women's script, a written language that was used solely by women in the Song dynasty (960–1279), have been found in Jiangyong, southern China. In addition to the study of women's script, some philologists have begun analyzing gender elements in characters of the Chinese language.

Scholars from other academic fields have also contributed to the development of women's studies as an independent discipline. After winning the debate over the very necessity of this discipline, many scholars have further discussed the object, methods, and relation between women's studies theory and women's problems in society. Several textbooks about women's studies theory have been published, such as *The Basic Concepts of Women's Studies,* edited by the Hunan Women Cadre Institution (1987), and *The Rationale of Women's Studies* by Duan Huomei (1989). Other important publications include *Eve's Search* (1988) and *Gender Gap* (1989) by Li Xiaojiang.

Women's studies programs from the 1980s to the present are obviously different from women's groups and their efforts one hundred years ago. On the one hand, these younger female scholars no longer have to struggle for basic legal rights for women; their studies are based on the equality already achieved. On the other hand, in challenging the patriarchal ideology that is far more invisible and intangible, modern-day women's studies scholars are facing a tougher task that requires an acute gender consciousness. At this juncture, this newer generation of scholars realizes that the purpose of women's studies is not only to study women and extend research into each traditional discipline but also to establish the methodology of a new independent discipline. Compared with previous studies about women, the women's studies movement in the 1980s started an attempt to value women's experience and women's subjective perspective, then to review ideas about women's equality and liberation from this new viewpoint.

Especially in contemplating both the ideas first raised during the women's liberation movement one hundred years ago and those raised during women's legal emancipation since the 1950s, women scholars have made several theoretical gains. First, women's studies scholars now challenge the concept of equality that is based on simply ignoring the differences between men and women. These scholars now recognize that the guiding principle of "whatever men can do, women can do also," while inspirational, in fact helped to conceal a male standard for women's equality. In other words, women's equality meant that women were equated with men. A male standard, however, only creates an illusion of equality, since women ultimately have no distinct gender identity within the context of so-called liberation. Thus, these scholars now conclude that the first task of women's liberation is to allow women themselves to discover who they are, where they come from, and how much they have been influenced by distorted, patriarchal images of their gender. This is the first step in breaking through the patriarchal line of dominant ideology.

Second, these women's studies leaders now recognize that women alone are responsible for their own liberation. They have indicated that one large stumbling block in Chinese women's progress toward their own emancipation, in fact, has been that many Chinese women have been wholly passive in the liberation process. This passive character was evident not only within the context of Chinese women's liberation initiated by male politicians within a male-run political system but also in cases when even so-called liberated women were habitually treated as objects to be protected; to complicate matters, women themselves often grew to expect this protection as a given. That is the main reason that when Chinese society suddenly withdrew its protection—such as the guarantee of women's employment—and sacrificed women's concerns to serve the greater economic demands of China, women began to panic and feel that they had fewer alternatives. Through their own efforts, women's studies scholars now anticipate that women's studies as a discipline will help transform this mind-set—moving women from passive objects to active subjects in order to achieve their own complete liberation. Actually, the role these very scholars have played in developing women's studies programs is an excellent example of how women can and should take charge of their own self-awareness and independence. Especially compared with the women's movement of a hundred years ago, women have been the major leaders in the development of women's studies in the 1980s. Male scholars have voluntarily participated and continue to help women, yet most are still invested in traditional male-centered ways of thinking. If only unconsciously, these men still approach women's issues with a patriarchal attitude and thus fail to understand the critical and creative significance of women's liberation as distinct from human liberation. Therefore, male academics still have a distance to travel before they can comprehend what women's studies scholars aim to accomplish: to dismantle the patriarchal tradition and provide a new, gender-balanced point of view to the world.

Third, this group of women scholars has begun to rethink the relation between women's liberation and women's employment; specifically, they realize that women's employment and ultimately women's economic independence are prerequisites of but not the only conditions for women's liberation. In other words, the employment of a woman cannot guarantee her complete freedom and independence. This conclusion is based on the debate that has flared up over the loss of jobs for women, especially those in the cities, since the mid-1980s. There are two general sides of the debate: those who believe that women should stay home as housewives and those who insist that women should keep working in the public sphere in order to maintain their independence. Neither side has adequately explained this unemployment trend affecting women. Looking for possible answers, some women scholars are trying to connect

185

the trend with China's relatively low economic performance; in a country with inadequate national income and work opportunities, the employment of women can bring benefits as well as burdens. For instance, since society cannot provide adequate conditions and equipment to make housework easier—the availability of washing machines, for instance—most women have to shoulder a double burden when working both in and outside the home. Women's studies scholars, on the whole, do not argue that women should go back to being only housewives. They do maintain, however, that under certain social conditions, overemphasizing the significance of women's employment to women's liberation may bring the opposite result and create misunderstanding of liberation. This opinion sounds different from the Marxist belief in the causal relation between employment and women's liberation propagandized by the Communist Party for over forty years. But the scholars who explore the idea do not claim that they are opposing Marxist thought; instead, they emphasize the undeveloped economy in China, which limits the possibility of practicing Marxist ideas. We can conclude, furthermore, not only that these scholars have no intention of challenging Marxism at this point, but also that they did not really challenge Marxism in the first place by encouraging further theoretical elaboration.

Women's studies in China undoubtedly has been influenced by ideas raised by Western feminists. Feminist essays and books have recently been introduced in China, including Simone de Beauvoir's *The Second Sex* and Betty Friedan's *The Feminine Mystique*. And yet it is interesting to note that the term *feminist* is seldom used to describe women's activities in China, whether governmental or nongovernmental, academic or general. Few women are willing to call themselves feminists; we have not found such a word anywhere except in translations or articles introducing Western feminism. Instead, in Chinese women's studies, the word *feminology* is used, and it rarely implies Western feminist theory.[4] For the Women's Federation, the term

---

4. The English word *feminology* is the translation for Chinese terms *fu-nü-xue* or *nü-xing-xue*. *Xue* is roughly equivalent to the English suffix "-logy," used for naming disciplines of research. *Fu-nü* and *nü-xing* both mean "woman" or "female gender." Two Chinese terms, *fu-nü-xue* and *nü-xing-xue*, can be translated into "women's studies." But the reason we use *feminology* is that feminology sounds closer to Chinese women scholars' ideas that women's studies can be founded as an independent discipline.

feminism is obviously seen as part of a bourgeois ideology and thus against the principles of Marxism. For scholars in unofficial women's studies groups, however, avoiding the term *feminism* or not identifying their work as "feminist" is a deliberate and voluntary choice rather than a political consideration. Such scholars respect Western-based feminist theory, and yet they still believe that Chinese women's studies has its own background and circumstances unique to Chinese history and social reality. Western feminist theory is certainly valuable as a rich source of reference, but a Western feminist tradition can hardly provide standardized answers to all Chinese women's questions. Ultimately, Chinese women's studies scholars believe that through their own ways of seeking truth, they may be able to contribute to the Western tradition of women's studies.

What are their own ways of seeking truth? Women's studies scholars are speculating about the further development of the discipline. Under the double pressure of social reform and traditional culture, these scholars believe that those working in women's studies in China must address the following topics in order to make rapid progress.

A. They must face women's problems resulting from economic reform for two reasons. First, Chinese women do need help—not help through receiving something but through self-knowledge, one important key to women's liberation. Second, the development of a theory of women's liberation needs to be grounded in reality.

B. They must work diligently to continue various programs concerning women's studies, thus bringing feminology into the normal orbits of teaching and research. They must make theoretical generalizations about women's problems in order to raise their study to a philosophical level and thus enrich the science of humanity.

In order to reach these goals, women's studies scholars maintain that it is important to notice the unique circumstances of contemporary China. Some of them are using a method called the "theory of stratification." The main idea of this method is to study women by dividing them into various groups according to their occupations—peasant women, working women in the cities or towns, and intellectual or professional women.[5] The scholars suggest that women in these three

---

5. The term *peasant women* refers to women who are engaged in agriculture in rural areas. Because of the Communist Party's dichotomous idea about class divi-

groups are very different from each other: they have different levels of liberation, different attitudes toward liberation, and different forms of development, although they all face somewhat similar problems. The differences are significant to such scholars for two reasons: one is that in evaluating Chinese women's liberation without noticing such differences, one may easily draw the wrong conclusions or fail to reach adequate explanations for some ambiguities; the other is that the differences show the empirical complexity of reality, which challenges theories and methods, therefore providing the possibility of their development as well.

Women's studies groups also plan to further women-centered cultural studies. The center for women's studies at Zhengzhou University, for instance, is preparing to found the first women's museum in China; in the interim, the affiliated scholars are compiling a series of books called *The History of Women's Oral Narration*. The center for women's studies at Beijing University is building a women's library in Beijing. In association with the Ford Foundation, several women scholars and local branches of the Women's Federation are involved in a project called Women's Childbirth and Health in some selected provinces. The Women's Federation is also organizing a wide-reaching study, "The Investigation of Chinese Women's Social Status," which is the largest survey on women since 1949.

The United Nations' Fourth World Conference on Women's Events will be held in Beijing in 1995; clearly, this is a very important event for Chinese women's studies programs. Women's studies scholars feel greatly inspired by this event; their research is prospering in many ways. Besides the activities they have already begun in making the world know Chinese women better—including their attitudes and opinions on some universal concerns of women, such as the environment, education, childbirth, health, and violence—many women's studies scholars are preparing the papers and speeches for the nongovernmental forum of the conference. The National Women's Federation has also organized a special committee for the preparation of the conference; one plan is to set up five exhibitions on the history, culture, and progress of Chinese women.

sion (bourgeois and proletariat) in terms of political respect more than just economic consideration, peasant women in contemporary China are always categorized as working-class, together with women who work in the factories; however, for the purposes of research, according to the nature of their work and their actual economic situations, peasant women and female factory workers are often treated as separate groups.

If you go to China today, you may not recognize any signs of a women's movement. There are no demonstrations on the streets or in the schools; no women are loudly declaring their resistance to men and society; no such words as *women's movement* even appear in the media. Women's study groups and activities, however, are quietly permeating people's lives. Without statements, slogans, and other radical actions, the women's movement in contemporary China is emerging, and its influence is felt not less but more than any women's movement yet in Chinese history.

The discipline of women's studies, generated in response to women's problems in society, is a pioneering force at the heart of this invisible women's movement. The social significance of this newfound discipline can be seen in many ways: female scholars have created a space for women beyond the mainstream male-centered ideology; women's studies has enlarged public space beyond the control of political power; women's studies is changing the structure of the traditional humanities by challenging masculine values and standards; and, finally, women's studies is changing Chinese women, especially their psychological dependence on men and society.

REFERENCES

Beijing Women's Federation and Beijing Women's Studies Institute, eds. 1992. *Women's Studies in China from 1981 to 1990*. Beijing: Chinese Women Publishing House.

Du Fangqin. 1989. *Evolvement of Women's Value in Ideology*. Zhengzhou: People's Publishing House in Henan.

Duan Huomei, ed. 1989. *The Rationale of Women's Studies*. Beijing: Chinese Women Publishing House.

Gao Xiaoxian. 1990. "Female Population Mobility and Urbanization." *Rural Economy and Society*, June.

Hunan Women Cadre Institution, eds. 1987. *The Basic Concepts of Women's Studies*. Harbin: Northern Women and Children Publishing House.

Jing Yihong. 1990. "The Sluggish Urbanization of Rural Women Labor Force." *Women's Studies*, March.

Kang Zhengguo. 1989. *Ballad, Poetry and Amorousness*. Zhengzhou: People's Publishing House in Henan.

Li Guojin. 1988. "The Analysis of the Average Age of Women's Childbirth." *Population*, March.

Li Xiaojiang. 1988. *Eve's Search*. Zhengzhou: People's Publishing House in Henan.

———. 1989. *Gender Gap*. Beijing: Sanlian.

Li Ziyun. 1985. *On Contemporary Women Writers*. Beijing: Sanlian.
Lü Meiyi and Zhen Yongfu. 1990. *Chinese Women's Movement, 1840–1921*. Zhengzhou: People's Publishing House in Henan.
Meng Yue and Dai Jinhua. 1989. *Emerging from the Horizon of History*. Zhengzhou: People's Publishing House in Henan.
National Women's Federation. 1989. *The History of the Chinese Women's Movement*. Beijing: Chunqiu Publishing House.
Sun Shaoxian. 1987. *Women's Literature*. Shenyang: Liaoning University Press.
Tao Chunfang. 1985. *Chinese Women's Past and Present*. Beijing: Beijing Publishing House.
Xing Hua. 1989. "About Periodical Employment for Women." *Women Theory Study*, January.
Yang Zhongchuan, and Wang Caizhen 1989. "The Study of Chinese Elder Women Population." *Chinese Demography*, June.
Yue Shuo. 1989. *Delayed Tide—Contemporary Women's Literature*. Zhengzhou: People's Publishing House.
Zheng Guizhen. 1987. "The Quality of Female Population and Social Development." *Population Information*, March.
Zhu Chuzhu, ed. 1991. *The Population of Chinese Women*. Zhengzhou: People's Publishing House in Henan.
Zhu Mingmei. 1988. "Women's Employment in Primary Socialist Society." *Women's Activity*, August.

FROM *THE ARK*

Zhang Jie

There was a rumbling outside and downstairs someone called, "The coal cart is here!" Jinghua quickly put down her wood plane and ran downstairs. By now, just about all the households in their block had given up using coal briquets and changed to gas heat. But they had never managed to buy a gas cylinder, and now the price of a cylinder plus cooker had gone up to more than one hundred yuan, far more than they could afford. But burning coal was really tiresome. The coal deliveries were so unreliable that sometimes for days they had no coal left to burn; yet if they had wanted to buy more coal at a time, they would have had nowhere to store it. The people in the local coal depot refused to sell to them if they went there themselves. Liu Quan had tried to call over and over again to ask for an earlier delivery and it was only now that they had finally agreed to come. The person Liu Quan had dealt with on the telephone had always been a man, but it was a woman who made the delivery, a small, feeble-looking woman. What had happened to all the men? Probably they were left in charge of putting off customers who came or phoned in.

It was just about to rain and a westerly wind blew the black clouds in rolls across the sky. The coal dust from the delivery cart blew into Jinghua's face, stinging her eyes, but the woman delivering the coal continued with her task of unloading, seemingly unaware of the change in the weather. Then Mrs. Jia came out of the building carrying a dustpan full of broken pieces of briquet and said, "That last delivery of coal was full of dust—it just crumbled when I touched it. Could you change some for me?"

The delivery woman just continued to shovel the coal as if she had heard nothing. Mrs. Jia laughed awkwardly, tipped the

Nelly Rau-Häring

Zhang Jie

broken briquets onto the cart and helped herself to four fresh ones. Fast, and as though she had eyes in the back of her head, the delivery woman swung round and retrieved two of the briquets from Mrs. Jia's pan, then continued with her work without saying a word. She stood on tiptoe and strained to reach the last briquets as she emptied the coal cart at the far end. Mrs. Jia went on grumbling to herself, the smile no longer visible on her face. "Such a big pan and you'll only let me have two briquets. . . ." She continued to take a briquet here, a briquet there, until she amassed a small pile of her own.

The delivery woman, very tired now, but still aware of Mrs. Jia standing behind her grumbling and watching, chose to ignore her. Jinghua jumped up onto the coal cart and helped her unload the last of the coal. The woman still remained silent, but just as she was about to leave she said to Jinghua, "When you need another delivery of coal, just phone up. My name is Zhou."

The wind became stronger, carrying with it the cool smell of distant rain. Jinghua had to move all the coal in before it rained. Her blouse was puffed up by the wind and as she worked the sweat began to trickle down her back. Mrs. Jia, meanwhile, kept watch over her small pile of coal and continually glanced at her wristwatch in agitation. "What can I do? The family will never get out of work before it starts raining and I cannot carry it up the stairs." Mrs. Jia had a pair of "liberated feet," or feet which had been unbound, and although walking was no serious problem for her, carrying the coal upstairs would have been difficult. So Jinghua naturally had to help her, knowing full well that at the next meeting of the neighborhood committee she would report to all those other old women, "The other day, you know, they didn't turn their light off until after twelve. Still seeing off visitors in the middle of the night." Or, "The other evening they still hadn't turned their lights on by eight. What do you think they're hiding in there?" The gossiping was like Mrs. Jia's "liberated feet," a legacy of the past. Whether Jinghua helped her move the coal or not, the gossiping would still go on. One had to be realistic: Mrs. Jia needed her help, so Jinghua helped her.

Both of their households were on the third floor and they had five hundred briquets of coal between them. This meant that Jinghua had to make a total of fifty trips and by the time she had finished she felt utterly exhausted, ready to collapse in a heap on the concrete floor. All the while Mrs. Jia prattled on and on, though Jinghua felt so tired that her ears ached and she was unable to take in a word of what she was saying. "Comrade Cao, don't go yet . . . come and wash your hands in here. How about some tea?"

"Don't worry, I've got soap and water in my flat," Jinghua replied, lurching off like a drunkard. But when she got back to the flat, she found that the hot water thermos was empty. There was nothing particularly remarkable about this, since it was often empty. However, she regretted it now. She turned on the tap and scrubbed her hands with a piece of soap, but her fingernails remained filthy. She could really do with a nailbrush. . . . Then, as she turned around, she suddenly felt as though someone had stabbed her in the back. She fell to the floor in front of the sink. Even the slightest movement was agonizing and she could not move her legs or feet to get up again. When she began groaning, Maotou bounded over and walked round and round her, miaowing anxiously and stretching out her neck as if calling for help.

"Don't make such a noise, Maotou," Jinghua pleaded. "Nobody can understand what you're saying. It's all right, thank you. . . ." As if she understood what Jinghua was saying, Maotou stopped miaowing and with a frightened look on her face pressed herself close against Jinghua's chest, as if she were keeping guard over her.

The thunder followed immediately after flashes of lightning, rolling in through the window and seeming to explode above Jinghua's head. A fierce gale shook the doors, trees, and telephone wires, howling and crashing as it went. As if God had at last lost his temper, the storm broke mercilessly over the world, while the earth seemed to shake and groan in protest. The rainwater blowing in through the curtains quickly formed a pool on the floor. Soon Jinghua's legs were soaked and the damp cold of the concrete floor seeped up through her body making her teeth chatter violently. She could not just go on lying here, she must somehow crawl to her bed. She raised herself up with her arms and tried to push herself along, crying out with pain. Maotou started miaowing again and wrapped herself around Jinghua's legs. She couldn't move any further so she stopped struggling. Who could help her up onto her bed? How she needed someone with a strong pair of arms, but she knew that no such person was likely to appear. As she lay helpless on the floor, she was acutely aware that she would never again know what it was to be loved by a man, but would live the rest of her life alone. Why was it like this? It seemed as if all three of them were separated from men by some unbridgeable chasm. Was it because men were historically more advanced than women—or women more advanced than men—so that they could no longer find any basis for communication? Well, if this was the case, then neither men nor women could really be blamed. No one could help or change the historical circumstances that had gone into creating these distorted positions.

She remembered a foreign film she'd seen the previous year, A Strange Woman. There was nothing especially strange about her—what she wanted from men seemed perfectly justified, but it was said that the film had met with considerable criticism. The things that women sought were exactly those things that Jinghua and most other thinking women looked for. No matter what race, nationality, or language, these seemed not to matter—the problem was one of universal dimensions. Jinghua thought one day she would write a study of this problem. . . .

She tried again to move and couldn't get as far as the bed, but she did just make her way to the sofa. She pulled down a small quilt and put it beneath her back to protect herself from the cold floor. It would still be a long time before Liu Quan got back from work, but when she did Maotou would get up and run over to meet her. The pain was hard to bear but she knew

Selling coal in the street

very well that even if she shouted nobody was likely to turn up in a downpour like this.

At last Maotou bounded out of the room. It was not Liu Quan but Liang Qian who came in, looking as if she had just been fished out of a river, her raincoat dripping all over the floor. Jinghua at once felt her pain ease. "What on earth are you doing here in such a downpour?" she asked. "Aren't you staying at the dormitory?"

"Good lord! What on earth is wrong with you?" said Liang Qian, squatting down next to Jinghua without even taking off her coat. Then, realizing that her coat was dripping all over Jinghua, she took it off in a flurry and threw it onto a hook on the door. After the third attempt to lift Jinghua, she said, "put your hands round my neck and we'll try it this way," and then she half-carried, half dragged her up onto the bed. She clasped Jinghua's icy, unwashed hand and said, "We'd better get you to the hospital."

"In this rain? Don't worry, there's not much they can do for me there. I'll be fine again in a few days' time." Now that she was on her bed Jinghua felt a lot better.

"You really should see a doctor. Look, your hand is still shaking. I'd better go and get you something warm to wear."

She took a cotton jacket and a pair of clean trousers out of Jinghua's wardrobe, but trying to change her clothes was too painful for her. When she lifted up the quilt Liang Qian noticed that Jinghua's feet were still covered with fragments of coal. "Ah! Now I know what you've been up to." Then she went to get some hot water to wash Jinghua's feet.

"I'm afraid you won't find any hot water there," said Jinghua weakly.

Liang Qian opened up the stove to make a fire and then put a pot of water on to boil. The lid of the pot hadn't had a knob on it for a long time and the hole on top looked like the mouth of a volcano. She found a cauliflower in the corner of the room, cut off a piece and used it to stop up the hole. When it came to household matters she felt clumsy and inept, so once she had set the pot to boil she felt as if she had made a major achievement. "Wait a moment while I go and call a cab," she said. "We should get you to the hospital right away."

"It's raining too hard now. Don't worry." Jinghua did not have the patience to go to the hospital; she was quite content to wash her feet and lie in her warm bed. "They'll only give me pain killers and send me home again. What's the point? Just plug in my diathermy machine for me, won't you, and put it against my back." But she wondered who could look after her at home? Liu Quan was still busy with her American delegation, and with her transfer due any day now, she couldn't very well ask for leave. At the moment, Jinghua couldn't even do small things for herself, like going to the bathroom.

So it was decided that Liang Quan would stay home and take care of her. Luckily Liang Quan's work was just about finished—the sound mixing had already been completed and now all that remained was for the film to be approved. She braved the rain today in order to especially invite Jinghua to go and see a preview of her film. Just now, speeding through the storm on her bicycle, she had felt exhilarated, as if she did possess the strength and stamina to press on after all. Few women could enjoy such a feeling of freedom. True liberation was more than gaining improvement of economic and political status; it was also necessary that women develop confidence and strength in order to realize their full value and potential.

"What a pity, Liu Quan and I will miss seeing the film tonight." Jinghua said.

Liang Qian adjusted the diathermy machine beneath

Jinghua's back. "Don't worry . . . it will go well and you'll have another chance to see it. Just rest now."

"How can I help worrying? I know that this film is your baby."

Yes, it was Liang Qian's "baby." When she had given birth to Chengcheng, she had felt this way too. At that time, she still hadn't understood the responsibilities of motherhood and Chengcheng's arrival had caught her quite unprepared. Now she was unable to find any trace of herself in Chengcheng, but her film, in contrast, contained much of what was her. One generation is connected to another merely through blood ties, but a work of art is a direct reflection of the artist and through it the artist may live on. What did it matter that Bai Fushan had cast her off like a piece of old clothing, or that Chengcheng might not grow up to be a person of exceptional value to society? In her work she could find her own kind of security.

Liang Qian's eyes lit up, making her look unusually pretty, as if two lights were glowing in her soul. The rain had stopped and the sky, washed clean by the storm, was filled with a clear soft light. The sound of dripping from the roof became slower and slower, and all around lay the tranquility of the calm following the storm. "Look, a rainbow." Liang Qian pointed to the horizon.

Jinghua strained round to try and look out of the window. "It looks so near, as if you could touch it." She loved rainbows, how they could transport the imagination to the beautiful world of fairy tales.

Liang Qian stared out into the twilight, moved by a feeling of peace. Her mind wandered back through the past, and into the future where further troubles and bitterness might await them, and through it all they would become even more mature. She did not want to give Jinghua any false words of comfort or encouragement; they were no longer children and the truth was that the time would inevitably come when Jinghua would be paralyzed and unable to get out of bed. Jinghua herself knew this better than any of them, though it was never spoken of. But Jinghua's spirit would always stand erect and she would certainly leave her mark in history. If she ever got around to writing that thesis she had been planning, she would certainly shake up those people who were still bound up by the rules of conventional wisdom.

"Jinghua, you mustn't go on with your woodworking," she said suddenly. "If you do I'll throw out that plane of yours!" Liang Qian patted Jinghua's back with the diathermy machine.

"Ouch! Don't hit me! What else can I do if people won't allow me to write? Whatever I say, there is always someone ready and waiting to attack me." Jinghua felt her anger rising.

"It's tragic," said Liang Qian, "that those people have completely lost their progressive spirit. They carry around the identity of a Communist Party member, but have long since forgotten the meaning of Marxism. Or perhaps they never really understood it in the first place. Anyway, even if for now they enjoy a momentary status, they are bound to be laughed at by later generations. You really shouldn't degrade yourself by bothering about them."

Liang Qian rarely spoke in such a direct and serious way about her work and Jinghua's interest was aroused. Everybody had their troubles, but if you could get past dwelling too much on them, life might be more rewarding. She remembered seeing a crane in the forests with a bald patch on its head and had been told that once the crane became mature that bald patch would turn red. Sooner or later, their heads would grow a patch of red too and then they would be able to soar higher and higher. . . .

"How do you want me to be?" she asked Liang Qian.

"I want you to write, write, write. . . . I want you to make a contribution toward revolutionary theory, or if you can't do that, I want you to support those who can, and not let them struggle on alone."

"I'm afraid your hopes for me are a bit too high."

"You can do it." Liang Qian looked at the tormented figure of Jinghua lying on the bed, at her sunken eyes, her unwashed, blackened feet, and her tattered clothes. How long could she go on like this, in pain, barely able to live her life. The image of a nearly burned down candle passed through her mind. But could she say to Jinghua, "Give up the flame?"

"Please go on 'recharging' me," Jinghua said. Whenever one of them had found herself in trouble and was feeling low, the other two would "recharge" her, and this word had become part of their vocabulary over the years since childhood. Endurance was a quality which marked their generation and they were proud of it.

"All right then, I'll try." Jinghua's eyes sparkled as they hadn't for years, in the way they did when she was a child, full of life and mischief and plans for some delightful joke.

Translated by Stephen Hallett

FUNÜSHALONG: THE WOMEN'S SALON

Lu Danni

With the progressive development of reforms in China, a whole range of what are known as "women's issues" has entered the public debate. A flood of literary works, studies, articles, periodicals, and theoretical books has appeared. More and more people are becoming interested in women's issues. Since the May Fourth Movement, women's studies has reached a high point, and the fact that nongovernmental women's salons have now sprung up clearly demonstrates this. They are being spontaneously organized by women and are forums for the discussion of women's issues.

In Changsha, Hunan Province, women workers founded the first women's salon in 1985. They discussed marriage problems of women in their thirties. In the same year, Li Xiaojiang of Zhengzhou University, Henan Province, organized a nongovernmental women's studies group that planned the First Women's Studies Conference, with participants coming from universities and research institutions in eight provinces and cities. They presented recent developments in and materials on women's studies, as well as personal opinions and plans.

The first women's salon at Beijing University began on 30 May 1988. A recurrent discussion topic is women's history in Europe and the United States. Among those who come to the women's salon of Beijing University are not only Chinese and foreign women who study and work here, but also women from outside the university. Some come regularly, others on the spur of the moment after hearing about the salon. Typically, about twenty women come each time and discussions and conversations are conducted in Chinese and English. Each meeting addresses a particular topic, and there is a presentation by one of the women who has done work on the topic.

The following topics have aroused the most interest and resulted in the liveliest discussions: Is the Western women's liberation movement the only right way? Have women in the West really attained a position of equality with men? Do women in modern-day Chinese society have equal rights and are they liberated? How are they to solve newly emerging problems?

In present-day Chinese society, women are still not highly valued; the traditional view that "only a woman without knowledge is virtuous" is on the rise again. Another common slogan announces that "women must go back to the home." Also, the more education a women has, the harder it is for her to find a husband. Most Chinese men want to marry a woman who is less capable than they in every respect. Though a "strong woman" is thought of as respectable, she is not regarded as lovable or as a "real woman." Such views raise conflicts for women. How can women be progressive and at the same time maintain traditional inferiority? Is there a perfect model of femininity for our time? If so, what is it supposed to look like?

The atmosphere is very lively in the women's salon: everyone participates in the discussion, and they all feel they are learning a great deal. The discussions are also essential motivation for raising the standards of women's studies and for broadening public interest.

Translated by Ilze Mueller

DAI QING: A PORTRAIT

BEIJING, 1989

Elke Wandel

Women's salon—Funüshalong, as it is called in Chinese—sounds like a beauty salon, or perhaps a cafe exclusively for ladies. At the entrance of Beijing University, China's elite university for the humanities, campus police stop me today. I have to show an identity card and tell them whom I plan to visit—an uncustomary questioning procedure, at least where "long noses" (Westerners) are concerned. But on the day before, students had decided to hold a nationwide boycott of classes and to found an independent student association.

Suddenly, I feel as though I were on my way to a conspirators' meeting. In the visitors' list at the main gate, I write that I want to visit a doctoral candidate who lives in the student residence hall here. I am allowed to pass.

The park-like campus of Beijing University still shows few signs of green. I attribute a slight scratchiness in my throat to the yellowish gray dust carried to Beijing by sandstorms from the Gobi Desert each spring. Past the university's pagoda-style water tower looming near the campus pond, past the memorial for Edgar Snow, I bike to the Humanities Department, housed in a venerable structure with an inner courtyard.

About thirty women have gathered tonight in one of the dark, musty seminar rooms of the university. Every two weeks, committed women students, faculty, and scholars have been meeting for discussion. They talk usually about women in Chinese history, the women's movement in Japan and in the United States, or simply talk with other women about on-the-job discrimination.

Full of excitement, the group waits for tonight's speaker: Dai Qing, a little over forty years old, perhaps the most prominent among the dissident Chinese women journalists and writers of her generation. Born during the war between Japan and China, she lost her father when she was a child. He was posthumously made into a revolutionary martyr. Dai Qing was adopted by a top military commander, Marshal Ye Jianying, who later played a major role in overthrowing the Gang of Four and became president of the National People's Congress. Because of her privileged position as a cadre child, she knew prominent public figures. Thus, she had access to inside information while enjoying special personal protection, a circumstance that cannot be underestimated in China, considering how courageous her writing has been.

She studied at the College for Military Technology in Harbin, Heilongjiang Province, then worked for the Department of Space Travel. During the Cultural Revolution she fell out of favor; subsequently, she was regarded as a counterrevolutionary and was sent to the countryside to do physical labor. After her rehabilitation she returned to Beijing—to the Department for Internal Security. Rumors that circulated about her in Beijing's cultural scene probably date from this period: Dai Qing, it was said, was working for the secret service. She learned English at the army's Foreign Language Institute of Nanjing and began to write in 1979. While her career seems eventful, it was not unusual for a cadre child—even for a female one.

Since 1982, Dai Qing has worked for *Guangming Ribao,* the most popular daily among Chinese intellectuals. Her merciless reports and penetrating analyses of political events have shocked readers. In particular, one report, called "Expectations," whose central theme is the disappointed hopes of Chinese intellectuals, proved to be an inflammatory focus of politico-cultural discussion.

One of her goals is to write about the past truthfully, though such revelations prove painful. She vigorously challenges official dogma about the history of the Chinese Communist Party. Her interviews of prominent reformers and dissidents add to the historical portrait and draw fire from the establishment. She has also signed a petition for the release of all political prisoners.

Her vehement commitment during the protest against the Three Gorges Dam project on the Yangzi River brought Dai Qing the reputation of being China's first environmentalist. Critics have described the project as an unprofitable political ploy, complaining about its disproportionately long construction phase (from twelve to twenty years), considering the resettling of close to a million people to be untenable, and warning of unforeseeable climatic changes and the possibility of erosion and earthquakes. However, this, the hottest of all Chinese environmental topics, is also an extremely explosive political subject because it is particularly close to the heart of a very special energy expert—Li Peng himself.

Women's Salon. Could it be that Dai Qing is a feminist as well? She hardly fits into a Western mold of a feminist. But there is no doubt that she is deeply concerned about women-related issues. In her lecture, she speaks about a series of articles she has written in which she uses individual lives, not isolated cases, to address women's problems that most people would prefer not to bring to public attention. For instance, in one article she portrays the life of a woman who has just been released from a reeducation camp, and in another, she describes the fate of a divorced woman who decides to remarry but encounters almost insurmountable difficulties because she is a woman.

In one of these portraits, Dai Qing tells the story of a nine-year-old girl who is raped by a stranger. On an icy cold winter evening, the child is standing in line, freezing, waiting to buy milk for her family. The tall man behind her spreads his warm, wide army overcoat and wraps it around her. She thinks he wants to protect her from the cold. But suddenly she loses her footing; she is lifted up, dragged over to a pile of cabbages, and beaten until she loses consciousness. When she wakes up in the hospital, she feels the pain not only of her bleeding vagina but also of the memory of a traumatic experience. Her mother and her grandmother tearfully bewail the loss of her virginity. The girl is worthless now, they lament, there is no hope for her, no future. Passionately, Dai Qing takes the side of women who are victims of violence and injustice. And she accuses a society that sacrifices the future happiness of its children for its rigid moral principles.

In another report, she "looks back in anger" at the years of the Cultural Revolution. In 1966 a woman student, who was then twenty, had written a letter to Mao in which she openly criticized the injustices she saw. She mailed the letter and poisoned herself. Her suicide attempt failed, the young woman was "saved," but was immediately sent to prison—for thirteen years.

Dai Qing treats her targets scathingly. She constructs powerful sentences, giving special pleasure to those listeners who have already learned to appreciate her sharp pen. Through the thick lenses of their horn-rimmed glasses, near-sighted older women miss none of Dai Qing's spare, expressive gestures. The younger students' hands fly across their notebooks. Here, there is definitely more to learn than in the usual lecture.

In the epilogue to one of her books, Dai Qing writes: "China is as it is today, after four decades of peaceful reconstruction, because whenever the people should have cried out 'No' in order to avoid grave political errors, there was nothing but silence."

After the death of Hu Yaobang, people broke their silence, first at the universities, then in the offices, department stores, editorial offices, and factories. They began hunger strikes. Dai Qing interviewed female and male students who refused to drink even water during the days of the Gorbachev visit to China. She supports the goals of the student democracy movement, but questions their methods, knowing the iron fist of the government. Dai Qing saw the impending trap and offered to act as mediator between the demonstrators and the government. The students declined her offer. Is it that they decided not to trust anybody over thirty?

In the early morning hours of 4 June, the military stifled the students' cry for freedom and justice in a cruel bloodbath. And even though Dai Qing had not approved of the protests, which were extreme even for Chinese circumstances, she was horrified and sickened by the reaction of the government and the party leadership. That same day, she publicly resigned from the Chinese Communist Party, an extreme insult to the old guard and an unmistakable act of support for the democracy movement.

Suddenly, but not unexpectedly, Dai Qing disappeared at the end of July. Now she occupies a cell in the infamous Qincheng Jianyu, the Beijing prison for VIPs, through whose "narrow gate" have passed many other critical intellectuals.

Translated by Ilze Mueller

3
WOMEN TODAY

Nelly Rau-Häring

In Tiantan Park, Beijing

PHYSICIAN

Lin Yamei

In 1953, after I passed my exams at the Medical College in Chengde, I joined the first generation of doctors of the New China. At the time we were twenty to twenty-two years old. We felt like soldiers joyfully following the call of the nation—to the front line, the border, out into the countryside.

I was assigned to a small clinic in Inner Mongolia, far from all civilization. Often I would ride ten, twenty kilometers (6–12 mi.) on a donkey or on horseback to help with a difficult birth. Once I even had to dismember and remove a fetus that had been dead for two days in the mother's womb. Another time I rode into the mountains to help a woman who had a very narrow pelvis give birth to her first child. I had to turn the child's head to get it out. Had I not been available, the family might have tried carrying this woman one hundred kilometers (60 mi.) to the nearest town, though the trip—there was no bus or train— might have killed her. Her family thanked me again and again and invited me to share their millet and cabbage, the best thing they had for a guest. Since they had little salt, the food had little flavor. Still I enjoyed the meal, for I had done a good deed.

In the countryside, I soon acquired a good reputation, since I was often able to save children who had pneumonia and tuberculosis. In such cases, I had to live with peasant families for extended periods in order to give children shots and medication around the clock.

Two years later I was transferred to a town clinic in which I looked after the employees of a trucking company. The work of long-distance truckers is very hard, because they are often on the road for twenty-four hours a day, sometimes for weeks on end. Their main complaints were stomach, lung, or bone diseases. In order to be on call at all times, I lived on company grounds. Every day I treated fifty to sixty patients, not only workers but also their families. In my free time, I would often take the children home with me and treat them there.

Here I also met a worker whom I later married. After that my life changed completely. Like men, I too had had a lofty goal in life, but then I had four children, one after the other. The children, the many household duties, the husband, were not compatible with my former plans. As a result, I had many arguments with my husband, for I could no longer organize my time with as much freedom as before marriage. I had no time to continue my education, or to go to a dance or movie once in a while.

When my husband was transferred to this company in 1955, he began to work as a mechanic. We fell in love because we saw each other frequently, and, being young and inexperienced, paid no attention to whether we shared common goals, interests, or hobbies. We did not realize this until after our marriage, when we both had a hard time. I like to read, and when I do, I forget the world around me. After marriage, there was no time for reading. As soon as I opened my beloved books, my husband would begin grumbling: What is the sense of reading, he'd say, why don't you do something in the kitchen instead? My husband loved to sit around with the guys after work, smoking and shooting the breeze, but I would no longer put up with that.

Despite the difficulties, we stayed together.

Now that I have helped fifteen hundred workers in the company over the past thirty years, I am content and happy after all. Today the children are grown, except for the youngest, who is retarded. The eldest three are workers, married, with children of their own. Now our family is quite big, twelve people in all. Our income, too, has gone up over the last years, and so we have a fine life.

My time is still at a premium. I need a lot of time to continue updating my medical training, for I hope I can help even more people with more knowledge and with the help of modern technology.

Translated by Ilze Mueller

PAINTER

Zhang Xiaofei

I am a Chinese artist. I was born in 1932 in Beijing. My father taught at a secondary school, my mother was a housewife. We lived in a quiet ten-room house with two inner courtyards, which were full of lotuses, oleanders, lilacs, many different trees, and ornamental plants. I had a sister and lots of relatives. I was a skinny, quiet girl, and a good student. Unfortunately my mother died when I was thirteen. When my father remarried, it meant the loss of family security for me.

After I graduated from lower middle school, my parents did not want to spend any more money for my further schooling. I was supposed to get a job or go to a teachers' training college. So I took the entrance tests at two teachers' training colleges: in Tianjin and at the State College of Art in Beijing. After passing both, I decided on the State College of Art, which also gave me a scholarship, two packages of flour a month, and enough to live on. For extra money, sometimes I tutored the daughter of a doctor and helped her do her homework.

Outwardly I seemed quiet and sedate, but inside I was seething with the passionate desire to lead a life off the beaten track. After Beijing was liberated, I left the college and enthusiastically followed the army south, to Nanjing and Wuhan, through Hunan Province to Sichuan and Tibet. I was one of a few women soldiers at that time. I had no desire to hide myself away among women. I liked being direct and open, and I loved to play ball with the soldiers, to go horseback riding, to go on patrol, even to shoot.

After a few years I returned to Beijing and continued my art studies. I took classes with famous masters, always did well, and was hired by the college after I graduated. My work was exhibited in national and international shows, and was published in books. I often traveled in order to paint, and that was how I got to see almost all of China.

With regard to my personal life, a few men who were fond of me liked my gentleness and amiability. Two men had declared their love for me in letters I never received, for they had been stolen. Both of them had someone else tell me about it, after they had already been married for many years, but by then it was much too late. I remember when I was nineteen, an honest and intelligent regimental commander had fallen in love with me. One time, in Sichuan, he accompanied me part of the way on horseback. But in those days a decent man simply did not declare his love directly. Later, at the college, I had an admirer for a whole three years. The way he looked after me was so sweet. If it was cold, he would buy me a scarf and woolen socks. If I went to the countryside to paint, he would see to it that I had a straw hat and a flashlight. He was a truly kindhearted person, but because I paid attention to outward appearances—he was a little shorter than I—I let matters take their course and allowed another woman to snatch him away from me.

After that I was courted by a university professor. His wife had killed herself, leaving four children aged seven to eleven. He was not in the best of health, though he was in his thirties. Whenever others talked about him, they would say that any woman who married him would have a bad time of it. I did not actually intend to marry him, but since he knew how soft-hearted and gullible I was, he pressured me so much that we got married within a month.

Married, I was a servant to him, one he did not have to spend money on and who went to bed with him besides. Daily I cleaned the four rooms, took the children to school, picked them up again, and attended parents' meetings. In addition to the four children, I also had to look after his old mother. We had financial problems, but I made sure we had clothes and other necessities; I spent my whole salary on the family. Since he already had four children, I gave up the idea of having children of my own. Despite all the things I did for him and the family, I myself did not receive the same treatment. It was not long before I began to regret the marriage, for my friends turned away from me, and I also lost the sympathy of many people at the college.

The Cultural Revolution was a catastrophe in which many people were killed and Chinese culture was destroyed. Out of fear, my father destroyed part of his collection of famous pictures, which he had gathered over many years; he handed over the rest, along with the good clothes and jewelry, to the confiscation center of the Red Guards.

Because of my husband's position, I was constantly exposed to harassment. For five years, I did not see him and did not even know if he was still alive. Then the colleges and universities were closed, and all the teachers and students were sent to the rural areas. In a village in Henan Province, we were organized into a company under military supervision. Every day soldiers would escort us to work in a field that was twenty kilometers (about 12 mi.) away. During these marches we had to sing without interruption, or recite quotations by Chairman Mao or Deputy Chairman Lin (Biao). The work was tiring and dirty. We had to plant rice seedlings, haul dirt, and collect manure. Even when people collapsed from the heat—up to 105 degrees Fahrenheit (about 26°C)—rest was out of the question. I was the fastest worker during the wheat harvest and on the threshing floor: there was no job I couldn't deal with. Daily, after the work in the fields, we had to bring eight loads (sixteen buckets) of water for the group and the landlord.

It was not the physical work but the psychological abuse that destroyed people. Even before daybreak, we had to assemble and go on a cross-country run, which was followed by an exhausting workday. In the evenings there were "criticism and self-criticism meetings," and at night, no matter how late it was, we had to make written "confessions" about everything. The idea was not to let us sleep. I was the target of severe criticism and was allowed to speak with no one except my interrogators. I need hardly mention that I was not allowed to paint during the ten years of the Cultural Revolution.

In 1974 I returned to Beijing. My husband was not rehabilitated until 1979. When we were reunited, the years of suffering seemed to be over; I wanted to raise my head and enjoy some good times. However, my kindness was rewarded with ingratitude. During a senseless argument, my husband suddenly demanded a divorce, which upset me so much that I became ill. Still willing to compromise, I took time each day to cook and take care of the family, which had increased to nine persons, what with the children getting married and the grandchildren. On top of everything, I still had to teach. The apartment was very crowded, I had no room for anything. My son and daughter-in-law bullied me, and sometimes they would chase me out of the apartment in all kinds of weather.

At the beginning of the winter of 1985, my husband finally dropped me for good. In the divorce proceedings, not one lawyer was willing to represent him in this immoral matter. Even the attorney of his university, who finally did represent him, sympathized with me.

Divorce is a terrible thing for a woman over fifty who has no children of her own. In Beijing there are a lot more women than men, and the men quickly remarry after a divorce. Women, on the other hand, have a hard time, and so it's no wonder there are newspaper reports about women committing suicide after a divorce. The years of misery had caused my health to deteriorate severely. I lived in a dilapidated old house that could barely withstand the roaring winter storms. I was too weak to make a fire. Fortunately, I had a good reputation as a painter, and so, time and again, admirers would come and visit me and help me light the fire in the stove. It was as though heaven did not want to abandon me.

I had been terribly unlucky, my situation seemed hopeless. But my artistic work saved me. In these difficult circumstances, I summoned all my willpower and studied English and French for three years. I painted a lot, in oil and in the Chinese tradition; I did calligraphy and carved seals. My paintings were successfully exhibited in Beijing and other cities. Shows of my work were organized abroad as well; thus I had a chance to see other countries. For half a year, I traveled through Asia and Europe. It is unusual for a Chinese woman my age who has no family or friends abroad to be able to travel alone, at her own expense, on a professional tour.

I taught at a university abroad for one year. The students welcomed me and took care of me every way they could. Thus, I felt close to people again. The students did not want me to leave. The entire student body asked the university administration to extend my contract. I was deeply touched. I felt I should belong to the whole world. I shall work where I am needed. It seems to me as though my life's work is only just beginning and that all my former privations were only a prologue.

Translated by Ilze Mueller

STUDENT

Wei Hong

I had just turned fifteen when I received permission to go to college. My father, in tears, exclaimed: "How long I have waited for this day!"

I grew up in a family of intellectuals, my father was a geologist. At the time, during the Cultural Revolution, only the children of workers, peasants, and soldiers were allowed to attend college, regardless of aptitude. As children of intellectuals, we were greatly disadvantaged; we were considered the "stinking number nine" class (as opposed to workers, peasants, and revolutionaries, who were grouped in the first class), and stood little chance of getting a higher education. According to the slogans of Chairman Mao, we were supposed to go to the countryside and become peasants. My older sister spent three years in a village, and after finishing middle school, I would probably have faced the same fate—it almost broke my mother's heart.

The first national college entrance exams held after the fall of the "Gang of Four" took place in 1977. That meant that students' academic qualifications counted again, not merely their background. From our unit, only my sister and I made it. She was admitted to a technical college, and I was assigned to Tongji University in Shanghai because my exam results were well above average. This meant I had to pack my bags and leave my parents for the first time. I spent three days on the train to Shanghai, all by myself. I was supposed to study there for five years and stay on as a college professor for seven more years. I get very sentimental when I recall those days.

Every college is surrounded by high walls, and everybody must show an identification card at the entrance. Lecture halls, libraries, cafeterias, offices, and labs are all located within the campus walls. Students live free of charge in dormitories that have four or five floors, with about fifty rooms on each floor. The rooms are about ten by ten feet, on the average, and are shared by six to seven students, though there are usually eight bunk beds. The room contains a bookcase, washbasins, and a large desk with a drawer for each student. There are separate communal bathrooms and showers with cold water; hot water must be brought from the cafeteria.

One roommate is responsible for the room, which must be swept daily and cleaned thoroughly once a week. Since there was no washstand in the room, we had to go to the communal washroom to brush our teeth or wash clothes. Living in such close quarters forced us to be considerate of one another. We had to study in the classrooms to avoid disturbing our roommates, for if only one girl was studying in the room, none of the others could listen to music or chat. It was not always easy to find a common denominator for seven girls!

I was known as a night owl. Though the lights went out at about 10:00 P.M. in the communal rooms, and at about 11:00 P.M. in the dorms, there were always a few lecture halls that remained lit. As soon as my roommates returned, I would gather my books to go out and study. In the morning I would barely manage to get out of bed in time for classes; not even the daily cleaning chores could wake me—my roommates never understood.

All the students lived in dorms for the duration of the five-year course of studies. Food was served three times a day in the cafeteria. There were four hours of scheduled classes in the mornings, the afternoons were free. At lunchtime the cafeteria was deluged by students; everyone wanted to be the first, though sometimes you had to wait for at least half an hour. If you were out of luck, the food was gone by the time your turn came and you had to start standing in another line all over again. Many students used this time to read. I always went to eat later, when the biggest rush had passed, though by that time the food was cold.

Each semester lasted five months, and there were two breaks: three weeks in the winter and five in the summer. After the final exams, we would buy our train tickets and head home to our parents. Mine lived in the northeast at the time, some 1,400 miles (about 2,250 km.) from Shanghai, a train ride of more than sixty hours. But some students' parents lived even further away; they had to plan on spending half their vacation time just traveling!

Though everything at college was regulated, there was a lot

of competition. Every morning one of the girls from our room would go to the lecture halls to reserve seats by placing books on them; you had to do the same thing immediately after class for the afternoon. I was the youngest student in my class; the oldest was twice my age. I did not have much life experience, but I was a good student. In one math exam, for instance, only two students achieved one hundred points; I was one of them. Fellow students would frequently turn to me for help.

Our German class was taught by a teacher who had never been abroad, and all our study materials originated in China. Though we had few occasions to talk to Germans, our interest in the language was so great that we created our own linguistic environment. One of my roommates and I spoke German to each other during meals, before going to bed, and while shopping or washing clothes. We even had our own rules: if you used a Chinese word during these conversations, you had to pay one *fen* (equivalent to 0.01 yuan). I soon realized that women did better in language classes than men because they could imitate sounds much more rapidly, an important requirement for learning a foreign language.

One of our roommates played the violin. Her music made us pensive, though we would also sing to it, so loudly sometimes that our neighbors complained. At four in the afternoon we would all go to play volleyball, and some games were so exciting that we would simply skip dinner. On the weekends there were dances in the main auditorium. Sometimes we were given tickets for free; at other times we had to buy them. It was better to find a suitable partner beforehand, because the male students were too shy to dance with female students they did not know. On Sundays the dorms were empty; some students visited their relatives, others went out with their boyfriends, still others went for walks or shopping. If you bought anything, you had to show it to your roommates who, of course, never held back any comments!

To ensure that students focused exclusively on their studies, the rules stated explicitly that we were not to fall in love; otherwise there would be repercussions when we were assigned a profession. This meant that couples would be separated and sent to different cities or to remote mountain regions. But it was useless. In the evenings couples holding hands were just about everywhere—on the lawns and park benches, even in the bushes. The regulations did not stop them, but if you were caught, it was recorded as a "moral lapse" in your personal file.

215

And that had a negative impact not only on your further course of study but also on your life, for the stigma remained with you regardless of the work unit to which you would later belong.

Yet it was almost impossible to meet in the rooms, because the women and men lived in separate dormitories, and there were numerous checkpoints to ensure women students' security. Visitors had to register and were not allowed to stay after 10:00 P.M. If one of us had a guest, all the others had to leave the room; if two of us made a date for the same time, we would simply put up a partition. But it was more fun to meet in the park, at the movies, in the dance hall, or in a cafe to taste a little bit of "freedom."

Translated by Ulrike Bode

TEACHER

Xu Quanzhi

This year I turned thirty-five. I have been a middle-school English teacher for ten years now. Every class I teach has about fifty students, half of them girls. When I look at myself critically, I think that I am not suited to this work. I am fairly quiet and think more than I speak. I am quite placid, and it's hard for me to be assertive with my students, even fifteen-year-olds. But I have to work in order to survive. It takes energy and effort to get along with students. I try to make each class as lively as possible. I set a high standard for myself, but I don't put all my energy into my work—I give much to my family.

My husband is a journalist, and my daughter is six now. My husband is a year older than I. For him, work is what matters most. He can spend half a day sitting at his desk without a break. He'll go on reading and writing at home even after work is over. At first I was amazed to see someone work that much. Isn't that kind of life boring year in, year out, I often wonder. But he's been doing it for years.

Of course he doesn't help me with housework. After I finish teaching, I buy some vegetables, cook them at home, and when I carry the steaming bowl to the table and shout "Come and eat!" he finally appears. Before my thirty-fifth birthday, I reminded him that I would like a present. He hasn't given me a birthday present since we've been married. Although I know that he is not familiar with this custom, I wanted to teach him to observe it. On this particular birthday I spent half the day with a girlfriend, and I was hoping I'd get a little present at home. At home I found my husband in bed—with a stomachache. He never even mentioned my birthday. It almost broke my heart, because I realized nothing would ever change. This coldness and insensitivity will accompany me the rest of my life. Next year I'm going to give myself lots of birthday presents. After all, it's my holiday!

Actually I don't enjoy spending a lot of money, but I do think that good food and good clothes brighten your life. Of course there should be a little bit of savings in the bank, for emergencies, but my husband counts every last *fen*. My monthly salary is 170 yuan, and my husband earns 250 yuan. All the household expenses are paid with my money. He pays only for our daughter's violin lessons. He also pays for his constant smoking. Once my money is gone and I ask him to pay up, he makes a long face and starts to grumble: "How can you just throw your money down the drain, you never have enough, do you? When a woman doesn't know how to handle money, the household isn't properly taken care of!" Such remarks always hurt me deeply, and I wonder how I am supposed to manage: For eggs I pay 20 yuan a month, pork is 30 yuan, fish is 20, and vegetables are 30 yuan, and besides there are the expenses for drinks and liquor when we have company. And then I'm supposed to buy books and toys and a little candy for the child. And the rent—all that with my 170 yuan. How am I supposed to save anything on top of that? When this happens, I hate my husband for whom it is always save, save, save, and justify yourself for every fen you spend. That makes me miserable. But strangely enough I have never thought of divorce. He may not be handsome, but he has a certain presence, he's very correct with friends and colleagues, and he's always the center of attention. Although I don't have particularly nice clothes, and my daughter's clothes, too, are hand-me-downs from her friends, I'm happy that I have a good husband by my side. I am able to trust him, and that's why I love him. He'll always be the first happiness in my life.

The second happiness in my life is my daughter. Because China has such a large population, every couple is allowed to have only one child. According to state regulations, we can have only one child, our daughter. I feel a bit lonely having only one child. But what can you do?

Every day after work, no matter how tired I am, I take time for her, tell her stories, look at picture books with her, and listen to music with her. When she was six I signed her up for swimming lessons. Although we live in the capital, with a population of ten million, there are hardly any swimming pools. To take my

(Private collection)

A teacher

daughter to the pool, I have to travel half an hour by bike. Before she started the course she had never been in the water by herself. On the first day, excitedly my daughter put on her new bathing suit and stood next to the pool. The swimming teacher was quite young. She had to teach ten children. She carried one after another into the water, and because the teacher was there, my daughter wasn't scared. The next time, the children had to go into the water alone. Fearfully she clung to the teacher's hand and began crying loudly: "Dear teacher, let me get out of the water!" And she swallowed a lot of water. Because the child was so tense, the teacher slapped her. All the people who were watching were sorry for my little girl. I hid in a corner and began to cry. I didn't know that learning to swim was so hard. But if she doesn't manage to take this first step, she'll never learn to swim. That night our daughter got a fever, and I gave her medicine. The next day, she didn't want to go swimming any more. I knew that if she didn't go now, she would be afraid of the water all her life. I was determined to help her overcome this fear. I told her that if she didn't go, the teacher would come to our house and punish her. Then she was very scared and went with me like a good girl.

That day she went into the water alone, and five days later she could already swim four hundred meters (440 yds.). The more she swam, the more she enjoyed it. At the end of the course, twenty days later, they had a race, and she came in first. I'm even happier than my daughter, because I provided her with this opportunity. If it hadn't been for my efforts, she might never have gotten around to it, like me, who still can't swim at thirty-five. I can't ever make up for what I've missed, and that's why I do things differently with my daughter.

My daughter is at school six days a week. On Sundays there is no school. At the end of November we went for a trip to "Fragrant Mountain"; the last emperor of the last dynasty loved to hunt there. The mountain is about five hundred meters (1,650 ft.) high and covered with old trees—cypresses, pines, and maples. In the fall, the scent of the cassia trees almost makes your head reel. The leaves of the maple trees turn red and cover the mountain like a carpet. The landscape is wonderful. We didn't want to walk on the paved road, so we tramped through the woods. Our daughter ran ahead, and my husband followed behind me. I was making only slow progress, for at times I was crawling on my hands and knees. My daughter made fun of me and yelled, "Like a silly bear." I'm sure I looked funny. When we reached the top, my daughter's happy laughter made me really happy.

I only have one child to love. She'll grow up and leave home. Oh, how lonely I'll be then.

Translated by Ilze Mueller

TEXTILE WORKER

Yu Mengtao

I am forty years old. In China they say that what you haven't achieved by the age of forty, you'll never get in this life. There are three of us in our family: my husband, my twelve-year-old son, and myself. My husband and I are both the same age. He works as an electrician at the Beijing airport. My son is in sixth grade. Our apartment is in a housing project near the airport. We used to have a one-room apartment, but this year we were allocated a two-room apartment. Overjoyed we moved in. Finally, after fifteen years of waiting, my wish had been fulfilled. The two rooms together measure twenty square meters (about 24 sq. yds.), and if I count the hallway, kitchen, and toilet, we have a total of forty square meters (about 48 sq. yds.). The apartment is on the second floor, and what makes it really perfect is that the windows face south. My supervisor at work, who's been with the company since 1953 and is now retired, only recently got an apartment like ours—we were so lucky!

I started working at the Beijing Textile Factory twenty years ago, and all these years I've always worked in the fabric-weaving section. Business is good for our factory; we can hardly meet the demand. And then there's export, too. We work around the clock in four shifts. Each is responsible for thirty-six looms, and each must produce eight hundred meters (about 880 yds.). After six days on the job, we have two days off, but the machines must never stop. (The people get a break, but not the machines!) Our work is very strenuous. We get no vacations, only one or two days off during the holidays. Our factory employs over seven thousand people, mostly women. I love my work. Over the years I have gotten used to the noise of the machinery and have improved my dexterity.

Unfortunately my apartment is so far from the factory that I have to get up at 5:00 A.M. when I'm on the day shift. It takes me fifteen minutes to get everything done and leave the house. I take the commuter bus to the city; I change buses twice and get to the factory at seven. I have breakfast on the way when I change buses—a fried pastry and a pancake. I bring my lunch with me from home. I make it ahead of time every night, pack it in a lunchbox, and the next morning all I have to do is take it with me. We do have a cafeteria at the factory, but I can't afford it, and besides I think it's a shame to spend so much money for food. Work finishes at four, and I take the same bus lines back to my house. I get home at six. If I'm on the night shift, I don't go home—I spend the night in the factory dormitory.

My husband has a much easier life: his place of work is not far from our apartment. It takes him fifteen minutes by bike to get there. He comes home before I do in the afternoon. He does the shopping every day; he cooks and looks after our son. It's been working out really well for over ten years now. When the boy was little, my husband also had to bring him to nursery school and pick him up. Those are his responsibilities, and I'm very grateful to him for looking after me and supporting me.

Right now I'm earning 150 yuan a month, and my husband makes 200 yuan. For rent, electricity, and water, we pay 20 yuan. Most of the money goes for food. Naturally we can't buy clothes very often. We also rarely have people over and just as rarely go visit friends and relatives, except on holidays. We support my parents-in-law with twenty yuan a month.

Even on Sundays I don't have much time for myself. That's when I have to do my household chores, including the laundry, because if I want to save money I really have to do everything myself. That's how we can save 30 yuan a month. Once we've put aside one or two thousand yuan, we can buy some electrical appliances. We've already bought a refrigerator, a washing machine, and a radio; now all we need is a color television. To buy that, we have to save quite a lot of money. We also have to start thinking about the expense of our son's wedding. And then, of course, I'd like a few nice dresses for myself. Since I'm forty now, I have to be careful about how I dress, or I'll start looking like an old woman.

Translated by Ilze Mueller

SOLDIER

Li Aijun

On New Year 1977, I finished secondary school. Since all the universities were closed as a result of the Cultural Revolution, I had two alternatives: I could go "to the countryside and into the mountains"—i.e., to a village—where I would be educated by the poor and lower middle peasants and "cultivate the soil." Or I could join the army. Since I come from a military family, I chose the second alternative. I had just turned nineteen.

With my heart in my mouth, I put my uniform on for the first time. What would life be like in the army? I had no idea. The corps to which I had been assigned was stationed in a lonely little village near Changli in Hebei Province. After an eight-hour train ride I finally reached my destination. When I got out, an officer came and commanded, "The leaders of the enlistees are to take their people to division headquarters. Fall into five lines!" A platoon leader sternly ordered, "From now on you are to listen only to my commands. You are part of the intelligence division. I am your platoon leader. I shall now bring you to your quarters. Forward march!"

The quarters were bare, steel girder frame barracks at ground level. The bitter January cold chilled us to our very bones. Sixteen women soldiers shared one room; none of us knew each other. We came from large cities like Beijing or Guangzhou, or from Henan and Jiangsu Provinces; only a few came from the countryside. There were two *kangs* (oven beds). Ten women slept on one, and six on the other. I went outside to wash my face. It was icy cold. I looked up at the sky, at the stars, and there was nothing I wanted more than to go home to my parents.

We ate three meals a day: for breakfast, steamed corn buns

Women soldiers

with pickled vegetables and a bowl of cornmeal porridge; at lunch we ate rice and fried dishes. Because of the daily training in the open air, I got chilblains on my hands, ears, and face within a couple of days. Sometimes the skin on my face would crack and bleed while I was washing it. A soldier's life was hard!

After two weeks I got my first pay: 6.75 yuan. (Male soldiers got 6 yuan, and women soldiers 0.75 yuan more as a hygiene bonus.) On our day off, I asked the platoon leader for a leave of absence. I went to the bank in the village and opened an account with my pay and the money that my parents had given me. I felt satisfied.

Army life is very monotonous. During the day we marched in step, or in goose step. We drilled and drilled. At night it was practice drill and long marches carrying a heavy pack. In our free time we memorized army and barracks regulations. We not only had to take disciplinary exams; our barracks duties were also inspected. This was a big headache for me, for the blankets and quilted overcoats had to be folded into exact squares.

The last part of our training was shooting with live ammunition and a semiautomatic weapon. While shooting at a hundred meters, I got good results in three rounds with twenty-seven points. Three days later the company commander informed me that I was to take part in the qualifying contests for the artillery sports games. Taken by surprise, I asked, "How many people were picked?" "Only five during this training session." When I heard that, shivers ran up and down my spine. It was really good to be part of the sports team; besides it meant you got a 1.5 yuan bonus, and it was more interesting than training. But suppose I were picked and failed to win—and with everybody watching too—what then? The most important thing was not to get worked up unnecessarily.

After supper a field officer and political commissar came to fetch me. We took the targets and went down the mountain to set them up at twenty-five meters (about 28 yds.). When we drew lots, I drew second place. The first rifleman missed three out of five shots. It's my turn now, I thought, and felt sure I wouldn't even hit the target. But I took the pistol in my hand just the way the political commissar had shown me and aimed. My arm was shaking. I held my breath, one second, two seconds, three seconds—thirty seconds, "Bang!" the shot went off. After the shot my ears were deaf, my hand and arm felt numb, my eyes were watering, I felt totally exhausted.

Shaking, I held the pistol: "I'm not going to shoot any more. I've never done any shooting with pistols, and my ears can't take it either."

Two officers walked over to the target, had a look, and then waved to encourage me: "Not bad, keep shooting. It's late, and there are three more people waiting."

So I kept shooting and left the place feeling I had been a failure. Much to my surprise I was the best with three times ten and twice nine points. I could hardly believe it. The company informed me that I would be part of the division team at the final elimination. I went to the training shooting range by truck. There, three trainers of the thirty-eighth Army were in charge of us. After my experience at the qualifying contest, I was no longer scared. In the next rounds of the final elimination, I got 372 points, and so I took part in the third artillery sports games in Shacheng in May 1977.

I'll never forget those four months. They left me with a lot of lovely memories. Every day we had collective training, cross-country running, calisthenics, and weight lifting. Then we trained in small groups. Not till evening did we have time for ourselves. We spent the evening together: some would sing; others would play the mouth organ; it was just like home. I enjoyed spending time with the trainers, especially the one in the rifle category. He was tall and came from the northeast; he was also from an army family. He was very nice, and because he knew my neighbors—they were the relatives of a good friend of his—we would always get together after training and talk.

Time passed quickly, and the competition date came closer and closer. I thought of nothing but achieving success and going home as soon as possible. The women's pistol group of our team got first place, and in the individual competition I came in third. Pleased, I ran to the hostel where the trainer in the rifle category lived. When I opened the door, I saw him sitting bent over his desk. Suddenly he jumped up and embraced me. I was shocked, because it was the first time in my life a man had kissed me. I hadn't expected that. Quickly I freed myself from his arms. I was very careful about Rule 2 of the general army regulations: "Soldiers may not enter into a relationship with each other," and Rule 8: "When a man and a woman speak to each other, a third person must be present." After all, I was a soldier. I put on my cap, went to the desk, and looked at what he had been writing. It was a love poem. He said that when it was finished he would give it to me to remember him by. I burst into tears and was filled with incredible sadness. I knew we had to go our separate ways after the competition was over. I was afraid others might see us together and quickly ran back to my hostel. On the day he left, I went with him to the station. It was May; there was not a cloud in the sky and flowers were in bloom. My heart was heavy, and I didn't know what to say. Just before the train left, he said to me, "Let's exchange fountain pens." I cried. When we gave each other the fountain pens, our hands clasped each other firmly for one long moment.

After my return, I was assigned to the divisional hospital. At first I took a five-month course in nursing. Now I was back with women, which I didn't really like. Not a minute went by without my thinking of the rifle range and my two beloved pistols, which I had long since given back. Most of all, I missed the trainer in the rifle category.

I concentrated totally on studying. When the course was finished, we went to Tangshan. There we took an autopsy course. I witnessed the great suffering after the severe earthquake in Tangshan. That was another profound experience. At the end of the course, I thought I could work in the hospital. But because of a work reassignment, I was sent to the hospital kitchen. Actually I didn't like it. But what's a soldier to do but obey? Later my friends would tell me, "Your cooking isn't bad."

Four of us cooked for fifty patients: an experienced cook, two assistants, and I. I lit the fires, so they all called me the stoker. We got along fine. A hospital diet is not easy to prepare. If an operation ran into the evening, we sometimes had to get up again at night to cook food. There were three different-sized stoves and an oven. Coal was provided, but I had to make sure we had kindling and wood. Daily I would get up at dawn and light the stoves before the cook and the assistants arrived. When the patients had eaten, we would all wash the dishes, clean the kitchen, and go on to prepare the next meal. After lunch I would go out into the woods to gather kindling wood. Sometimes I would enjoy a long walk in the woods, looking at the distant mountains, watching for birds, and remembering my experiences during the target-shooting training. ". . . In our free time during training, we would shoot at mosquitoes, birds' nests, we would shatter bricks, bottles. . . . Laughter, songs. . . ."

I feel I have grown up and matured. When my army days are over, I'm going to take off my uniform and return to Beijing.

Translated by Ilze Mueller

ARCHITECT

Wang Xiaohui

I'm an architect, but my whole life doesn't revolve around my profession. I am somehow torn. I love this profession, but I also love my many sidelines: writing, photography, painting, and television work. However, I can't simply pretend I'm no longer an architect. It's not always possible in one's life to make the right choice when you're at the crossroads. There is a lot in life that can't be undone, like a brush stroke in Chinese painting. You see, in Chinese water color painting, not a single line can be corrected, whether it has turned out well or not, and every brush stroke has an element of chance about it. My choice of a profession, too, was a combination of necessity and chance. To explain that, I need to go back to my teen years.

At age eighteen one is full of illusions, full of hopes. But during the Cultural Revolution it wasn't like that. There was no future, no hope, nobody made great demands on life. If you weren't sent away to the countryside, you could call yourself very lucky. It was out of the question to choose your own profession. We had to take the job to which we were assigned. It was impossible to get into a university if your family hadn't been "red for three generations." And in those days, universities were scarcely worthy of being called by that name. Life during those years was typically boring. In that atmosphere it was hard to find even a spark of *joie de vivre,* or even to breathe. Fortunately I knew how to play the accordion, so I was detailed to play in an orchestra and was thrown together with other young people who were interested in culture. I also did some composing myself, and the pieces were performed.

The only place I wasn't allowed to do that was at home. My mother is a composer, and the most painful experience of her life was that she was not allowed to be a musician. To want to be a musician in those years meant to risk your life.

So that it wouldn't occur to me to study music, and so the Red Guards would not search the apartment, she even kept the piano under lock and key for years. But I would compose in secret and play my pieces for my friends. In accordance with the times my pieces did have revolutionary and martial titles; even so, this activity was an oasis in the cultural desert for me. True, this oasis was small, but I was able to survive in it.

When the Cultural Revolution was over, we felt as though we had awakened from a dream. Suddenly universities were giving entrance examinations again, but there was a lot of competition, for now ten times as many young people as usual were waiting for a chance to continue their studies. I was lucky to be one of the few who passed the exam and was suddenly faced with a problem—I had to choose a field of study. The arts were my only love. I would have preferred music or photography. Or—and this was my fondest wish—film directing. Film is a sort of synthesis of all the arts, and I could have applied all my interests here. But my parents wanted me to study something technical. A career in the arts, as they had discovered during the past years, depended too much on the political situation, and the political situation could always change. So I chose the subject that seemed the most artistic of the technical subjects: architecture. To study architecture I had to go to Shanghai.

A Chinese woman has many duties in life. One of them is respect for her parents. For many young Western women, it may be natural simply to do or not to do what they feel like. It's different in China. A "good daughter" fulfills the wishes and expectations of society. As a "good daughter" I became a hardworking student, although the dry technical material often did not interest me. And not only because of my parents, but also out of ambition and because of practical considerations. Only if I had good final grades was there a prospect of graduate study or of getting a job at the university. It was only within the university that there was a chance that I could choose my own field of work, and only life at the university offered a little leisure and vacations. I hate being under pressure, and so I had a hard time keeping my many wishes in check and focusing on my studies. It was a difficult life, but I felt good when my parents were proud of me or when a professor would point to me as an example for others to follow.

At that time, one of our graduating class was to be chosen

for a scholarship to Vienna. Because of my outstanding grades, I was chosen. Everybody envied me then, but when the school of architecture lost the scholarship, I felt like a balloon with all the air let out of it. I had already given away a lot of my books and clothes because I was ready to go abroad. Now I had to go back and make up for lost time so that I could still take the exams to get into graduate school. I was so exhausted that I wondered if there was any sense in taking the exams. There were too few openings, and I had to compete with the top students. In China, merely graduating from a university is already a fantastic achievement for a woman. Why should I insist on striving for higher things? But again my parents pressured me. I knew what was expected of me, and again I gave in, gritted my teeth, and finally made it.

Now I had really reached the end of my strength. I felt as though I had been sick for a long time. I went home to stay with my parents for a while and slowly recovered again. I met friends I hadn't seen for some time. They were almost all married now, had children, and were content with leading simple lives. To them, I seemed to come from another world; suddenly there was a deep gulf between us. This was especially true for the men, who did not want to associate with a woman who was "above" them.

I, too, wanted a family, but I couldn't have lived as my former friends did. Only—what could I do instead? I had done a lot better than they, I could be proud of myself, but what had I really achieved? My entire life up to this point had been a life according to plan, a life under pressure.

During this time, when I was feeling so empty, so exhausted and almost old, I met a former teacher, a painter. I told him how I felt, and he asked me how old I was. "Twenty-six," I answered. "Oh, that's the best age to tackle something new," he said. "Take me, I'm sixty-two, and there is still so much I want to do that I don't know where to start. You must figure out what you really want and set about doing it." That's when I decided to do only what I really wanted.

In China it's extraordinary even to set your mind on something like that, let alone to carry it out. Ideal and reality are even further apart in China than elsewhere. To change careers is almost impossible, and this is especially true for intellectuals. They belong to the state and the "work unit."

The Chinese have a stereotype of women who are successful at their studies. These "strong women" are seen as "bluestockings"—near-sighted, dressed in old-fashioned clothes, stiff, and humorless—who are interested in nothing but their profession and are regarded as "sexless"; I didn't want to belong to this category. I wanted to be successful, but I also wanted to be feminine, I wanted the rest as well.

They say that professional women have a harder time of it than men from the start. I agree, but I do think a woman also has certain advantages over men. What I find most unpleasant are the resentment and low opinion that intellectuals often have of each other. As a Chinese university teacher, if you have no outstanding abilities and make no bad mistakes, nobody will tell you what to do. Eventually the seniority system makes you a professor. But if you are not satisfied with the routine and want to do something out of the ordinary, you become the target of attacks. That's why the Chinese have this proverb: Don't stick your neck out, just pull your tail in, and nothing can happen to you.

Once, when a Shanghai restaurant was being renovated, I had a couple of unusual ideas for it, and when it was finished, the restaurant was featured on television and in the newspapers, and many people came to see it. When interviewed, I asked journalists to omit mention of my name and to simply say the restaurant was designed by someone from our university. Still, I sensed the envy and resentment of many people who knew the design was mine. If people weren't able to find fault with my professional work, they would focus on my private life: that I was too "free," that I wore too many "foreign" clothes, that I was too arrogant. In Shanghai I was the moderator for a series of programs on famous historical buildings all over the world. Colleagues said critically, "She's eager for fame; she ought to concentrate on her field instead." But many people who wrote to me had suddenly developed an interest in architecture. To be honest, this was also a way for me to get closer to the world of film and television, in which I saw the job of my dreams.

Today I am in the process of establishing myself in a world where I constantly have to keep deciding on new directions. It often helps me to remind myself of the old Chinese proverb, "When the cart comes to the mountain, a road will always turn up."

Translated by Ilze Mueller

YANGERCHE NAMU: SINGER

Xia Jiufang

Yangerche Namu (born in 1967) is well known in China today as a member of the Central Minorities Ensemble for Dance and Song. She has made it her lifework to familiarize Chinese audiences with the songs and culture of her people, the Mosuo. Her name is as beautiful as she is herself: in her language, Yangerche Namu means "jewel goddess."

She grew up in the border area between Sichuan and Yunnan Provinces by Lake Lugu. This lake, according to a Mosuo legend, was created when a goddess dropped her mirror from heaven. The hospitable Mosuo, or Yongning Naxi, as they are also called, live on the shores of this lake. Namu is the third daughter of a family which, like most families by Lake Lugu, is matriarchal. In these families it is the daughters who continue the line of succession, and property passes from a mother to her daughters.

Namu has inherited the talent of her mother, who is a well-known singer. In her teens, Namu worked on a farm and in road construction, until at seventeen she made a decision to leave the idyllic life by Lake Lugu. With two hundred yuan that she had borrowed, she set out on foot. After she had walked for days through the lonely mountain landscape, a trucker gave her a ride to the district administrative center, another hundred kilometers (about 62 mi.) down the road. From there, not knowing a word of Chinese, she found her way clear across China to the teeming city of Shanghai. She slept on the floor of the guesthouse of the local conservatory until, in May 1984, she was able to audition for her entrance examination. The examiners were enthusiastic. Namu was accepted as a student and, thus, became the first from the land of women to go to college. It was not easy at first. She had to learn Mandarin and find a

Private collection

The singer

way to finance her studies, for her family, which subsists mainly by bartering, could send her no money. Only a few ten-yuan notes were left of the original two hundred, and she had nothing but a track suit and her traditional Mosuo costume. But she managed to find work. In the morning she would go to class, in the afternoon she would give children singing lessons, and at night she would appear in dance halls. Often she was almost dead on her feet, but she even managed to earn enough to send some money to her mother.

In 1988, Namu began her last year of studies. She now had to decide what to do after graduation. Although she did not particularly like life in the city, it was out of the question for her to return to Lake Lugu. Of course, that did not mean she no longer cared about her homeland or that she no longer thought of her relatives. If she had stayed, she would no doubt have had to work in road construction, but she had made it her goal to introduce her people and their songs to the Chinese public. Her audiences should learn about the "faraway paradise" on Lake Lugu. Indeed, people all over the world should get to know the rich culture of the minorities in China, which is all too often overlooked. That is why she decided to go to Beijing, the heart of China, the center of Chinese culture. In her fourth year of studies, she went to Beijing a total of six times to look for a steady position, five times to no avail; the sixth time, she was accepted into the Central Minorities Ensemble for Dance and Song and was given a Beijing resident's permit.

Namu's first appearance with the ensemble was a huge success. At the Spring Festival of 1989, she appeared in the light entertainment program of Central Chinese Television and, thus, became nationally famous. In the meantime, she has already recorded her third cassette. In addition to working in the ensemble, she collects folk songs, and some day she would like to organize a lecture series on the music of minorities in China.

Namu is still very young, and many of her future dreams may yet come true. Self-confidently she says, "Why shouldn't women be able to do things?"

Translated by Ilze Mueller

FRUIT GROWER

Li Jianzhen

This year there will be a bountiful apple harvest. The branches bend beneath the weight of the fruit, as though they wished to welcome us. They are the pride and joy of our whole family.

I was born in Jiuzhao, a fertile mountainous region with plenty of water. The land is particularly well suited to apples. I come from a poor peasant family with lots of children, and even as a child I would fervently hope for a good harvest, because a good harvest promised a better life. When I was seventeen, I was married to a husband who was twelve years older than I. I had five children, three sons and two daughters. I had to think twice about every penny I spent.

After the founding of the People's Republic of China, my family joined other families to form a production brigade. In 1958, when the communes were founded, we were collectivized. Men and women worked together with equal rights. While the men's work was harder, women were stuck with all the housework. My husband, for example, left the house early, and I would stay at home, since the children were still very young. Every morning at the crack of dawn, I had to make breakfast, wash the dishes, straighten the house, do the laundry, sew and mend clothes, feed the cattle, et cetera. Every year we fattened a pig that was slaughtered for the Spring Festival—it would then weigh 150 pounds (67.5 kg.). A small part of it (head, feet, and innards) was eaten during the Spring Festival; the rest was cut up and salted in a big barrel, which had to last till the next year. I kept ten hens and was able to trade the eggs for staples like soy sauce, salt, vinegar, and matches. There were no eggs left for us to eat.

When company came, it was always a big problem. One

time, the father-in-law of one of our sons came to visit. We borrowed a couple of pounds of rice from a neighbor, kept our eggs, and bought a bottle of soy sauce from the deposit money on three bottles. We have a proverb: The rich are scared of fires, the poor are scared of guests.

We were rarely able to buy clothes. In those days, the main problem of peasants was how to get enough to eat. The basic rule for clothes was: three years new, three years worn, three years mended. You ate grains and vegetables, but no meat. The housing situation was even worse. Seven of us lived in a mud hut that was 247 square feet (about 22 sq. m.). We used dry brushwood for cooking and heating. All seven of us slept on a *kang* (oven bed), a third of which was reserved for drying grain. We also had problems with water. The house was on a mountain, and every day we had to carry our water up from the valley. We would wash our clothes down by the river.

In 1982, as a result of the land reform, land was again distributed among the peasants. My family received nine trees per person. Each family now does all the work themselves, but those who produce more also have bigger profits, which not only motivates us but brings advantages for the whole country. If I remember right, the first two years after the reform were not too productive, but there was a big harvest the third year. Every family was able to harvest a lot of apples; some even had to have a horse and cart to bring in their harvest. Last year we were able to buy a television set, a bicycle, and a water pump. On top of that, we saved three thousand yuan. For the first time, my second son was at the bank counter where you deposit money, not the one where you borrow it. All my sons have bought themselves television sets, tape recorders, and sewing machines in the last years; they have even built themselves new houses. They have lamps and electricity in the house. And on our own farm we dug a well.

Because our income is larger, we are doing better all around, the family lives happily, and there are hardly any arguments among the married couples over money. The wives of my sons often say, "We women are really liberated."

Translated by Ilze Mueller

PIANIST

Chan Wei

I am a pianist with the Central Orchestra, and I am fifty years old. My husband is a violin professor at the Central College of Music. We have two daughters, both over twenty. Recently many of my friends have been saying to me with a good-natured laugh, "Little Bao, you're lucky. Your husband was promoted to full professorship, and you have become a first-class musician (which amounts to the same thing as a full professorship). Your daughters are studying in the United States. Truly enviable!"

Though such words ring like sweet bells in my ears, my hair has become prematurely gray for this family and this career. I come from a family of teachers and have loved music from the time I was young. I had piano lessons at the school where my father taught and always did extremely well. In 1952, I passed the entrance examination for the secondary school that is affiliated with the Central College of Music. In 1959, I finished my piano studies and was assigned to play with the best orchestra in the country—the Central Orchestra, in their soloists' group, in fact. I was a soloist and an accompanist, and appeared in performances for two or more solo instruments. Often we would play in factories and mines, for the army and in the villages. Sometimes we would give two or three performances a day. This was a lot, but the applause of the audience made us forget all the hard work. In China, I have played in all the provinces except for Tibet and Taiwan; I have also done concert tours in eleven countries, where I was warmly welcomed by foreign friends.

A one-hour concert performance takes from five to six hours of rehearsal. For a solo concert, you have to practice considerably longer, sometimes from one to two months. For a good concert, I need a lot of energy. There was no time for housework or for the children. Before a concert, my understanding husband would take on the burden of the household and the children. I must say that without his support I would not have been successful as a performing artist.

The household chores were done on the side. In the morning, the laundry would be soaked, and the vegetables would be washed and stored in a basket; then at noon the food would be prepared in a big hurry, and at night the laundry would be washed. We rarely had time to sit down and rest. When the children were little, we would give them music lessons at night, play music for them, or help them copy musical scores. In our three-room apartment, each of us had a corner of our own. Even the bathroom and the kitchen were used for practicing. Sometimes we would make music together, and in our free time we would listen to music as we cleaned house.

In spite of all the hard work, we also have pleasures. We are delighted that our older daughter Feifei has received three prizes at international violin competitions and graduated with distinction from the Central College of Music. Our younger daughter, Xinxin, twice received a prize in national violin competitions and was an A student during her six years at school. Both of them owe their great progress largely to my husband, their father and their teacher. He had very high expectations of the children and would not allow them to spend money foolishly. A few years ago, our joint income was just 144 yuan, and with that we also had to support my parents. My husband grew up in an orphanage. He doesn't smoke or drink. Since he was little, he has always been thrifty, and he didn't change even when he studied abroad for six years in the fifties. Today our income is higher, we're doing a lot better.

One flaw in our otherwise perfect life is that for many years now we have rarely done things for fun, such as sports or entertaining, not to mention spending money on clothes. We were too strict with the children for fear they might develop bad habits; their life was too cramped. The way we live seems rather monotonous. Now that our children are no longer at home with us, we have a fair amount of leisure, but old habits die hard. In future, we plan to take it easy, look after our health, and we hope we will have an opportunity to visit our children abroad.

Sometimes my husband and I play a sonata together at home to drive away the feeling of emptiness and loneliness since the children left.

Translated by Ilze Mueller

PENSIONER

Yang Guifen

L ife flows by like a swiftly moving river. The approval of my retirement seemed to come up suddenly. When you're back in the house again, after a long working life, you have plenty of time to think about your past.

At the age of eighteen, after I graduated from secondary school, I became a member of a group of dancers and singers in the provinces. In addition to performing in towns, we often went to the countryside to help the peasants in the literacy campaign. The Communist Party asked us to make friends with the peasants, under the motto "Three Things in Common": eating together, living together, and working together. This phase of my life, when I was constantly on the move, passed quickly. At twenty-three, through friends of mine, I met my future husband. He was a newspaper editor at the time, three years older than I, five foot nine (about 1.73 m.). He was friendly and nice. A year later we got married. After marriage, a very affectionate relationship developed between us; we had three children, two daughters and a son. This happy family gave me a wonderful life, but our happiness did not come by itself, we had to work hard for it. Our joint salary was not high; it was not enough for us to be able to afford a servant. I had to look after our first child myself, keep house, and go to work. Things were a mess. Luckily, my mother moved in and helped with the daily work. I found a job with the same paper as my husband and could come home during breaks to nurse my baby. After work, the laundry and cooking would be waiting for me. The children were born at three-year intervals.

At thirty, I could have used some time to pursue other interests, but I never even got to go to the movies. When my husband saw how busy I was, he would occasionally take the children to nursery school or even do the shopping. He did everything to make my burden bearable and to help me develop professionally.

No matter how busy we were, in our spare time we would take the children to the Imperial Palace, to Beihai Park, or to the zoo. That's how the years between my thirtieth and fortieth birthdays went by. In 1972, my mother died. I had often thought that one day, when I no longer had to work, I would take all the housework off her hands. It's too late now.

When I retired, I didn't feel very happy. Close to forty years of work were over, and I had to say goodbye to colleagues and friends with whom I had worked day in, day out. I wasn't used to living this way, and soon I felt the isolation of being at home. But the state retirees' department did all it could to plan interesting activities for us. There are four hundred retired people living in our residential district of Beijing alone. We have a multipurpose hall we can use—there's a reading room with books, periodicals, and newspapers, as well as an auditorium and a gym. Every day, many elderly people come and play table tennis, billiards, mah-jong, or chess. In the fitness room, we have exercise and massage equipment. A short while ago, I took part in a sports competition. Although I lost at table tennis, I got a small consolation prize for taking part.

As a person gets older, good health becomes more and more of a concern. We can go to the hospital for regular checkups. I took a three-month course in *qigong* (breathing exercises) with a famous teacher. Every morning and evening I repeat the exercises, which help relieve minor ailments. For example, a couple of years ago I was having problems with my knees. Going to the doctor didn't do any good. Now that I'm doing my breathing exercises, I can walk long distances again. My memory loss is gone, too—without medication. I especially enjoy disco dancing, which we do two mornings a week. As we dance to the music, all our day-to-day troubles seem to disappear. At our last New Year celebration, everybody loved the song, "When We Were Young"—memories of our past were reawakened, and we all took our reminiscences home with us.

Translated by Ilze Mueller

MY PATH TO WOMANHOOD

Li Xiaojiang

A Youthful Fantasy

Thirty years ago, I was full of fantasy and budding idealism. But my ideas had nothing to do with women. In fact, I was quite blind to the connotations of the word "womanhood." Most of my childhood and adolescence were spent within the confines of various campuses. While at school I was a boarder, and during the vacations I used to go home to my parents. My parents were often transferred from one university to another: Jiujiang, Nanchang, Shanghai, Changchun, Shenyang, Beijing, and finally to Zhengzhou—the end of their journey. By accompanying them on a migratory journey that traversed almost the entire length of China, I had the opportunity to see many beautiful places across the country and form friendships with a lot of interesting people. However, my early years were so confined to university campuses that I felt quite isolated. Thanks to the tranquil environment of campus life in China and a political climate characterized by a national *esprit de corps* emphasizing class struggle, neither I nor my four sisters experienced discrimination as girls or labored under any of the humiliations women are traditionally destined to suffer. Despite the fact that China's women were still victims of social biases (because of which my parents continued to want a male heir), we were raised in relative freedom.

In my opinion, the experiences of contemporary Chinese women are quite different from the conventional pattern. Women enjoy almost full "equity," as circumstances and social conditions allow. Contemporary Chinese women have shared equally with men in all the weal and woe that befell the country. For the duration of at least a certain historical period, conven-

241

tions and traditions receded before the onrush of the revolution. While repelling the bourgeoisie energetically, the proletariat also stamped out many manifestations of feudalism. The term "feudalism" in Chinese distinctly connotes norms governing the relationship between the sexes. "Feudalism" does not refer to anything political in nature, and "feudal" is used as an epithet for a person who holds a conservative stance on gender relationships. All contemporary Chinese women—urban and rural—engaged in physical or intellectual labor, were subject to a political environment that propelled them into a new pattern of life, a pattern labeled "the age of liberation."

Though four decades have elapsed, and much of our lifestyle has reverted to what it was like then, the life of the present-day Chinese woman has not generally deteriorated. What my father once said concerning the status of contemporary Chinese women still seems appropriate: "Thanks to the four decades of 'liberation,' the social strata in China that has undergone the greatest change in terms of status are women, actors, and actresses." Living in a social community marked by a sense of equality makes it rather difficult to identify one's own "gender status." Of course, I know my own gender, but I confess I had no idea of the quality that might distinguish one gender from the other. I was quite ignorant about what distinguishes a woman from a human being or from a man. Indeed, in my younger years, I might have even turned out to be an opponent of women's studies! In my childhood, I behaved more wildly than is normal even for a boy; I liked to climb trees, scale walls, and shoot pebbles from a catapult. I hated wearing shoes and was against having my hair combed. I was fond of sports, singing, and romping, but was reluctant to be involved in an athletic contest where I had to abide by rules or in a performance that called for make-up. I was not deliberately imitating the behavior of a young boy; rather, I was striving for the common human desire for freedom and the need to feel free of restraint. While for three decades I have trudged the long path typical of the contemporary Chinese woman, the desire for freedom and the propensity to be rid of any restraint remain with me.

Femininity and Sexuality

My awakening to my femininity was synchronous with my sexual maturation. My reaction was drastic. I had extreme contempt for femininity and longed for a way to rid myself of any trait that could be termed as feminine. In the years between my awakening and now, I have come across a great many women who had mental experiences similar to mine. These feelings have led me to try to understand the experience of today's Chinese women. The evening before my graduation from primary school, two girl students in my class, who were both a bit older than the rest, flatly said that they were not interested in going on to secondary education. They were determined to begin work in a textile factory. Their decision made me feel very sad, but they remained quite unperturbed. One of them even came to comfort me, saying, "Come, come! Don't feel sad for me. I've been bored to death by life at school. It isn't a girl's fate to become a scholar. She's bound to get married in due course and give birth to children. And as for struggling with men for a career, she's up against more than her match there!"

I remember that evening as lit by faint moonlight. Seven or eight girls in the graduating class sat on a carousel in the school playground. After the two older girls had announced their determination to forsake their pursuit of a secondary education, the rest of us turned mute. A funereal silence reigned over us. At that juncture, I wanted to shout back at the two girls, "I won't believe in fate!" but I felt gagged. I just bit my upper lip so hard that it bled. Inwardly I took an oath, "I swear that I shall surpass all my male classmates in the pursuit of a brilliant career. I am going to convince you of the falsehood of your blind trust in fate." To this day, I can feel afresh the salty taste of blood oozing from my lip.

During the course of my secondary education, most of the girls in my class began to menstruate. Girl students had a nickname for menstruation: "bad luck." When a girl student had her "bad luck," she was exempt from attending physical education and from doing manual labor. Boys jealously complained of girls' privileges. When choosing a model student, boys, more often than not, would reject girl candidates on the ground that they were too self-indulgent when it came to physical exertion. At that time, I was on the side of the boys rejecting girls, on the same ground. I thought a girl should have the guts to strive to be a boy's equal in everything and ought not to offer such a feeble excuse as "having the menses." Some of my female classmates retorted, "Since you have not met your 'bad luck' yet, you can afford to be smug."

I regard the day of my first menstruation as monstrously ominous. It was during the early stage of the Cultural Revolution. On that day, my father was hauled out to parade in the streets by Red Guards; he was in disgrace. He was dragged along, tied with a rope; a placard with humiliating and abusive words hung from his neck and dangled on his chest, and an ugly fool's cap was crushed on his head. I walked stealthily in the midst of a throng on the sidewalk, as I had on several previous occasions, following my father from a distance as he completed his mortifying march. Abruptly he came to a standstill for no apparent reason and was instantly shouted at and shoved along by some of the Red Guards following him. One of them poured a big bottle of ink over his head. My heart shrank at such a grim sight and, driven by impulse, I was on the point of rushing to his rescue when I felt a drastic twinge in the lower part of my abdomen. A flow of hot liquid trickled down the inner sides of my thigh. Suddenly, it dawned on me what the flow meant, and tears began to run down my cheeks. It was an instant of bewilderment: The ink that was poured on my father's head, my menstrual discharge, and my tears churning like a whirlpool. I seemed to be engulfed. I felt a deep sense of humiliation in my status as a woman and as a daughter. In those days, I was disgusted with myself for being female.

Rejecting Womanhood

As I matured physically, I developed a craving to become more and more like a boy. I tried to read all the biographies of great men I could find and strove to strengthen my willpower. I deliberately sought to torment myself in the same way as Laharmeitov (a character in the novel *What To Do?* by Russian writer Chernishievski). When a roaring gust of wind rose, I would stay for hours on end where it blew the strongest. I would expose myself to the sun during the hottest days of summer. I would swim in the river during the coldest spell in winter. Years later, when I was assigned to settle down in a rural area, I continued to torment myself so as to harden my willpower. Though I had never before worked in the field, when I was sent to live in the countryside, I insisted that the executive chief of the village production brigade give me the most strenuous farm work, assigned as a rule only to men. Consequently, I volunteered to handle almost all the heaviest and most tiring farm chores in the village: Carrying on my shoulders a pole with two big bales of reaped paddy hanging from it, climbing to the top of an immense stack of paddy in the sheaf in order to make the stack conical, handling a primitive instrument (called *jiang* in Chinese) for sowing wheat seeds, and other terrible, physically exacting farm chores that have been left untouched by the average village woman for millennia. In the freezing days of winter, I carried water in pails suspended from a pole on my shoulders, going uphill, with a total load of more than seventy-five kilos (about 165 lb.). Only God knows how many times I fell on the slippery ground with my waterload and only God knows how many times I rolled, with my pails full of water, down hillsides crusted with snow and ice. I was often totally soaked with spilt water, with shoulders first bruised and then broken by my poles. Even then I almost never shed tears.

I was challenging my own fate and my "gender status." I chanced upon Irving Stone's *A Sailor on Horseback*. I read it and then forced myself to follow the example of Jack London. I applied myself assiduously to reading books in order to increase my own stock of knowledge. My self-imposed discipline continued beyond the days I lived in the countryside and had to work in the field from dawn to dusk, to those when I was assigned as a factory worker and had to work in the daytime and take part in sports matches in the evening. As an amateur sportswoman, I persevered for more than a dozen years in this strenuous self-education. In those years, I slept for only five or six hours each night. During the dozen or so years of self-education so arduous many men found it unbearable, I never flinched, and I finally emerged victorious. Together with other resolutely enterprising people of my generation, I struggled to shake off the yoke of our hostile fate and succeeded in tiding myself over a decade in which our nation was on the verge of total collapse.

University Years

In 1979 I enrolled at Henan University. At that time, I had had only eight years of schooling. In Chinese society, it is permissible for a woman to strive as strenuously as a man to carve out a career for herself. So long as she works hard to build her career, there is every likelihood that her achievement will match a man's. After the decade of turmoil had ended, life in China gradually returned to normal and became stable and peaceful. Both in the days when I was pursuing my postgraduate studies and when I became a teacher, I never experienced any major discrimination because of my gender. After my postgraduate career, I was designated an instructor and taught on the campus of a university. Before long I was promoted—before my originally scheduled time—to the rank of associate professor by a special order from the university authorities. I had surpassed my male colleagues in the competition. At this time, I devoted all my zeal and time to studies on women which, as a branch of knowledge, was completely neglected by academic circles in China. I plunged into it quite alone and have been pushing ahead energetically in this field of study ever since.

After I got married, I soon discovered that I was hindered in every direction when I sought to think and act in keeping with the willpower, independence, values, and conduct of my unmarried days. My husband and my son, household chores, and my family's social connections could all turn out to be one sort of obstruction or another if I persisted in following my earlier path. They tended to take up almost all my time and energy, and foiled my attempts to pursue my plans independently and without restraint. On the other hand, it would have been like a death sentence had I been forced to part with my husband and family. Thus, I acted the way a traditional woman would have acted in the matter of indulgently giving and receiving love: I have been extremely indulgent in selfishly drinking in conjugal love and selflessly bestowing maternal love. I believe it is my own fate that has preordained me to behave like this. And my own fate is typical of the lot of many Asian women. As long as I was unwilling to part with my husband and family, I had to assume all the consequences that stemmed from this unwillingness. And no sooner had I volunteered to assume all the consequences than I realized I had been lured into another trap. I was forced to play two roles at the same time, to carry a load that was twice as heavy as that usually carried by a man.

All modern women are doomed to fall into such a trap. Most are now wallowing in it silently and in a docile manner. It is not that someone has necessarily endeavoured to entice women into such a situation. The existence of this trap, and of the trapped, seems to be quite a "natural" occurrence. But they are actually not all that "natural." In the long run, I came to realize that the dual role women are obliged to play in everyday life entails dual philosophies of life. Such a duality splits a woman as a social entity and deprives her of the capacity to present herself as the perfect "ego" in both family and social life. However, the question that baffles me is why women alone are made to suffer in this manner?

I believe that nobody will come forth with a ready answer to this question. For in modern society only men are entitled to come forth with answers to social problems, but men know precious little about women, especially contemporary women. And women, instead of finding an answer to this question, either evade it or curse their own lot aimlessly and wantonly. Perhaps we are haunted by the fear that men will look down upon us if we confess to the truth of this question. But then, I feel that women too are ignorant, devoid of answers. I have arrived at this conclusion only after reading for many sleepless nights. My conclusion troubles me, but in ways that have roused me to become enterprising and single-minded in the pursuit of women's studies. Women are a complete enigma to me. The role they have played in history and society, and the cultural development of humanity, is an enigma, one that has oppressed us, fooled us, degraded our status, and made our lot more unbearable.

I hope to discover why women have been so tormented and full of disgrace. In an age that boasts equality between the sexes, why do women lead a painfully laborious and depressing life? My own experience has already shown me that differences do exist between the sexes; still, I want to understand the real causes of the view that men are irreversibly superior to women. As a woman who has had to go through much, I believe all women ought to be brave and enterprising. Despite the fact that women's inherent status and value have been completely obliterated by historians, I harbor the hope that my academic studies may contribute to the rediscovery of that status and value. And only by making such an appraisal can I become fully independent, confident, and competent as a woman scholar, and exert myself to dive into a study of humanity.

A Hard Path to Womanhood

When I first aspired to study womanhood in my own capacity as a woman, I expected that other women and the academic community would lend a hand. I never anticipated that these very groups would deliberately block and hinder my pursuit. The only legitimate women's organization in China is the All-China Women's Federation. I expected the federation to help me answer some of my questions by supplying me with relevant data to facilitate my study. Therefore, I wrote to ask them for materials I needed urgently. I also wrote to some acclaimed women leaders for their support in developing women's studies. I have not received a single response to these appeals and by the time my first paper on women was published, women leaders were so upset that my work was drowned under a sea of disapproving voices.

Academic polemics in present-day China are generally tied to a particular political orientation. Some authorities or officials seem to want to use their power to reshape truth. Owing to the fact that the All-China Women's Federation was largely a political facade and scorned by people from all walks of life, my pursuit of women's studies was likely to have only a slim chance of survival. Then, as luck would have it, the leadership of the federation changed and brought in fresh new elements. Women intellectuals in the prime of their lives were promoted to leading positions as editors and reporters. And they were determined to be of use to other women. These women have now become my true friends and help in publicizing my efforts by providing financial and moral support.

Another hindrance to my efforts in women's studies came from the academy, which chose to remain silent. This silence was a contemptuous defiance of women and women's studies. Scholars, in their twenties, thirties, and forties, especially those who had taken the lead in developing reforms in their disciplines, responded to women's issues as "little whines" uttered by the weak who were still mentally enslaved by feudal tradition. This was because they were obsessed with complications existing in the macrocosm, major fields of knowledge, the world community, and man. I have been tempted to feel sorry for contemporary man. It is widely known that in the 1919 May Fourth Movement almost all advanced male thinkers addressed themselves to the liberation of women: Lu Xun, Shen Yanbing, Chen Duxiu, and Li Dazhao, to mention but a few, were exemplary in that regard. But the leading reformers of our day have chosen to shun the study of women. There was no university or college that would take the lead in offering academic degrees or faculty positions in women's studies. It was not until 1986 that any periodical or institution dedicated to women's studies came into existence in mainland China.

The pretext used to camouflage this lack of attention was simple: So long as women are a part of humanity, any study related to them ought to be placed within the category of human studies. It was deemed redundant, therefore, to establish an independent branch of knowledge or a specialty. I recall a symposium on literature, when a rather celebrated professor taunted me, saying: "Literature bears no gender, you know. It would sound absurd for it to split into two departments, one for men and the other for women. Literature is not a latrine that can be dedicated to one sex only." Implicit in his words was his opinion that I intended to rouse our academic circles to a futile endeavor. There was also another pretext : Since women have special problems, women's studies ought to be favored with exclusive treatment. It should be placed in a special niche in the edifice of sciences and receive exclusive treatment. At a scholar's salon in Beijing, after I had finished a lecture on women's studies, a fairly renowned philosopher immediately protested: "I've hardly ever heard of this so-called women's studies. As far as I know, in Chinese history there has scarcely been any woman philosopher. And a great many philosophers in our history remained single all their lives. It seems that no woman in Chinese history has ever played a significant role in the field of philosophy." His protest suggested that developing women's studies was like building castles in the air.

Today obstacles such as these have largely disappeared. Although some influential elements in the leadership of the All-China Women's Federation still have a grudge against me, and I face contempt from major portions of the academy, the development of women's studies in China is no longer held in check. The people who have devoted themselves to the study of China's women have formed an organized contingent and built their own stronghold. In some disciplines, women's studies components are already included in collegiate curricula. They are warmly welcomed by the majority of our women intellectuals and highly appreciated by farsighted male scholars. No matter what the political situation in China may become, a number of persevering researchers have now vowed lifelong devotion to the cause of women's studies. They are working extremely hard to trace the history and current condition of China's women.

A Lifelong Commitment

In my postgraduate years, I majored in Western European literature. It was a "great leap forward" from the status of a high-school student assigned to live permanently in the countryside, or of an amateur basketball player and fitter in a factory. Many reporters have asked me to write about my life. They want a story about a self-taught woman. I have shunned them all as if I were fleeing a disaster. I hate the intrusion upon my privacy (as I also avoid involving myself in other people's private affairs). Besides, I do not want the mass media to present me as the stereotype of a self-taught woman. My work and studies are motivated by a conscientious craving to realize my own worth. In my opinion, when one decides on matters related to one's career or private life, one is motivated either by a penchant to explore or the need to survive. The latter, however, could become a constraint in that it hinders a personal zeal to keep on exploring.

For me, women's studies is neither the starting point nor the termination of my career. Our generation has now been pushed forward to the threshold of a new century and is confronted with innumerable *terrae incognitae*. I aspire to penetrate more and more of these unknown worlds and earnestly hope that I can set about my research right away so that I can soon solve many enigmas that are now puzzling me, my fellow countrymen, and contemporary humanity. But it is also very difficult for me to give up my deep commitment to women's studies. I have found that I need to give up all my previous hobbies, interests, and theoretical explorations in order to concentrate on women's studies. At times, it seems as if I am being dragged along by an invisible rope and cannot tear myself away from this field of study.

For me, developing women's studies is the fulfillment of a kind of duty. Such a duty may be regarded as an absurd obligation by Westerners. There is a Chinese saying, "Beginning is the most arduous part of any undertaking." Therefore, whoever is charged with the duty of making a beginning ought to make it successful. And one ought not give up the undertaking of which one has made a beginning. Over a period of time, I have come to realize more and more deeply that I have become one of the pioneers of women's studies in China. And I must function dutifully as one of the cornerstones of the edifice of women's studies. I am obliged to do so. My paper "Progress of Mankind and Liberation of Womanhood" was published in 1983. It was the first treatise on women published in China since 1949 and immediately caused a commotion. Some people howled vehemently for its suppression and labeled it as "anti-Marxist gospel." It is because of this treatise that scholars who later became the core of the "women's studies contingent" rallied to form a front. In 1984, my paper "China's Womanhood's Road to Liberation and Its Characteristics" was published. I put forward the argument that all the progress that has been made so far by the women's liberation movement in China has been an outcome of legislation too advanced for the political awareness of the populace. Moreover, I argued that the liberation of Chinese women has so far been an outcome of a social revolution, rather than of a feminist movement. These and other arguments I have made constitute the watershed between the "new" and the "old" school of research on women's studies. My arguments drew much crossfire from conservatives in the women's movement in China and were regarded as heresies. Yet they also attracted honest and kind friends and a group of women intellectuals who involved themselves with me at this time. The year 1985 saw the initial success of our tentative efforts to form some sort of organization and offer women's studies as an independent course for college students. In the spring of that year the Society of Women's Studies was founded. The Henan Provincial Futuristic Research Society sponsored the foundation ceremony. It is the first women's research institution in China and is not financed by government. In August 1985, the society organized China's first women's symposium in Zhengzhou. Higher educational institutions and research units in eight provinces in mainland China sent their representatives to the symposium. The representatives were, for the most part, young women scholars, the majority of whom had master's degrees. They came from more than a dozen disciplines.

In May and June of 1985, under the auspices of Wang Lihuan, president of Henan Provincial Institute for Women Cadres, a household management course was started. The course is the first of its kind in China; the participants were introduced to the topic of "Recognizing Our Womanhood" during the course. At first, the course was regarded as an eyesore by some conservatives, but it has since won support and trust from the vast majority of women in Henan Province. Liang Jun, an undergraduate student majoring in world history at Beijing Normal University, volunteered to abandon her original major and take up women's studies as her life career after attending the course. From then on, she has run courses, given many lectures on radio and television, and traveled through dozens of cities and provinces to deliver around a thousand talks on the subject of women's liberation. She has been doing her utmost to alert our women to their predicament and has won their hearts as well.

In September 1985, I began to offer a course on women's literature to the students of the Department of Chinese Literature and Language of Zhengzhou University. This was also the first of its kind offered at a university in mainland China and was a success because of the support of the Academic Affairs Committee of my department and the students who took the course. In a 1986 essay in the magazine *Women of China,* I proposed the establishment of a women's studies curriculum for the college or university. A proposal of this kind had never been put forward in mainland China before. Since then, disapprovals have been voiced. Some people have defiantly argued against establishing women's studies as an independent field of knowledge, while others have advanced their own views and proposals. It is quite natural that people's approaches to a new field will vary considerably, and that is not a bad thing. In my opinion, my proposal has induced other people to take women's concerns seriously. From the polemics surrounding the establishing of women's studies as an independent branch of knowledge I was able to gather information regarding categories and topics that I will include in *Serial Books on Women's Studies,* a multivolume publication I have been editing.

In 1987 I applied to the leadership of Zhengzhou University for the establishment of a university center for women's studies, and my application was soon approved. The creation of this center was a significant event. It was the first research unit dedicated to the study of women established on a campus. In the last two years, the Center for Women's Studies of Zhengzhou University succeeded in rallying women's studies researchers at dozens of higher educational or research institutions in different parts of China to coordinate efforts. Now the center has become the general base for women's studies in China. Its work arouses keen interest among those who work to focus on women exclusively and touches on topics related to more than a dozen branches of the humanities. It provides comprehensive comparisons between women and men. The materials supply more than enough background information and knowledge to substantiate a full curriculum for a major in women's studies at a college. With money from the Fund for China's Reform and Opening to the Outside World, we are planning to publish a periodical, *Women Intellectuals.* Women intellectuals are among the most advanced in Chinese society and ought, with perfect self-assurance and courage, to call upon the whole of the country's women to rally together. Such intellectuals can now act as the core force in the movement for women's liberation.

This is but a rough description of the journey my comrades

and I have taken in promoting the growth of women's studies in mainland China. We still remain pioneers in this field, and we are still at the initial stage of our pilgrimage. One consolation is that we have, after all, made women's studies sprout from the barren soil of China's land.

What will women's studies be like in the future? Our projects will develop on the basis of the successes of previous projects. It is probable that our future journey will be easier than our past. Perhaps unjustifiable pressures will be less often applied, and opprobrium will no longer be so profusely heaped on us. Nevertheless, I do not think I can be too optimistic. For a long while yet, women's studies will continue to be in its academic infancy and the development of its theoretical foundations will be shaky.

Although we may expect more and more scholars, especially women, to work in the field of women's studies, our society can hardly be expected to respond very enthusiastically to our call for vigorous development of the women's cause. This lack of response can be accounted for by two factors: the political climate and financial difficulties. So long as China is beset with enormous political and economic problems, its women and women's studies will find it difficult to develop and expand. Still, we can hope that the progress we have already made will not be wiped out. Whether circumstances are favorable or unfavorable, I know there will always be women who will stand by me, shoulder to shoulder, through thick and thin, and that is enough! On our pilgrimage to the shrine of freedom, they cannot dispense with me, or my work. With such mutual understanding, nothing in the world can constitute a permanent hindrance to women's progress.

A SERIOUS MISSION

Liang Jun

Self-Consciousness

I started my "real" life at the age of forty. Since then, whatever I have done is clear in my mind and unforgettable. But my life before forty is another story. I was born into a family of intellectuals; my father is an engineer and my mother a doctor. I am the only girl among six children. Like their peers, my parents are traditional although they have accepted some new ideas. As a result, in my education, new demands often competed with old concepts: My parents required me to do as well as my brothers; at the same time, they restricted my behavior to conform to the traditional virtues of the Asian woman. Consequently, I was taught to be tenderhearted and obedient as well as eager to do well and to be successful.

While I was growing up, people with a family background such as mine were discriminated against. In most cases, those who face such discrimination look on the world with cold resentment, and even hopelessness. Or they go along with the social norms and strive to mold themselves in a way that will make them acceptable. Being obedient but unwilling to be "backward" and out of step with the times, I naturally chose the latter method of adjustment—one that was easy to choose, but extremely hard to conform to. As a young woman born into an intellectual bourgeois family, I felt I needed to relate to workers and peasants. As a woman who was growing up during the era of "equality of men and women," I needed to fit into the standards created for men. While I regarded these as my lofty goal, I was apprehensive; I did not know what would happen to me. At that time, I only knew that I should seek, strive, and exert the utmost strength.

When I took part in voluntary labor, in spite of my menstruation, I stood with boy students in water above my knees, scooping up sludge from the river or transplanting rice seedlings. When the "four clean-up" movement was carried out in the countryside, I fetched water during the drought and carried manure to spread in the field with male peasants during the day; at night, alone, I crossed the mountain passes haunted by wolves to "call on and learn about the poor and lower middle peasants."

When I graduated from school, I was disdainful of male students who asked for an ideal assignment; I transferred without hesitation to Tibet, which is known as a place where "no grass grows on the mountains but stones move when the wind blows." There, I lived in a tent with holes on all sides, used my hands to eat half-cooked mutton with the herdsmen, and rode horses to keep sheep and cattle within bounds. I fell off my horse once and suffered a moderate cerebral concussion, but I did not stop my work. I also climbed a mountain five thousand meters (about 15,000 ft.) high, talking cheerfully and humorously despite a terrible headache; this gained me increasing respect from my male companions. At the time, I did everything with great enthusiasm, and did not feel tired. Illnesses did not deter me, and I did not regret my choice. I only thought that the dream that "women would live like men" had come to pass at last in my generation.

However, I am after all a woman with traditional roots. I planned to marry and bear children. I fantasized about having a warm, sweet family. So, like most Chinese women, I got married; I had a baby boy the following year. I became busier and experienced great happiness. Nonetheless, I soon started feeling overburdened with work at home and outside. "I will not give birth any more," I said to my husband, and I sent my son to kindergarten when he was three years old. But not long after that, I whispered to my husband, "Should we have one more child?" I soon had another baby boy.

It seemed natural, but I was no longer the person I had been earlier. From the "modern heroine," I had turned into both a professional person and a housewife, whose life was confined to working at the office and doing housework at home. All day long, I was in a desperate hurry and always felt exhausted. Gradually, my brave pledge to compete with men was abandoned as an illusion. I came to believe that a marital relationship could not remain balanced. Like a seesaw, one end rises and the other end falls. "So long as you are successful in your achievements, I am willing to do everything for you," I told my husband. If I delayed doing housework because of official business, I would feel ashamed and guilty, as though I had done something scandalous. My husband was sincere, straightforward, and kindhearted.

But in my innermost self, I wished to develop myself. It was hard for me to live this way, tied down to my double burden. Sometimes, when my husband did more housework, I blamed myself for lacking in enthusiasm. At other times, when I had to do more housework, I complained that my husband and children hindered me in my professional work. Because of my own emotional instability, there was often a grim atmosphere at home, and a "cold war" started between my husband and me. I shouldered the heavy load of work and life, unable to bear it and yet unwilling to abandon it. Day and night, I was worried, depressed, and resentful. My enterprising spirit was subdued and I felt prematurely old. I began to look for a less demanding profession, so that I could have more time to help my husband at home. Around this time, I was transferred from Henan Financial and Economic College to Henan Women's Cadre School.

I never expected that the new job would become a new beginning for me. Li Xiaojiang, an extraordinary woman, led me into another life. At the end of the spring of 1985, Li, an associate professor of Chinese language and literature at Zhengzhou University, organized the first household management course in cooperation with the Henan Women's Cadre School. Since I was new at the school, I knew nothing about Professor Li or the class. It was only out of curiosity and a thirst for knowledge that I went to Li's lecture.

What a vivid lesson on "Self-Consciousness of Women"! Professor Li stood on the platform, graceful and confident, without being overbearing. What were riddles for contemporary Chinese women were explained and clarified by her flowing words: the differences in physiology and psychology and in the historical process of evolution between men and women; the current inequality of men and women; the damaging interruption of women's lives (because of women's reproductive activity); the historical inevitability of tension arising out of the dual roles of women; the unbending pursuit of spiritual life among women; and so on. She pointed out boldly that equality between men and women is not the final yardstick of women's emancipation. All the problems of women cannot be solved by the founding of the socialist system. However, the formal recognition of equality (albeit based on men's norms in the 1950s) provided a starting point for Chinese women to assert their identity. Women live a hard and burdened life. Nevertheless, since we were born women, she said, we should squarely face our existence and value and accept the challenge.

The audience was overwhelmed by her sharp words, penetrating analysis, and original point of view. I still remember someone shouting in class "You are right!" One of the women, who was over fifty years old, said, weeping: "Teacher Li, why didn't you tell us all this earlier?" At that time, I did not express my feelings, because I suffered from a sense of inferiority. But I was greatly affected; it was as if I had seen a lighthouse on a dark sea. The depression sitting heavily in my heart for so long dissolved at once. I was eager to start my new life. I thought I should tell all women who were depressed like me what I had heard from Professor Li. I soon became acquainted with Professor Li and, as we saw more of each other, we became good friends. All the same, I look up to her as my teacher and spiritual guide, even though she is six years younger than I am. Reading Professor Li's works and talking to her are exciting experiences. She has opened out a new world for me—a new sphere of learning and a new realm of thought.

Certainly, I underwent an arduous process before I became aware of myself and of my womanhood. It is a common failing of the Chinese woman, and a remnant of history, to rely on her husband and child at home, or to depend excessively on the social environment for self-realization. In the practice of women's studies and education, I learned that women's emancipation is dependent upon women themselves. I did not dream or wait for a miracle any longer, but sought a path forward. I would not change my faith, no matter what the political climate was or how policies changed.

I give the impression of being a strong woman to those who meet me for the first time. In fact, I am quite traditional. I am turned off by the cold and negative portrayal of "strong women" in the newspapers. I am unwilling to sacrifice sweet domestic happiness for my cause, so I try to be a woman devoted to both work and family life. I believe active understanding is better than passive acceptance. The dual roles of women are essentially beneficial to the progress of women, given the social and material constraints of China. Further, the tension of the dual roles is an inevitable reality at this stage of history. Since we cannot get rid of the load, we may as well accept it of our own accord. Our generation of women has to pay the price for the emancipation of women in the future.

I soon rearranged my household work on the principle that both my husband and I should bear the responsibilities of the family. Our children also did what they could, which in turn increased their sense of responsibility and independence. I am grateful that my husband and sons are doing well. Now, in our family, when anyone has an urgent task, the others will do the housework voluntarily, without complaint.

One day, both my husband and elder son were away from home. My younger son was with me. I was so busy writing the draft of a lecture for that night that I had no time to cook. Quietly, my younger son prepared rice and fried eggs. When I left, he saw me off at the door, waving his little hand, "Good luck, Mommy." As I heard those words, my eyes filled with tears. That night, my lecture went especially well.

In March 1990, a conference on "Social Participation and Development of Chinese Women," organized by Li Xiaojiang, was held in Zhengzhou. As I was in charge of over 150 representatives, I was too busy to take care of the family. My husband was also preoccupied with his work. In his spare time, he came to help me, sometimes staying until midnight. At the meeting, my husband's attitude was much admired by the ladies from Taiwan and Hong Kong. I complain no more; men are not unchangeable. It is possible to change them just as we change ourselves from passivity to strength.

In recent years I have become more active, and more work is given to me. But I do not feel overloaded. On the contrary, I am happier. Old friends who now meet me say they can hardly recognize me. Through the process of learning about feminism, I have recreated myself. I counted my fortieth birthday as a new start to my life. That year, I devoted myself to the cause of women's education.

Awakening Sisters

My awareness of feminism is accompanied by my growing understanding of women's issues in China. In 1985, when reform of the urban economic structure was launched in the country, various women's issues came to the surface and intensified with the developing reforms. Women, convinced that they would gradually achieve the same position as men in Chinese society, now heard worried reports from all sides. Some 84 percent of the women in Daquzhuang Village of Jinghai County in Tianjin broke away from social production and returned home to be housewives; many women workers were retrenched and awaited relocation in various enterprises; several women cadres lost pitifully in elections at all levels of government organizations; women students, who were once regarded as the lucky ones, were rejected by employers; and the number of women intellectuals promoted to higher ranks decreased in scientific research institutions and universities. Why did this happen? The state becomes more progressive while women appear to be under increasing pressure! Why?

Puzzled and worried, women turned for support to their own organization, the Women's Federation. But the federation, too, was puzzled by the new policies. For some time, Chinese women questioned what was happening and wanted reasonable answers to their questions.

Just then, Li Xiaojiang held up the banner of Chinese women's studies. She gathered a contingent of scholars and organized academic discussions. She was the chief editor of the Women Studies Series, which was the first publication of its kind in China. Her other publications included *Exploration of Eve*, *Women's Way*, and scores of essays, which evoked nationwide response, especially from women. Nevertheless, the oppressed status of Chinese women is such that her theories must be popularized before they can be absorbed by the mass of women. This was a task I felt confident to take on. I decided to give up my specialization in world history and devote myself to women's education, to rouse educated women to realize themselves.

When I began my work, I found myself treading new ground. Chinese women enjoy the same rights to education as men; they enter schools or universities at the same time and receive the same education. Before the 1960s, there were several girls' and women's schools. During the Cultural Revolution, women's schools were combined with those for boys to ensure a balanced social environment and equal educational opportunities for both sexes. But there were no special organizations for women's education, nor were there schools offering a course on women's education. After the Cultural Revolution, however, some women's schools were restored or rebuilt. In these schools, all the students come from the Women's Federation.

The Communist Party's principal tasks and policies are taught there, but education for ordinary women is ignored. Under such circumstances, I had to break the traditional patterns of education to contact directly millions of women from diverse backgrounds. As for women's education, it is extremely difficult for a few educators to accomplish such a task because of variations that existed in educational levels. Fortunately, various women's organizations helped me out.

The Women's Federation gave me much help. It is the only organization of women with establishments at all levels across the country. Before the reform, the federation worked mainly for rural women and the urban unemployed. Under the pressure of reform, there was a growth in awareness. Breaking the structure of closed organizations, the federation strengthened ties with a variety of women and helped me to reach vast audiences. The women's sections of labor organizations present in most institutions also helped me a great deal. In the past, women's sections only existed in the labor unions of enterprises that employed mostly women workers. With the increased attention to women's issues during the economic reform, it became routine to establish women's sections in all unions. Without the help of these sections, I could not have met a range of women to carry out the cause of women's education.

The student union also played an important role. In China, students are basically separated from society as they form a community of their own. Women students are generally indifferent to other women. This psychological distance reduces their adaptability after graduation. Through the women's section of student unions, I was able to give numerous lectures, with good results. Moreover, many working women's groups, such as the Women Technical Workers' Association, Women Cadres' Association, Women Teachers' Association, and Women Medical Workers' Association, have been organized during the reform. These associations provided me with a platform from which to address women from a variety of professions.

Since 1985, with the help of various groups, I have gone to government organizations, hospitals, oil fields, railway departments, factories, and villages in the provinces of Henan, Jiangxi, Guangdong, Guangxi, and Inner Mongolia as well as in Tianjin, to report on different subjects that I have been researching, such as women's self-realization, the dual roles of professional women, the consciousness of female students, and "When You Grow into a Young Girl." It is astonishing how unclear the notion of womanhood is for most women, worn out as they are by the pressures of their daily lives.

Sitting face to face with them, I felt a strong sense of responsibility and mission. I knew that I wanted to help them resolve the complexities of their lives. One of the women cadres said, "Having listened to your lectures, we became conscious that we had not known ourselves as women, though we had done women's work for some decades!" Others said, "We have been accustomed to our present condition and have not made the effort to change anything anymore. What you said will inspire us to strive for a better life. We will have a foothold in society as women." Many rural women attested to the statement: "We are thought to be lighthearted and happy so long as we are rich. That is not so. We hope more people like you will be concerned with our cultural and social existence." Women students said, "We are lucky to have listened to your lectures before graduation." An interpreter said, "Having listened to your lecture, I am proud to be a woman."

Each of my lectures received warm applause, which reflected the urgent demand of women for education and the raising of awareness. Once, I visited an ethnic minority group near Hechi City in the Guangxi autonomous region. I was "kidnapped" by the cordial mayoress and made to lecture there for an entire day. Looking at the faces in the audience, I felt excited and stimulated. Now my mission in education over the past twenty years has extended into a new and vast field. How enormous is our country! Traveling up and down this land, day and night, is an important part of my life. I have frequently lectured in one place and left for another at night to lecture again the next day. On the way to a meeting, I was once delayed on the Yellow River Bridge at night. Although I was shivering with cold, it did not affect my enthusiasm for work. My strong adaptability resulted from frequent encounters with the unknown: I became used to any vehicles and to all kinds of hotels. No matter how tired I was, I would be full of life and enthusiasm whenever I walked onto the stage.

It is impossible for a few educators to achieve the expected results only by giving lectures. The mass media are an ideal educational tool. Consequently, I offered on television and over the radio a series of lectures entitled "The Road for Today's Women," "The New Woman of the Eighties," and "Women, Goals, and Family." These were well received. Many intellectual women wrote me to say they hoped to join the contingent and make their contributions toward enhancing the quality of life of Chinese women. Wang Haiyan, a college teacher suffering from cancer, wrote: "So long as I live, I will try my best for women's education. As a woman, I am fortunate to be able to do something for women." How great is the awakening of Chinese women!

Looking back, we have made spectacular progress in the pursuit of women's education, but thinking ahead, we are beset with difficulties. Women's education has not really established itself to the desired extent. All levels of women's schools need to be strengthened and reformed. Women's education has not been "aligned" with the national educational policy-making body. Without establishing a system with an ongoing policy, the pace of women's education might slow down soon after its initial momentum. It is necessary for women to work and strive for themselves. It is a great pity that with intermittent political struggles, the development of women's education suffers occasional setbacks. I realize that I shoulder a heavy and serious mission, and I shall face countless difficulties. In spite of this, I am willing to persevere in the hope that these small sparks will start a prairie fire one day.

4
LANDSCAPES AND CITYSCAPES

Wang Xiaohui

Suzhou

ON THE BEAUTY OF BEIJING

Renée Mark

B y the year 2000 Beijing will be the most beautiful city in the world," announced the *Beijing Daily News* in the early eighties. And the Chinese capital actually *has* undergone a radical change, especially during the planning of the 1990 Asian Games and while China was competing to be chosen as the site of the Olympic Games in the year 2000. During the early eighties, a drive from the airport to downtown Beijing used to take visitors down a bumpy road, past peasant carts pulled by donkeys and a never-ending line of bicycles, many of them elaborately loaded. Today, in the nineties, a visit to the city begins with a drive along a four-lane highway amid a stream of big-city traffic—VW Santanas and Toyotas. In the city, it takes more and more imagination every time you visit to visualize the ancient capital of the Chinese empire among stretches of high-rise buildings that have mushroomed seemingly overnight and expressways and by-passes interrupted only by cloverleaf intersections. At one time, the city landscape used to gleam with the yellow, blue, and green glazed tiles and ridge turrets of temples and palaces. Today the last of these ancient points of reference, in a city planned according to strict geomantic principles, can only been seen at a distance from the top floor of an office building, not looming above you, but hidden from view down below.

Upon arriving in our Beijing hostel, we foreign students hastened to add a few homey touches, like bast mats and colorful swaths of fabric, to the hostel's gray stone floors and once whitewashed walls, which had become gray and full of holes over time. Our Chinese fellow students had no understanding for this typically Western impulse. Not only that, but they would also point out to us with a pitying smile how foolish it

Nelly Rau-Häring

was to buy china dishes and chopsticks when you could use a spoon and bowl made out of the much more practical unbreakable light-green enameled aluminum in the cafeteria, as they all did. It is not *how* you eat but *what* you eat that counts: witness the many privately managed restaurants that are springing up everywhere. To be sure, the exquisite dishes, so expensive that only someone with an expense account can pay for them, are elaborately served, but even elegant restaurants use only plastic tableware. The country that once invented porcelain now produces tableware made largely out of synthetic materials. Even traditional rice-grain pattern bowls now come in plastic.

When searching for beauty in Beijing amid increasingly negative manifestations of big-city living, it is often a good idea to go longer distances by bike. Thus, by Rear Lake (Houhai) or along the moats around the Forbidden City, you may still find a vanishing phenomenon: the idyllic sight of songbird and goldfish breeders. In the lanes of the Dashalan shopping district, look for the weathered facade of the former imperial shoe and candy shop. And in the once lively flower district along the Street of the Celestial Bridge, you may discover a bright red ribbon in the hair of a little girl sitting in one of those roomy old wooden baby carriages.

Even ten years ago, it was clear that the young women of Beijing did not think in practical terms alone. You had only to look at the waitresses who worked in the hotels for foreigners. Standing in front of the tarnished mirror in the ladies' room of the Beijing Hotel, or before the mirror walls of the coffee shops in the joint-venture hotels (whose gleaming surfaces seemed at the time like something out of another world), they would giggle girlishly and fuss with their uniform and their perm—paid for by the hotel, sometimes forgetting the guest who was waiting for his salad and cheese. Until the late eighties, Beijing was a city where even in multistory department stores along Wangfujing, the main shopping street, you could not try on slacks, blouses, and jackets, but had to buy them over the counter wrapped in brown paper and tied with string. To this day the only personal hygiene available to many people here is a weekly coupon that admits you to the poorly lit public shower house. The large mirrors, then, are one of the rare chances a woman gets, after the pushing and shoving on the bus or in the cafeteria line at work, to see herself as a person with an identity of her own, from head to foot.

The chic women of Shanghai put down the women of the capital, calling them *tubaozi* (sacks of dirt). But even during the period of the "spiritual civilization of socialism," when according to government propaganda "beauty of the heart" was all that mattered, Beijing women attached a great deal of importance to their physical appearance. This was borne out by the loud vituperations of fashion-conscious women at the free markets; after ordering clothes they themselves had designed from one of the open-air tailors, they would make him rip out the seams of items they felt did not make the grade, not once but repeatedly. Nowadays, when even officially happiness is equated with being rich, a woman who can afford it no longer goes to a tailor, but allows herself to be seduced into buying expensive brand-name off-the-rack clothes in one of the glittering shopping centers, where she can now try on the slinky suits and frilly silk blouses.

The longing for beauty is now frankly acknowledged. At night, strolling through the streets, after the stores have closed and even noodle stalls have shut, you will still see signs of life in the beauty shops, at least in outlying districts. Women, especially the younger ones, spend up to three-quarters of their monthly income for a good haircut, and preferably a perm, in

Kosima Liu-Weber

Fashion show in Beijing

these ramshackle huts by the roadside, lit by a bare bulb dangling from the ceiling and filled with the sound of the latest hit music.

For those who have more money and who, equipped with a city pager and mobile phone, have seized their opportunity at an auspicious moment in the socialist market economy, the magic word in matters pertaining to beauty is the Palace Hotel. Here since 1991, Watson's Drugstore—modeled on a similar store in Hong Kong—has been selling brand-name cosmetics made in Tokyo, Paris, or New York for hard currency, often at many times the original price. When we express doubt about whether or not there is a market for such luxury items, the sales clerk points out that in the capital's sophisticated world of business, good manners require that one create a pleasant atmosphere by giving a selection of the latest shades of mascara or French perfumes. Yuppies (*yapishi*) are not yet a thing of the past in Beijing. No doubt the sales clerk is right. Her statement is corroborated by the fact that there is now a new Chinese women's magazine devoted entirely to cosmetics, and that the joint-venture enterprise of the Japanese company Shiseido in the special economic zone of Beijing is planning to develop products specifically designed for the Chinese skin.

I have often wondered why I enjoy going to Beijing again and again despite all my criticism. I think the answer is that it is a challenge to find something new, something promising on every visit, whether among the peddlers hawking books piled on tables placed on sawhorses at the roadside, or in a movie theater, or in the seclusion of an inner courtyard. This is what makes the long flight worthwhile.

Translated by Ilze Mueller

A shopping street in Beijing

THE BEIJING SILK ROAD

Anna Gerstlacher

Throughout history, China has been famous for its many inventions such as spaghetti, fireworks, porcelain, and especially silk. Often considered the most beautiful fabric in the world, silk will make a rich momento of your travels in China. The Silk Road, an overland route for trade with the Middle East, was heavily traveled during the Han and Tang dynasties. During the eighteenth and nineteenth centuries, scientists discovered the route and, in recent years, the tourist industry has also conquered the ancient road. A journey on the Silk Road is still an adventure.

The days when betrayal of the secret of silk was punishable by death are gone, as are the times when customers paid for their silk in gold. But a great demand still exists nowadays; after a drop-off during the Cultural Revolution, silk production in China has been increased to meet world demand.

You do not have to travel to the areas where silk is grown (Shandong, Sichuan, Zhejiang, and Guandong Provinces); you can find a remarkable variety of silk products in many shops throughout the country. But the easiest and probably the most economical way of fulfilling silky desires is to go to the "Beijing Silk Road"—or as Beijingers say, the Xiushui Market. Located in the Embassy district, near the Friendship Store, the market stretches from Chang'an Avenue to the American Embassy. Compared to the older Silk Road, the Beijing version has a short history dating back some ten years. Beijing merchants offer every silk product from negligees to winter coats, from classic silk dress shirts to airy blouses, and from scarves to patterned silk ties. But silk is not all there is for sale. The market also specializes in cashmere goods, antiques, pearls, and hand-carved wooden articles. Even if you have little time this is a one-stop, must-stop shopping area.

The Beijing Silk Road is an international thoroughfare. Languages from all parts of the world can be heard here. Wholesale traders flock here to buy in bulk, with a sharp eye on the bottom line. Here the bottom line is almost too low to be believed, especially if you speak some Chinese! The key to success at Xiushui Market's Silk Road is to bargain, bargain, bargain. The vendors expect to wrangle, so their original price is always high. If you feel too timid to bargain, you are paying too much. When prices at one stall are far below the rest, it is usually a bad sign. The vendors are generally fair and polite, but a few unscrupulous people can get into any crowd and nylon feels an awful lot like silk—in China as well as at home.

When you leave the market, your dominant concern will be how to get all your wonderful new purchases into that little suitcase you came with. But do not despair, the vendors are prepared. Just go around the corner where there are several stalls selling canvas or nylon bags, just right for travel.

BEIJING'S SNACKS

Liu Qian

According to history books, Beijing was the capital of the state of Yan three thousand years ago, which is how it got the name Yandu (*du* means capital in Chinese). Beijing's long history of being the capital during several dynasties has made it a city possessing lasting and profound cultural appeal.

For instance, well-known Beijing foods like *douzhi* (a fermented drink made from ground beans), lotus seed porridge, and dried dairy products have been around for more than a thousand years. Today you can find more than a hundred kinds of snacks in the marketplace. No wonder people say the Beijingers know how to enjoy life.

I still remember the scene twenty years ago when I lived in Beijing for a short time. In the hazy early mornings, waiters from snack shops would push small handcarts into the residential areas loaded with hot *douzhi*, sesame seed cakes, and other foods for breakfast. The early risers would go with their pots and jugs and surround the carts. Soon, their tables would be laden with fried cakes made of glutinous rice flour, deep-fried dough cakes, *tang'erduo* (a kind of sugary fried dough) as well as hot *douzi*, or bean milk. By that time the sun had risen, and the warm atmosphere would fill the morning. Many years after I had left Beijing, I could still remember the warmth of Beijing's mornings.

Some people consider Beijing's snacks to be simple fare, but which possess strong local flavors. The snacks differ from dinners in the ways they are made, sold, and eaten. Both fixed food stands and peddlers sell snacks. For instance, the peddlers selling *pagao* (sweetened rice flour cake) in the lanes can often be heard calling, "Pagao, very chewy. . . . Bean jelly, hot and sour. . . ."

These snacks are usually easy to make and should be eaten immediately after they are cooked. Consumers of this fare are generally ordinary people. In addition to breakfast, many people enjoy these snacks to satisfy a between-meal hunger while shopping or spending time outdoors. Some regard snacks as part of the folk culture.

There are many accounts of the origin and development of Beijing's snacks. One explanation asserts that snacks originally made for the palace gradually became popular among the masses. Beijing was the capital during the Yuan, Ming, and Qing dynasties. At that time the food trade in the country was prospering. Apart from the palace delicacies, the snacks were also available in great variety; meat pies and lotus seed porridge of the Yuan dynasty; dragon's beard noodle of the Ming dynasty; and small steamed bread made of chestnut flour, pea flour cake, and sweet-sour plum juice during the Qing dynasty—more than two hundred kinds of snacks existed.

Another account indicates that during the Ming and Qing dynasties, when the imperial examination system was carried out, many southerners passed the examination and went to the capital to be officials. Many snack recipes traveled with them to the capital.

Moreover, the Man, Mongolian, and other ethnic groups introduced many snacks to the capital such as different types of buns and *saqima*, a kind of candied fritter.

Up until the late Ming and early Qing dynasties, Beijing's snacks had gained popular reputations, but they were still enjoyed only by imperial families and nobles. It is said that at that time some palaces issued special passes to some famous snack shops, asking them to send their products regularly.

It was not until the revolution of 1911 that Beijing's snacks became favorites among the common people. For a time, snack shops mushroomed in the city and did a brisk business. Popular were Jushunhe's *fuling* cake and Duyichu's fried triangle cake in Dashalan, Qianmen Street, as well as Jiulongzhai's candied haws on a stick in Xidan Street. Jushunhe's preserved fruits even won an award at Panama's International Fair. Those old shops gained fame for their unique skills.

Some people have estimated that there are more than three hundred traditional snacks in Beijing and divide them into six categories: steamed and boiled, fried and baked, glutinous, liquid, meat, and fruits. For instance, *aiwowo*, one of the Beijingers' favorites, belongs to the glutinous category. Ancient people described its recipe: "Steam the white glutinous rice and fill with assorted stuffing. It looks like stuffed dumplings but they do not need to boil. The Muslims call it *aiwowo*." There is a story about *aiwowo*. Early in the Ming dynasty, *aiwowo* was a delicacy for imperial and official families. Li Guangting from the Qing dynasty wrote in a book titled *Explanations on Folk Proverbs*: "In the Ming dynasty, an emperor liked to have this food and named it *yuaiwowo* (*yu* means imperial). Later, people omitted the *yu* and called it *aiwowo*."

Take the peach-shaped longevity cake as another example. It existed early in the Song dynasty and belongs to the steamed category. Old Beijingers traditionally present this cake on somebody's birthday. It is said that a huge peach-shaped cake that contained one hundred smaller ones was prepared on Emperor Qianlong's birthday.

So to describe Beijing's snacks as "living fossils" of the capital's thousand-year history is not an exaggeration. But nowadays people like to celebrate birthdays with Western-style cakes, instead of the traditional peach-shaped cake.

Today, Beijing's typical snacks are encountering the rapid changes of the time. Many traditional snacks can no longer be found in the market. Some old Beijingers have appealed to retain the city's pride in its food. Meanwhile, snacks from other parts of the country are pouring into the capital. In Donghuamen Street, Dongdan, Xidan, and other downtown sections, signs or streamers advertising snacks with northwestern, Sichuan, and Guangdong flavors hang on many stands. Old Beijingers treat them coldly, but the young ones are ready to try them. Even the big newly built hotels have joined in. In a five-star hotel, people can also find a snack stall. Old Beijingers have resigned themselves to the idea that many snacks have seemingly finished their turn.

People can enjoy the snacks anywhere at any time in Beijing. In the summer, the city becomes a world of snacks. When the evening lights are lit, mat-awning snack stands are everywhere. The smell of food is so delicious that few passersby can resist the temptation. So, they try quick-fried tripe, light fried dumplings, and spring rolls (a thin sheet of dough, rolled, stuffed, and fried) one after another along their way. Hey, guts, don't get too full! If you want more, come back tomorrow.

A Note on Tongzhou

Tongzhou is located at the east end of the hundred-*li* (33 mi. or 53 km.) street in Beijing. The area is a hub that links Beijing, Tianjin, and Tangshan. It is also the starting point of the Great Beijing-Hangzhou Canal. A gathering place of merchants since ancient times, Tongzhou's food culture continues to flourish. The snacks found in the area are local specialities; others combine the flavors of northern and southern China.

The Tongzhou Festival of Dainty Snacks has been an annual event since 1990. Each year a street is blocked off solely to exhibit the making and selling of traditional favorites. Heirs and heiresses to the making of some long-standing and famous specialities attend the festival to demonstrate their skills. Tourists from China and abroad are attracted to the event each year. The festival has helped to boost Tongzhou's economic development.

Translated by Chen Shanshan

CHINA BY TRAIN

Julia Mollée

W hen the semester at the Beijing Language Institute is over at the end of January, we have a vacation that co-incides with the Chinese New Year. During this time, people in China travel a lot. Chinese New Year, also called Spring Festival, is comparable in significance to Christmas. Thousands and thousands of Chinese travel to visit their fami-lies after a long absence; family members often have to live apart for years.

At the language institute, we, too, are allowed to travel only during our vacation; we cannot get travel permits during the school term. Near one of the many ticket counters in front of the Beijing central railroad station, I take my place in the long line of waiting people. Suddenly, somebody tugs at my sleeve and tells me that these counters are only for the Chinese, while the counter for foreigners is inside the station building. I quickly go and find it. The lobby is pleasantly empty and clean There is more space. The ticket office itself, however, is bustling with hectic activity—there is only one counter for foreigners. Here, there is also a long line. I see other foreigners and, judg-ing by the quality of their clothes, some Chinese officials. There are three classes of people here: the "normal" Chinese out on the square in front of the station, their compatriots standing in-side in the warm, and we foreigners.

I had planned to travel to Sichuan Province, known for its spicy cuisine and particularly lovely landscape, but tickets to Sichuan are already sold out. I quickly decide on Fujian Province, which is directly opposite Taiwan. The ticket agent offers me a ticket in the "soft sleeper" car for the long journey, but I buy a "hard sleeper" ticket instead, because I do not have a lot of money.

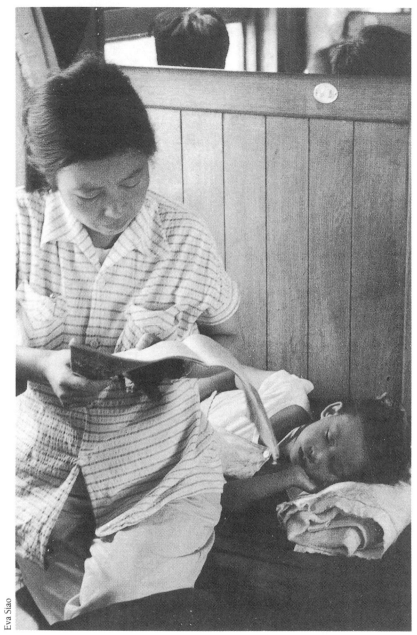

Eva Siao

Hard seats

The state-owned Chinese railroad distinguishes four classes of tickets, and therefore prices: "hard seats," the lowest price class; "hard sleepers," which reserves the right to a hard bunk; "soft seats;" and "soft sleepers." The last two classes are the most expensive and nicest, if you are going a long way. The "hard sleeper" class is basically different from the "soft sleeper" class. In a "hard sleeper" car, several open six-bed cubicles are arranged in a row, each with two three-story bunk beds facing each other and close together. The head end of a sleeper is by the window and the foot end next to the corridor, which is regularly mopped with a wet rag.

Since distances between major Chinese cities are immense and trains travel slowly, it is a good idea to have a bed where you can rest. While traveling by day, people who share a "hard sleeper" cubicle usually sit on the two lower bunks chatting about their families, the landscape, or their latest acquisitions, as the mood happens to strike them.

The "soft sleeper" class, on the other hand, meets the need for more privacy. A compartment with four cubicles, each with two upholstered bunk beds, can be closed when necessary, and offers several other conveniences. "Soft seats" and "soft sleepers," however, are within the means only of foreigners and well-to-do Chinese.

In the "hard seat" category, the least expensive of all categories of rail travel, you literally sit on *hard* seats. Every millimeter of space is used. Moreover, there is luggage, bulky and heavy for the most part, stowed away so cleverly that it does not come tumbling down. Those who do not find a seat on the benches, in spite of shoving and pushing, sit on the luggage, spend the journey on their knees, or, if worse comes to worst, have to stand. Time passes most quickly when you play cards or sleep.

Every car has a little sink for freshening up. These sinks are not in a separate cubicle that can be locked, at least not in the two cheaper categories of cars. They are public.

The toilets—which *can* be locked—consist of a hole that opens directly onto the tracks, with outlines marked on the floor on both sides of the hole for one's feet. The farther the train travels, the dirtier the toilets get. They are probably not cleaned until the train reaches its destination.

Three days after buying my ticket, I get to the station punctually before the train's departure. Quickly I find the platform for the train to Fuzhou, capital of Fujian Province. Again I get special treatment: railroad employees take me to the waiting room for foreigners and officials. Pretty wicker chairs stand in a row between little tables with lace doilies. Tall porcelain cups with covers and tea leaves in little paper bags offer refreshment. There is hot water in big colorful thermos jugs standing on the floor near the tables and regularly refilled by women station attendants.

Soon I board the train and as it slowly begins to move, I stand at the corridor window and look out at the city in which I have spent several months. I am not sorry to leave.

Meanwhile, I make myself comfortable on my bed. There is even room for my backpack. Curiously, I observe the men and women who are to be my neighbors. They, in turn, look into my eyes frankly and smile at me encouragingly. We begin a timid conversation, which soon breaks off for it is late. They get ready for bed. At ten, the light is turned down, but it is still possible to find your way around in the dim light that is left on. We have forty hours to go until Fuzhou. The monotonous rattle of the train slowly rocks us to sleep.

Six o'clock in the morning. Crackling loudly, the loudspeaker wakes us up with music. Shrill announcements reverberate through the car. With a jolt, I sit up and ask the others who are already sitting on the beds, "What's that racket?"

They laugh and reply: "That's the radio, and the speaker is right next to your bed!"

I try to find the button to turn the radio down. Unfortunately there is none—the program continues at the same volume. Now I can make out dialogue. My traveling companions laugh and giggle, point at the speaker, and call to me: "It's a comedy show—don't you understand the jokes?"

"No," I say, "they're talking much too fast!"

At some point, much later, the noise dies down. Everyone is wide awake. Now I am the focus of interest. Their curiosity seems boundless. They want to know everything about me.

"Where are you from?"

"What are you doing in China?"

"How old are you?"

"Are you married?"

"Do you have children?"

"What is your name?"

"Why are you traveling through China alone?"

I have the impression that the women would not like to

change places with me. Are they afraid of this kind of freedom? Not only on this occasion, but during other trips through China as well, I have observed that Chinese women seldom travel without male protection, and if they do they are accompanied by a mother, sister, daughter, sister-in-law, aunt, or woman friend. Both women and men give me to understand that traveling alone is dangerous. I do not understand. Is their fear groundless, or have they really had bad experiences?

At mealtimes dining car employees run through the train selling portions of rice and meat to some of the passengers, who push the food into their mouths with chopsticks they have brought with them. Others eat during official hours in the dining car. A cook asks me to come to the dining car at 2:00 P.M.— and not a minute before. When I get there, I see only the staff of the dining car cleaning the tables that were in use. Am I to eat there all by myself? Shortly afterwards, another "long nose" enters the car. Aha, another special treatment! We get into conversation. I exchange practical information with the Englishman— tips about good and cheap hotels, transportation, routes, landscapes, and places worth seeing. For example, it's important to know the maximum price you should pay for a bicycle rickshaw if you do not want to be cheated.

After a forty-four hour journey the train punctually arrives in Fuzhou. From Beijing to here we have enjoyed a wonderful, sometimes bizarre landscape. During the journey, we have gotten to know each other a little and offered each other tea, fruit, and sweets. Our conversations have always remained on a friendly, noncommittal level. No one told me his or her entire life story—as has often happened when I travel by train in Germany. That is not customary in China and it is not polite, least of all with a foreigner. Political topics are also avoided as a rule. I remember another train ride. A young woman had confided some of her political views to me. Shortly thereafter she was asked to go to another compartment by a man in plain clothes. I never saw her again.

We are tired after the long journey, but in Fuzhou and its environs we shall all go to sleep in a real bed that night. When I arrive at the station, I ask my way to the hotel that was recommended to me. With my student identity card, I get a discount and am given a bed in a dormitory.

The night is terribly cold and damp. In southern China there is no heating. In the hotel bar, I drink a brandy against the cold, and in my bed I wrap myself in all the available blankets. But the cold keeps me awake. The day after tomorrow, I shall leave the People's Republic, and so I lie there thinking about the long train ride, about China and "the Chinese."

Translated by Ilze Mueller

TRANSFORMATIONS IN
CONTEMPORARY SHANGHAI

Lida Junghans

S hanghai is rapidly becoming China's showcase—a place where the possibilities of "Market Socialism with Chinese Characteristics"* can be revealed to the national and international public.

The architectural monuments being rapidly erected throughout Shanghai's districts suggest conspicuous consumption on a citywide scale. And while the sumptuous, well-capitalized buildings are persuasive indicators of Shanghai's status as a flourishing center of business and trade, it is also true that they are being built as part of a gamble, in order to inspire confidence and lure foreign investment. It is well known in the People's Republic that many of the wealthiest tycoons in Southeast Asia and the world are, in fact, ethnic Chinese who left the country in a series of migratory waves, which began when the Manchus overthrew the Ming emperors to found the Qing dynasty in 1644 and saw another high tide in the years around 1949. Extraterritorial Chinese wealth confirms an intuition widely shared by many Chinese citizens, which is that the Chinese are very talented at doing business, and that the Shanghainese are especially gifted at the art.

There is a sense that only disadvantageous political policies have prevented Shanghai from enjoying its rightful place as the most modern Asian metropolis—a reputation initiated in the early part of the century when imperialist business interests from Great Britain, Japan, Russia, the United States, France, and Germany built highly profitable industries on Chinese soil. The architectural remains of this history give Shanghai a unique at-

---

*This phrase has been used to describe the contemporary political-economic system for some years, but its meaning has never been firmly established.

mosphere that has alternately been reviled and celebrated by subsequent leaders. These days foreign investments are coveted as the city's managers sink scarce resources in the construction of sites that they imagine will attract entrepreneurs with sentimental associations to the Shanghai that was once the capital of glamour, sophistication, and industry in Asia.

The dazzling architectural surface of the Shanghai that is home to business, banking, tourism, and trade contrasts with the simpler interiors of the city that are the homes and workplaces of its residents. A recent report published in the *Far Eastern Economic Review* revealed that the price of prime office space in Shanghai and Beijing had surpassed the rates for comparable spaces in Paris, London, and New York. In China such news is interpreted as a sign of progress and modernity, as if the unfettered workings of the property market represented a great accomplishment. These figures loom strangely next to the statistics on income and rent of the average Shanghai worker/resident. In 1993 a typical working couple, each employed by a state enterprise, had a combined income of approximately 800 yuan per month, or about U.S. $94, of which roughly $3.75 went to housing costs.

The local and transnational economies that coexist in the urban space of Shanghai produce interesting tensions and pressures in the lives of the people who navigate the crowded city streets. For many, Shanghai's new identity as the cultural capital of an internationalized, marketized, modernized China signifies the re-emergence of distinct patterns of spatial and social hierarchy that exclude them from the landscape of prosperity.

One of the trends that the commoditization of space has caused is the destruction of many of the city's older buildings and their replacement by high-rent office space. The razing of buildings that had housed working people has forced the relocation of many Shanghai residents to high-rise residential blocks in the numerous suburbs that are springing up on the city's periphery. Housing has primarily been the responsibility of the work unit, and currently many work units do not have the cash flow that would enable them to construct adequate housing in the suburbs for their workers. When work units do have the means to accommodate their personnel, it is frequently far from the workplace, thus requiring workers to make long commutes across the expansive city (commutes of one and one-half or two hours each way on bicycle or buses are not uncommon).

In interviews with railway workers conducted in 1993, many people told me of how the neighborhood across the street from their workplace had been replaced by speculative real estate projects. People who worked on board trains complained that their work unit had no clout in the city and, therefore, failed to shield them from the stresses of this time of transition. In Shanghai, the sense of the railroad as providing insufficiently for its employees contrasts with the way this "iron rice bowl" was perceived before the recent reforms, when it was one of the most secure and high status of all state jobs.

In conversations with women and men who are career workers in the state sector of the economy, I learned, for example, that whereas in many towns it is considered advantageous to be a permanent railroad employee, in Shanghai working for a locally based enterprise is considered to provide greater benefits. Both of these opportunities, however, pale in comparison to the prospect of working in a joint venture or a wholly foreign-owned subsidiary.

A woman who had been honored for many years as a "model worker" in her capacity as an elementary school teacher to the children of railroad workers spoke with obvious pride about her future daughter-in-law (fiancée of her second son). This young woman had a plum position as an aerobics instructor in a foreign hotel. The prospective mother-in-law expressed exasperated impatience, however, with her eldest son who, upon his honorable discharge from the military, made a lateral transfer into service for the railroad. His job assignment in the luggage and freight management division situated him in a place to receive favors and to reciprocally allot the scarce commodity of space in cargo containers, but he dully refused to participate in these practices, which are taken by many, his mother included, as part of the everyday workings of the system.

These vignettes, unremarkable on the surface, nevertheless starkly illustrate the disparate systems of value that shape the experience of life in contemporary China. An ideology that had stressed *pingdeng* (equality) is now reviled as having been an irrational detour from the path of progress and development. Socialist values have, for all practical purposes, been replaced by an ethic that naturalized the unequal distribution of opportunities to thrive, profit, or even survive in the market environment.

In Shanghai a young woman with looks and talent can hope to trade on her assets—to gain a place in the sector of the economy that appears to have a future. But for those whose places were fixed in the less lucrative sectors of the economy during times when the prospect of exercising in an international hotel chain for a living would have been inconceivable, the emerging inequalities give all of Shanghai's gleaming symbols of modernity an ominous significance. To encourage the skeptical to embrace the new opportunities provided by the market and to join in the profitmaking, headlines in state-run newspapers urge the public to "*huan naojin*" (literally, trade in brain muscles, or change old ways of thinking). But for the people who grew up reading a different rhetoric in the papers, "old ways of thinking" are intimately linked to the material conditions in the world of their experience.

HANGZHOU: IN SEARCH OF
A PARADISE LOST

Dagmar Borchard

The news that I would be spending both spring and fall in Hangzhou made my Chinese friends envious: "In heaven there is paradise, on earth there is Hangzhou," they would say, clearly enraptured. Hangzhou, a city on the Qiantang River in eastern Zhejiang Province, was famous for its beauty as early as the seventh century, during the Tang dynasty. Marco Polo, who visited the city in 1280, was enchanted and praised its splendor, the friendliness of its inhabitants, and the charm of its landscape. If I ever decide to settle in China to study poetry, it will have to be in a cottage on a mountain with a view of the West Lake, the jewel and pride of all Hangzhou. Legend has it that it was created when a pearl fell from the sky. There are folk tales about each hill, pavilion, pagoda, and temple in Hangzhou; in China, along with advanced age in a tourist attraction, this is a certain indicator of quality.

Those who doubt the existence of fairies and their supernatural abilities to transform themselves into mountains and cliffs can retrace the footsteps of many famous travelers and daughters and sons of this city, whose ghosts might reawaken when you read their poems in one of the pavilions or teahouses by the lake. The city has always attracted famous personalities, especially poets and painters, who sought the inspiration of the magnificent landscape. During the Song dynasty, Li Qingzhao and Zhu Shuzhen, two of China's important women poets, lived on the banks of the West Lake in the thirteenth century. The few poems of Zhu that have survived (most of them were apparently burned by her parents after her death) perfectly capture the West Lake's moods. The Su Dam is named after a Song poet, Su Dongpo, the city prefect of Hangzhou, while the Bai Dam honors Bai Juyi, scholar, bureaucrat, and famous poet.

And Qiu Jin, the feminist revolutionary who was born in nearby Shaoxing, is buried by the West Lake.

Spring and fall are the best times to come here (even more so than in the rest of China), because it is then that Hangzhou's perfume is at its best. March brings out the camellias (called "tea flower" in Mandarin), and it is the season for outings to the cherry gardens where fathers proudly pose for pictures with their little kings and princesses (each only child dressed to the nines, of course, and spoiled by the entire family) in front of stunning backdrops of pink cherry blossoms. When it gets a bit warmer, the weeping willows around the lake sprout tender green leaves, and the magnolia groves in the botanical gardens exude the scent of spring. In the fall, the slightly sweet scent of the blooming osmanthus (called *guihua* in Mandarin, a word frequently heard in September and October) envelops the city. Osmanthus sugar (*guihuatang*), which is obtained from inflorescence, is one of Hangzhou's specialties and can be bought in all teashops.

Apart from being one of the best-smelling places in China, Hangzhou is also renowned for the exquisite tea that grows on the hills surrounding the West Lake: the famous Dragon Well tea (also called *longjing* tea), the best and most expensive tea in all of China. All Chinese families and Westerners knowledgeable about green tea are very happy to receive a small box of good longjing tea from Hangzhou. Depending on the quality, a small box can cost up to 100 yuan, if you prefer the first leaves of the spring harvest, which are sold after 10 April. Fine white hairs on the surface of the dried tea leaves indicate that it is especially good. Since the dissolution of the people's communes, the tea is once again harvested by families, and it is sold mostly by women in the vicinity of the Dragon Well Village. Even skilled bargainers cannot bring down its price, for the women know the value of their green gold. This tea tastes especially good if it is brewed with water from the Dragon Well spring or the Tiger spring.

On my first day in Hangzhou, I usually take an early morning walk along the lake. Visitors inclined to walk around the entire lake are advised to start with a good breakfast, for example on the terrace of the Hangzhou Hotel that is second only to the Beijing Hotel in terms of its renown and the flair of the good old days when China was not yet overrun by foreign tourists. In the afternoon (at the latest), the influence of the German-Austrian hotel management becomes most evident in Black Forest cake and apple strudel. I often rent a boat to ride to "Small Paradise," an island in the West Lake. It consists mainly of a bank reinforcement with four smaller lakes on the inside, covered with lotus blossoms in July and August. To the south, three stone pagodas rise from the water, and on full-moon nights the moonlight is mirrored through the openings of the three stone figures *Santanying*. Chicken wrapped in lotus flowers is a Hangzhou specialty not to be missed, as are the soups made with lake plants.

It is worth renting a bicycle to explore the area. Since Hangzhou is also one of the main tourist attractions for Chinese, bicycles cost as much as five yuan a day. Many newly married couples dream of honeymooning by the West Lake, and the city is also a popular spot for conferences (*kaihui*).

The Lingyin Temple cloister and the Pagoda of Six Harmonies are wonderful places easily reached on a bike. And you can spend an entire day in the Yellow Dragon Park, watching the presentations of classic Chinese opera (in Hangzhou, music connoisseurs can appreciate *jueju*, the local opera from nearby Shaoxing) and of traditional music in the different pavilions. Classical Chinese orchestra music comprising a two-stringed violin and a bamboo flute is offered in a grotto at the rear of the park. In yet another area, girls dressed in traditional robes play the *guzheng*, my favorite instrument. It sounds like a deep dulcimer, and its music has the effect of a stream or a small waterfall, for each note rolls like a pearl from the instrument's twenty-seven strings.

But modern developments have not spared Hangzhou. The souvenir stalls by the lake offer as much *kitsch* as can be bought anywhere else in the world, in this case catering to Chinese tourists' demand for thermometers shaped like the stone pagodas that mirror the moonlight. Small wooden figures—mainly from classical Chinese tales, such as Little Pig or Monkey from the pilgrim novel *Travel from the West,* but also classics of Western cartoons, such as Mickey Mouse and Goofy—can be bought for two yuan. And those who dream of old Hangzhou can buy a small (truly annoying) bamboo pipe that imitates a river bird's shrill cries for one *mao* (one U.S. cent).

The modern women of Hangzhou are fashionable in silk blouses and suits that reflect the latest Western styles, bought with several month's pay in one of the private shops around Jiefang Street. The shop owner's remark that certain pieces were actually intended for export and that they are available in

Hangzhou (a mere provincial capital, after all) thanks only to his special skills is, of course, designed to counter the reluctance of the undecided. Fashion consciousness is in the air, for Shanghai is not too far away. The silk shops of Hangzhou on the *hubin* (lakeside) promenade are jammed from morning to night with groups of women, animatedly discussing fabrics and patterns. Decisions take time, for qualities must be tested, colors compared, and prices calculated. And all bemoan the rapidly rising prices of silk, which often costs twice as much as the previous year. Women who sew their own clothes prefer to get sufficient supplies of particularly beautiful prints before the rumors of yet another price hike come true next fall or spring.

It is primarily women who work in the silk mills of Hangzhou—the center of China's silk and brocade industry—under some of the most hair-raising conditions imaginable. Some of them have to dip their fingers into steaming hot water all day to unwind the beginning thread from the cocoons floating in the water. The threads of six to seven cocoons yield one silk thread. A tour of a silk factory (including the inevitable visit to its own store) is part of all group programs and can easily be booked for individual travelers through the local travel bureau. (The woman factory guide will barely conceal her displeasure if the tourists do not spend at least as much time in the shop as they did on the factory floor.)

The cosmetics counters of the department stores carry everything from nail polish to lipstick and eye shadow in the latest fashion colors and are always busy. A facial cream made from pearls ground in a mortar, which is said to keep skin young and smooth as well as to give it a lighter color, is an especially hot item in spite of its high price. Here, too, the women take their time before they decide to put down an entire month's salary for an assortment of eye shadow in six colors. Tip: Cosmetics make excellent gifts for Chinese women friends!

The appropriate way to leave "paradise" is by boarding the *Paradise,* a ship for foreigners that connects Hangzhou to Suzhou via the Emperor's Canal. The overnight trip in a soft bunk with a view of the busy life on the canal leads directly to the next paradise on Chinese earth, the garden city of Suzhou.

Translated by Ulrike Bode

GUILIN: FOREST OF
FRAGRANT BLOSSOMS

Anna Gerstlacher

I arrived in Guilin, a city in the northeast of Guangxi Province, on a warm summer's night on the train from Kunming. Traveling with a few other tourists and no guide, I was taken by bicycle rickshaw to the Lijiang Hotel, the only place open to foreigners. The next day brought my first view of the famed silhouette of hills that draws many travelers to Guilin—Elephant Hill, Mountain of Lonely Beauty, Mountain of Layered Silk, Fubo Mountain, and others. They are part of a hilly terrain that stretches in a tremendous variety of formations from southern China to Vietnam, Thailand, and Malaysia; the karstic landscape is concentrated along the Li River in Guangxi.

Guilin is a leader in many respects, including in the downsides of modern mass tourism. In the early 1980s, it became evident that if you were not careful, somebody would relieve you of your possessions. In the past, poets and painters visited Guilin to be enthralled and inspired by its extraordinary landscape; nowadays the city mainly attracts traveling businessmen who come to observe Guilin's latest developments and then apply them to money-making schemes elsewhere in China. The first night markets offering opportunities for trade were established in Guilin's streets in the mid-1980s. One of China's first discotheques was opened on the roof of Guilin's Lijiang Hotel and quickly became a popular nightspot. At the time, admission to the disco cost ten yuan—a fortune given the average monthly salary of eighty yuan! Now the all-pervasive background music seems to be thought of as a special service, be it in the Lala Cafe, in the Guilin McDonald's, or in one of the many restaurants that are supposed to stimulate the free socialist market by competing with one another. Although tips are forbidden by law, employees quickly recognized that they significantly improved

Nelly Rau-Häring

Advertisement for Guilin

their salaries and thus rapidly made them part of the equation, wherever and whenever the occasion presented itself.

The streets come to life late in the day, at dinnertime between five and eight. During the day tourists can enjoy the deservedly famous sights. The brightly illuminated Ludiyan (Reed Flute Cave) will never lose its magic, and the impressive view from one of the hills, none of which is higher than 330 feet (about 99 m.), will undoubtedly etch itself into the memories of those who have seen it. The walk through the bonsai gardens of the Seven Stars Park is less tiring but equally charming, and watching the panda bears at feeding time in the morning and evening is especially rewarding. There are gravestones and tumuluses of Ming royalty on the outskirts of the city. In contrast, however, to the distracting hustle and bustle of tourists in the famous Ming tombs of Beijing, here the visitor can contemplate this historic site in relative peace.

Tianxia diyi di (the best place under the sky)—that is how many Chinese describe Guilin even today. The conical mountains rose from the sea as a result of a giant eruption more than three hundred million years ago. For thousands of years, the green karstic hills have been mirrored in myriad waters, from green rice paddies to winding streams and the stately Li River. A few years ago, severe environmental pollution threatened all of this with extinction. Both the skyline and the hilltops were obscured by smog spewing from the smokestacks of Guilin's small industry, and the Li River was dying from garbage thrown overboard by the operators of sightseeing boats. Well-directed environmental measures have had surprisingly rapid effects: Guilin is once again *tianxia diyi di,* though with small blemishes.

The five-hour, fifty mile (about 80 km.) journey down the Li River past the magical mountainscape is a must for anyone traveling to Guilin; it can be done in groups (where everything down to lunch is perfectly organized) or individually (where you have to get everything yourself). Skipping lunch is not that bad, for such earthly needs can easily be satisfied later in Yangshuo.

As soon as the tourist boats and buses arrive, the town of Yangshuo is taken over by the visitors and innumerable stalls, where all of China (the gaudier the better) appears to be on sale. Only those truly versed in the art of bargaining will leave with fortifying mushrooms, bicycle bells, a dancing panda bear, or a tablecloth. Shortly after 3:00 P.M., when the buses of the State Tourist Office return to Guilin, the streets are transformed. Peace returns to Yangshuo, the stalls disappear as quickly as they were set up, and the laid-back rhythm of daily life reasserts itself. This is the best time for exploring the town and its surroundings. Rent a bicycle and spend a few quiet days in the countryside, which offers something in short supply anywhere else in China: respite and relaxation.

Translated by Ulrike Bode

Qiu Jin in Japan

SHAOXING AND ITS FAMOUS FEMINIST

Elke Wandel

The high-ranking officials of the town are outraged. Eyebrows raised, they peer out at the street. Faces that are usually so blasé lose their composure. Tea vendors, sellers of birds, and pastry cooks hold their breath: a woman in masculine attire! Her head held high, a sword at her hip, she rides horseback through the staring crowd. She cut off her long hair years ago. Her narrow, smooth hands betray her social background. The expression on her face is self-confident and determined. She is a thorn in the flesh of local administrators: Qiu Jin, China's most famous feminist, who passionately paved the way for the republican revolution. The place and time of the action: Shaoxing in the year 1907.

Shaoxing Today

Shaoxing is a small town in Zhejiang Province, which today can be reached by train from Hangzhou in a good hour. It is crisscrossed by numerous little rivers and canals, and even today much of the town's traffic goes by water. In the morning mist, as one walks through the picturesque streets and alleys, the inner city seems like a vision in a dream, a Chinese pen-and-ink drawing. Large and small semicircular bridges arch across the narrow waterways. Long narrow boats, whose rudder is operated by foot, glide silently over the surface of the water. As soon as the sun rises higher, the romantic transfiguration vanishes and gives way to sober observation: The canals carry not only boats but garbage as well. The canals serve as both sewers and sinks for washing chopsticks, rice bowls, and vegetables. The picturesque backdrop, a stereotyped image of "old" China, is tainted by dirt and stench.

A series of lakes and countless fishponds cluster around Shaoxing. The Eastern Lake (Donghu) is probably the most popular place for excursions in the area. With its rock formations, caves, little bridges, and pavilions, the park, which dates from the late Qing period, is designed according to the principles of Chinese horticulture. Teahouses invite guests to linger a while.

South of Shaoxing—at the foot of Mount Kuaiji—a popular figure of Chinese mythology is worshipped in the Temple of the Great Yu (Yu Miao). Legend has it that four thousand years ago a certain Yu overcame a flood that threatened to inundate the countryside. For a nation that has constantly had to struggle with either an overabundance or a lack of water, controlling huge volumes of water is an important theme in folk tradition.

The Orchid Pavilion (Lanting) is southwest of town. Fifteen hundred years ago, the great calligrapher and poet Wang Xizhi and his writer friends were inspired to write lyrical poetry here as they drank wine. The park in its present form dates from a later period—the sixteenth century. It is surrounded by a lovely bamboo grove.

Shaoxing is particularly well known for its excellent golden rice wine, whose quality is praised all over China. In the rustic setting of the ancient Xianheng wine tavern, which has a branch restaurant in the Shaoxing Hotel, guests can sample the best Shaoxing wine, accompanied by a cold snack. This delicious, aromatic "yellow wine" is warmed in a shallow metal pan, brought to the table in the same container, and sipped from large stoneware cups.

This hospitable tavern used to be a favorite haunt of Lu Xun, perhaps the most famous modern Chinese author. This master of satire wrote his essays and stories in the vernacular, as opposed to classical Chinese. With biting sarcasm, he criticized the inhumanity of a "cannibalistic society," as he called it. Born and raised in Shaoxing, he studied in Japan and returned to his hometown in 1908 to teach in a local school for a few years. It is therefore not surprising that his works contain many descriptions of Shaoxing, for example, of the tavern mentioned above. The house where he was born is only about a hundred meters (about 330 ft. or 110 yd.) from the tavern, and next to it are the Lu Xun Memorial Hall and the Three Fragrances Studio (Sanweishuwu), the private school that young Lu Xun attended at the end of the nineteenth century.

Qiu Jin

Another great figure who made history in Shaoxing is Qiu Jin, the feminist. A museum is housed in her childhood home in the Hechangtang. Visitors can see the room she had in her parents' house, with its original furniture. An exhibition consisting of photographs and letters, and her poems and newspaper articles, gives us a glimpse of the life of an unusual and militant woman.

Born into a moderately affluent family of officials on the island of Xiamen in Fujian Province, Qiu Jin learned as a young child of China's humiliation at the hands of foreign colonial powers that had settled in a few coastal towns in the nineteenth century. Qiu Jin's grandfather, who worked as a prefect in Xiamen, found this situation demeaning and finally, embittered, returned to his hometown of Shaoxing with his entire family. At fifteen Qiu Jin was a passionate patriot. However, her anger was directed not only against the "devils from across the sea," as the Western intruders were scornfully called, but also against the corrupt and wildly extravagant Manchu dynasty, which she, a Han Chinese, regarded as a foreign power. Even as a young girl, she developed a clear sense of mission and the determination to help justice prevail.

As her parents' second child, Qiu Jin profited by the fact that a tutor was hired for her older brother. With her mother's active support, she enjoyed a comprehensive education, not an exclusively gender-specific one. Although she did have to learn traditional women's skills like sewing and embroidery, she did not find them satisfying and soon exchanged her needle for a sword. She asked her uncle to teach her the Chinese art of swordsmanship, a special form of martial arts. She found physical exercise thrilling. It was an experience denied to the great majority of upper-class Chinese women.

When she turned twenty-one, Qiu Jin's parents married her off to a man from a very traditional family. She painfully realized the contradictions between her own liberal background and the more narrow-minded attitude of her parents-in-law. Though she soon seemingly became established in her new family after the birth of a son and a daughter, she felt repelled by her husband and found it hard to accept her subordinate position. When her father died, and her mother, brothers, and sisters found themselves in a difficult financial situation, her well-to-do husband refused to help. Slowly Qiu Jin arrived at the decision to look for new perspectives outside marriage. A breakup was inevitable.

In 1904, helped by her women friends, she left her husband and children, sold her jewelry, and booked third-class passage to Japan. A year later, in a letter to her brother, she said disparagingly of her husband: "This person behaves worse than an animal. I've never known anyone who is so shameless. . . . Before I allow myself to be treated like a slave, why shouldn't I stand on my own two feet? From now on I shall try to earn my own living—why should I stay married?"

Presumably, Qiu Jin's feet had been bound when she was a young girl, though probably not very tightly. There were a number of indications that she unbound her feet at the time of her trip to Japan. Thus, she first broke the bonds imposed on her as a woman by the family and by society; then she flexed her political muscles as well. In Japan she came into contact with exiled Chinese intellectuals who were planning to overthrow the Manchu dynasty. Soon she, too, began to write radical pamphlets and dramatic patriotic poetry, made fiery speeches, and gained prominence in the movement. Indeed, she was so determined and passionate a presence that she became a figure of reverence for many students. Years later her compatriot from Shaoxing, Lu Xun, was to remark, perhaps accurately, that Qiu Jin was applauded to death.

In 1906 she returned to China and worked in Shanghai as a negotiator between a number of conspiratorial groups and circles opposed to the emperor. While making a bomb, she almost got killed. Her commitment to the cause of women was still strong, but whenever she could, she linked it with her political goals. She founded the feminist newspaper *Zhongguo nübao* (Chinese Women's News), in which she inveighed against the cult of chastity, foot-binding, and arranged marriages; she worked on a lengthy autobiographical story in verse, "The Stones of the Bird Jingwei," which she left unfinished. She supported education for girls and taught at girls' schools in several cities. She told her students to exchange their silk skirts for military uniforms and urged them to take part in military drill to prepare for a potential insurrection. When the school administration found out about her revolutionary "learning goals," Qiu Jin was fired. In protest against Qiu Jin's dismissal, the school's headmistress resigned. She and two of Qiu Jin's women students remained her faithful companions and later helped document her life story.

In 1907, Qiu Jin began to teach at Datong School in Shaoxing, an educational establishment then regarded as a center for the activities of a secret society. With her students, Qiu Jin planned to capture by force nearby Hangzhou, capital of Zhejiang Province. The plan failed, and three hundred soldiers were sent to Shaoxing to arrest her. She was warned, but refused to run away. At the last minute she hid the weapons, burned the list of her students, and was arrested after a short struggle.

Two days later, on 15 July 1907, Qiu Jin was decapitated by the emperor's keepers of law and order. She was thirty-two. A memorial built for her in Shaoxing at the place of her execution is a dark gray stone obelisk. The statue that stands on her grave by the West Lake in Hangzhou is a worthier memorial to the premature death of this unusual and impressive woman. The white stone figure that represents China's first great feminist stands opposite the Hangzhou Shangrila Hotel, on the Isle of the Lonely Hill (Gushan), behind Xilin Bridge.

Translated by Ilze Mueller

FACING THE YANGZI RAPIDS
IN A RUBBER RAFT

Jiehu Asha

C hengdu, April 1986. Over six hundred young people from all over China have come to the capital of Sichuan Province to apply for a place in the first Chinese Yangzi expedition, organized by the Chinese Academy of Sciences. Rubber rafts will follow the 6,300-kilometer-long (3,915 mi.) river from its source to its mouth. The obstacles to be surmounted include a drop of 6,500 meters (21,450 ft.) and over seven hundred rapids. I manage to be selected. The expedition includes eleven scientists, twelve journalists, and twenty-two crew members. There are four women among the forty-five participants.

On 3 June, we fly from Chengdu to Lhasa in Tibet. From Lhasa we proceed in jeeps, then on horseback, and finally on foot. After ten days we reach the place where the Yangzi rises, the Jiangjidiru Glacier in the Gelandandong Mountains, at an elevation of over 6,000 meters (19,800 ft.). The expedition officially begins on 16 June at Tuotuo Lake, the source of the Yangzi.

The lake is shallow and in some areas only mud. Every day for ten hours or more we pull the boats barefoot through icy water. We do not have any rubber boots, and some of us get frostbite on our toes. The temperatures fluctuate widely, and a brief storm soaks us and our luggage, the only raincoat being used to wrap the cameras. At dusk, we set up our tents on the bank. Our sleeping bags are thoroughly soaked. A bowl of soup and a zwieback biscuit is our only meal of the day. Our provisions are tight and have to last until we reach Machang; there is no closer place to get resupplied. Four hundred kilometers (249 mi.) through an uninhabited region where bank notes are worthless paper, but our mood could not be better. The landscape fascinates us—an azure sky, snow-covered mountains, and glaciers are as if out of the realm of fantasy. We see herds of yaks and wild horses and flush thousands of fleeing antelope.

On the fourth day we reach the "death lake," where wolves howl near our tents all night long. On the fifth day, we are heading for the first rapids when suddenly two large black bears come charging down the mountain toward the boats. The reporter for Sichuan television, who is sitting alone in a little rubber boat, sees the beasts through his camera lens, lets out a cry, and drops the camera. Three shots. The bears turn around and flee.

To our great shock, the boat is now headed directly into the rapids; we do not have enough time left to get ready for them. We pitch and toss violently and lose the last four provision crates overboard. When we reach the shore and inspect our supplies, we find that we have only a small sack of flour left. For supper there is a spoonful of flour paste apiece. For two days we have had nothing to eat. It will take us about another ten days to get to Machang. Will we make it alive? Regardless, we all want to go on—we have no other choice. Aesthetic pleasures have ceased to interest us. No one recites poetry in the boats anymore, no one can enjoy the fantastic scenery of the plateau. Something to eat and a good sleep would be the deepest fulfillment. When we pull in to shore in the evening, no one is excited as in the first days; we just want to put up the tents quickly and sleep. But when your stomach is empty it is hard to sleep; hunger makes you restless. In the middle of the night I get up, slink around the tents, and hope to find something to eat. Finally, I go to the river bank, pull a waterproof container out of a boat, and shake it out, only to find a few cracker crumbs. I drink some water from the river and go back to bed, where I doze off and dream of noodle soup and other delicacies.

The daily boat ride has come to seem eternal and monotonous. As we row weakly, the only thing that puts new heart in us is talking about our regional specialties. Those from Chengdu tell of the snack shops there, someone from Chongqing raves about that mountain city's fire pot, a Beijinger goes on about how famous Peking duck is at home and abroad, and I brag about the original "tuotuo" meat dish of my Yi nationality from Liangshan.

There are plenty of wild animals, but we do not want to blunder into fresh difficulties. It is not that these animals are protected species, but that we are not good enough shots. If an enraged wild yak were to attack us, we would not be able to defend ourselves. Peaceful coexistence and mutual nonaggression are the only way to ensure security.

On 27 June, as we set out at daybreak, we hear bird calls in the distance and see thousands and thousands of birds circling in the sky. Up ahead is an island full of birds! We perk up and row with all our strength toward it. The entire island is covered with white eggs. We grab buckets and bowls and storm onto the island. Everybody crowds around the fire as the fragrant egg soup cooks. I have never eaten anything more delicious.

Fifteen days have passed with rain showers and hailstorms the entire time, and the expedition is making slow progress. The snowy peaks ahead of us seem only to get further away. Ugly vultures constantly circle over us, waiting for carrion. The sun on the plateau is so strong that it peels the skin on our faces off layer by layer. Lips crack, eyes become inflamed. Finally, when we almost look like red-eyed wolves, we come upon a green meadow with a herd of white sheep moving along like a cloud. Tents! People!

Just as we are, windblown and dirty as vagabonds, male and female no longer distinguishable from one another, we grab our things and run toward the Tibetans. When they see us, the women put their arms around their frightened children. Paying them no attention, we storm into a tent and look around. As we hoped, there is enough to eat, and we don't care how, tonight we will eat our fill. Relieved, we start taking off our equipment to rest a bit when we see a herd of horses galloping down the mountain. Although it is snowing, the riders, strong, aggressive Tibetans, are barechested. Each one carries a dagger at his hip, which looks incredibly impressive! I am stunned by the sight and let down my long hair, which I had stuck up under my cap, to show them that I am a woman, that we are not bandits. Since we cannot speak Tibetan, we use sign language to make clear that we want to trade something for food. We unpack a few medicines and pieces of jewelry to present to them. In return, the Tibetans are kind enough to give us some of their *tsampa* bread. That evening, as I lie in a warm tent under the Tibetans' warm sheepskin blankets I feel like I am in heaven and immediately fall asleep.

Early the next morning we pack our things back into the boats. No one wants to leave, for we are afraid we will not find any more people downstream and will freeze and starve again. But we have to go on. With heavy hearts we bid farewell to the Tibetans.

Jiehu Asha on the rafting expedition

Luckily, from then on we meet people every day and getting enough to eat is no longer a problem. However, meat is scarce and much desired. Once, a reporter and I set out in search of meat. At the door of a tent where a Tibetan man and his two grown sons live, we fold our hands before our chests politely and greet them in Tibetan. The Tibetans let us enter and offer us yogurt and butter. We eat enthusiastically, but how can we make it clear that we really would like to eat meat? My companion puts his hands on his head like horns and moo's like a cow. This is understood, but aside from a cool smile, there is no reaction. The reporter noticed that the two sons were staring at me and began gesticulating again. After he had thought over this proposal for a while, the old Tibetan finally grinned and his two sons laughed happily. It had just been agreed that I was to remain with the family as a daughter-in-law in return for the yak meat. I think, the ideas that men come up with! That we can now get some meat has nothing to do with whether or not I become the daughter-in-law, so I silently give my agreement and laugh, too. The old Tibetan stands up and pulls aside a curtain. There hangs half a freshly butchered yak. All eyes are

303

glued to the meat. The old Tibetan cuts off a few slices, dips them in salt, and cooks them over a yak-dung fire. Our mouths water.

After we had eaten our fill, we wanted to get going. But I had hardly stood up when the old Tibetan reached for my hand and indicated that the man could go, but I was to stay. The two sons barred the entrance like door gods. It took a lot of doing to get myself out of this jam and escape back to our camp. When the others saw the telltale smudges of yak fat around our mouths, they did not even ask how we had managed it, but took off like a swarm of bees toward the Tibetans' tent. The freshly cheated Tibetans were still furious and when they saw these strangers coming back for more, they set their dogs on them.

After eighteen days we finally reach Machang in the Quma District. The rainy period has begun and the floodwaters of Tongtian Lake—as this section of the Yangzi is called—rise suddenly. On the first day after we leave Quma District, a boat capsizes and seven people go overboard.

At noon we eat biscuits with one hand and bail water out of the boat with the other. The current is raging and the steerers have trouble holding course. Suddenly, the boats are in a gorge where the river drops sharply. The boat in front of us managed to navigate around the rapids, but when they look back and see the eight-meter-high (about 26 ft.) waves and the dangerous drop, they quickly row to shore and run up the mountain to fire a warning shot for us. But it is already too late for us to make it to shore. We have no choice but to grab firm hold of the life-lines. With six people aboard, the boat plunges into the waves. The little rubber boats tied to its side capsize immediately and only pop up again ten seconds later. Now there are only three people on board: Sha Ying, who still has a camera in one hand and the safety line in the other, Xu Ruiyang, and I. With no one steering, the boat turns sideways in the middle of the river. I try to turn it around with a paddle. I see something red near the boat, and at first I think it is my down pants, which I had taken off, but it is Wang Qi. We get him back in the boat, and shortly after we are able to pull Zhou Hongliang on board, too. Now only Liu Hui is missing. Finally we see him surface out of a whirlpool; he has lost his glasses. He waves his arm weakly and calls in despair: "I can't make it, save me!"

I pull off my jacket and am about to jump into the river when someone grabs me around the waist. Zhou bellows in my ear: "You can't get over there." I scream: "Liu Hui, to the left!" A huge breaker lifts him to the top of the wave and then mercilessly plunges him back into the depths. Our boat cannot be slowed; aside from the paddle I have in my hand, all of our equipment is lost. When we finally make it to quieter water near the left bank, we prepare a lifeboat. A hundred meters (110 yd.) away, we see Liu Hui surface, and two kilometers (1.2 mi.) further down the river we finally save him.

We lost fourteen cameras, film, and luggage worth over a hundred thousand yuan. Many of us have only the T-shirt and shorts we are wearing left. That evening over twenty people crowd into the two tents. Outside a rainstorm rages, and on the other side of the river masses of mud and stones slide thunderously down the mountainside into the valley. We are terrified.

By the next morning, the river has risen four meters and transformed itself into a wildly foaming muddy soup. We decide to head out at midday. Around each bend in the river waits a rapids and in every rapids the boats capsize; it is like a law of nature. When we capsize in the four-kilometer-long (about 2.5 mi.) Alei Rapids, the raging current and high waves make it impossible to right the boat. For more than ten minutes, we clutch the lifelines in the torrent. The rope cuts deeply into my flesh and I swallow a lot of water. I would like to let go, but that would be certain death.

The next segment of the Yangzi, the Jinsha River, flows through my home village. From the time I was a little girl I heard the eerie story of the river fairy who kidnaps people. In fact, the upper branch of the Jinsha River has claimed many lives. Yao Mashu, who in 1985 made the first attempt at the Yangzi in a rubber boat, suffered a fatal accident in the Tongjia Gorge of the Jinsha. Now, ten men from our expedition determine to attempt this section. When they emerge from the gorge at Yeba in Zhibaiyu District, seven people are missing. In Batang, we fish out of the river a red rubber boat and a few waterproof containers, but there is no sign of our friends. Stunned, we begin to search along the steep banks with the help of soldiers stationed there. I am so exhausted I could weep. The sun burns, I get a nosebleed, and I fall ever farther behind. Finally I manage to catch up with the others, who have just fished a life jacket and a paddle out of the water. Our faces darken at the sight of these familiar things. If our friends are still alive and we do not find them in time, they could freeze or starve.

For three days we climb around in the mountains in the burning sun, comb through the forests, lose our way. Our provisions are long since gone and we gather a few wild berries to still our hunger. The berries make us sick, and three of us have symptoms of poisoning. It rains again, and we wrap ourselves in our jackets and spend the night in a cave in the cliff. On the fourth day we see a rich, green field of grain, a few mud huts, and fruit gardens. We run to one of the huts, and the door is open, but it is utterly silent, no one is home. In the next hut, the same. The inhabitants are probably in the mountains harvesting or have gone to a market in the next valley, so we boil water for ourselves. After we have eaten a few nuts and had something to drink, we spread out some straw in the hut and lie down to sleep.

After five days we finally arrive back in Batang, full of hope, only to hear, "Kong is dead. We watched with our own eyes as he was torn away and we couldn't save him." I cannot make a sound. . . .

When we arrive at the famous Tiger's Leap Gorge, we see that it deserves its name: only a tiger could leap across it. It is sixteen kilometers (about 10 mi.) long and drops two hundred meters (660 ft. or 220 yd.). Its valley, three thousand meters (9,900 ft. or 3,300 yd.) deep, is not quite 30 meters (99 ft. or 33 yd.) wide at its narrowest point. It has eighteen dangerous rapids whose roaring can be heard at a distance of several kilometers. This gorge is a challenge to us all.

On 12 September, Sun Zhiling and Lang Baoluo step into their boat. Thousands watch from the banks as the little boat is dragged into the depths by a huge breaker, turns over, and splits apart. Sun Zhiling's head surfaces briefly and then disappears from view. Lang Baoluo, clinging to the wreckage, is driven toward a towering cliff, and, with immense difficulty, he manages to clamber on. He is trapped there for four days and nights until he can finally be rescued by a special army team from Chengdu together with volunteer helpers from the local population.

Wan Ming, a reporter for the newspaper *Junge Welt,* is killed by a rock while crossing under a waterfall. The same day a spectator falls off the mountainside. When we arrive at the village of Qiaotou, we learn that a truck filled with people has plunged into Tiger's Leap Gorge. In one day the Jinsha River has washed more than ten bodies into the gorge.

With growing anguish I have seen one opportunity after another to attempt the most dangerous rapids pass me by. What is the point of taking part in a rafting expedition without going through any of the "king rapids"? I was the first of the four to apply to take the trip through Tiger's Leap Gorge, and I will regret for the rest of my life that I did not get to go. However, the Jinsha River has more "king rapids" that have never been traversed.

After I have thought it over, I decide to ask the expedition leader one last time to let me go through the Lao Jun Rapids. I implore him, reminding him that we four women expedition members represent the women of China, and I am also a police officer and a member of a national minority. The Lao Jun Rapids are in Liangshan, the autonomous territory of my Yi people. I am the only representative of Liang region, and the entire region will be watching me. It is not possible *not* to let me go. At my urging and request, the command staff decides that Song Yuanqing, Yang Xie, and I will be allowed to ride the Lao Jun Rapids.

The Lao Jun Rapids, one of the "king rapids," are four kilometers (about 2.5 mi.) long and fall forty meters (132 ft.). More than six hundred cliffs jut out of the water from the mountains on both banks, creating enormous whirlpools. The cliffs are over ten meters (33 ft.) high and very sharp edged; we take an enclosed boat, and if it slams into a cliff it can easily disintegrate. Strokes of good fortune are especially important when passing through the Lao Jun Rapids. If we are lucky and do not land in any of the caves, it will be a great success. If we are driven into a cave, our colleagues will only be able to watch without the slightest possibility of saving us.

At 2:10 in the afternoon, the closed-cabin boat transports us toward the last "king rapids" of the Yangzi. As soon as we pass the first set of rapids, the boat tips and we are all thrown off balance. Shortly thereafter, the second rapids follow, and like a flash of lightning we plunge down a ten-meter (33 ft.) drop and crash into a cliff. The boat spins around, and water gushes through the portholes, up to our hips within moments. I hold the radio to my chest to protect it. My companions press their backs against the portholes to seal them, but the water keeps streaming in. We cannot bail and are in danger of drowning in the boat.

From outside we can hear only roaring; heaven and earth seem to collapse as if the end of the world has come. It is dark, the water is now up to our chests, and we have lost our link to the outer world because the radio has gotten wet. We have lost our orientation and do not know where north, south, east, and west are. I am convinced that we will die here today. In mortal fear we three have unconsciously joined hands.

While I am contemplating my fate, I hear Yang Xie say, "While we still have some strength, let's smash the boat and get out, we're almost out of air." I want out, too; seeing the sky while you are dying is better than suffocating in here. But then Song says: "Wait a minute," and from a distance we hear a siren that quickly gets louder. The storm boat! If we yell, we will be saved. In Tiger's Leap Gorge the storm boat had carried out successful rescues three times, so we have no doubt that it can bring us safely to shore. But the siren disappears. We all burst into tears. Don't these people know how much danger we are in? Do they want to test how much longer we can live? When we can no longer hear the boat, one of us cuts the rope that is wrapped around the porthole. We climb out and look for the storm boat. Gradually it becomes clear that it has been sunk by a breaker. The four members of the rescue squad take refuge on our boat. There are now seven people clinging to the roof, and we are propelled further down the river, tossed by every wave. We are utterly exhausted. Wang Yan, the group leader, decides that we should try to swim ashore. "No, we can't swim!" Mu Xia and La Yong cry in panic. "What? You're a rescue crew and you can't swim?" we bellow.

Gradually, darkness falls, a strong wind blows on the river, and we have no choice but to continue floating downstream. After about thirty kilometers (about 19 mi.) we see two wooden barges on the shore, from which people are illegally gathering state-owned wood from the river. For us they are angels of mercy. We all yell our heads off, calling for help. But the peasants do not understand what is happening. They point to us and laugh, their children wave pieces of clothing at us in greeting. The boat floats past quickly and a few hundred meters ahead we see giant rapids. We need only to hear the roaring of the water and see the foaming spray to know that these are no harmless rapids. At this moment we catch sight of a ferry on the bank. The ferry man realizes what is happening and rows very rapidly toward us, but only three people can board his small boat. We let the nonswimmers transfer and the boat brings them to shore.

"Let's go!" At Wan Yan's command, Yang Xie and I dive into the water. Immediately, my pants slip down to my thighs and it is impossible to either pull them up or take them off. My life jacket has lost its plugs and the air streaming out of it adds to the undertow pulling me downward. I panic and do not come back to the surface for a long time. When I do, Wang Yan and Yang Xie are already close to shore. I have lost all hope. Fifty meters, thirty meters, twenty meters, I am being driven toward the rapids by the current. I do not want to die, I want to live. The instinctive will to survive transforms my desperation into a last burst of strength. Ten meters, only ten more meters and I am swept into the last backwash before the rapids; I manage to swim to the bank and grab hold of a cliff. The people on the bank stare at me with open mouths, and without a word they throw me a root-bark rope.

Barefoot, we follow the people to their village. After the senior crew member has introduced us and the peasants learn that we have swum out of the Baihe Rapids, they receive us warmly. And even a girl along—they find that especially admirable. They tell us: "Until now, no one who has been caught in the rapids has come out alive."

The peasants here are poor, but they slaughter their only chicken for us. One of the women sees my long, tangled hair, bare feet, wet T-shirt, and sweatpants; she opens a trunk and takes out the embroidered shoes, embroidered jacket, and blue pants that she herself had worn at her wedding. She gives me these clothes to wear, combs my hair, and binds it together with a red wool cord. When I look at myself in the mirror, I discover for the first time that I am really quite pretty.

The next morning another high mountain waits for us. I am utterly convinced that in this life I will never want to climb another mountain. The village teacher shows us the way and over his radio we hear this report on Central Chinese Radio: "The Lao Jun Rapids have been successfully conquered by Jiehu Asha, Song Yuanqing, and Yang Xie, members of the Chinese Yangzi expedition." I am full of pride at this nonetheless I have to keep walking. Calm down, I say to myself, nobody is going to pick you up with a car.

After the last portion of the Jinsha River, from Leipo to Yibin, the dangerous section of the Yangzi expedition is over. One hundred and seven people who worked on the expedition come to a farewell celebration. I am the only woman among the fifteen rubber boat crew members, and I am very proud of having made it through this far. Past Yibin, the river becomes very wide. In its own way, the trip to Shanghai is a unique journey for me, crowned by a splendid triumphal reception prepared for us on the shore.

Pamela Tan

Huangnan scenery

Pamela Tan

A Tibetan and a Tu exchange greetings

THE SPIRIT DANCES:
GLIMPSES OF TIBETAN CULTURE IN QINGHAI PROVINCE

Pamela Tan

The name *Tibet* conjures up the mountainous land that borders Nepal and India, which the Tibetans themselves call the "Land of the Snows." This, however, is not the only place where Tibetans live. In ancient times the Tibetan kingdom stretched into what is Chinese Turkestan, or Xinjiang (literally, the new frontiers), and into much of western China. In the seventh century, the king of Tibet, Songsten Gampo, moved his capital to Lhasa and continued his military expansion. To improve political relations with his neighbors, China and Nepal, he accepted in marriage both the daughter of the emperor of China, Princess Wen Cheng, as well as the daughter of the king of Nepal, Princess Bhrikuti Devi. From the sixth to the ninth century, Tibet gained and lost a vast Central Asian empire. Large portions of China, including the modern provinces of Qinghai, Gansu, Sichuan, and Yunnan, came under Tibetan domination. The areas were settled by Tibetan soldiers who were garrisoned there and many Tibetans who migrated because the climate was less harsh than in the Land of the Snows.

Qinghai, known as Amdo in Tibetan, was once called Eastern Tibet. Here the people, particularly the nomads, retain their traditional lifestyle. Many places have been given the title of autonomous area, and one of these is the Huangnan Tibetan Autonomous Prefecture, or Rekong in Tibetan. Huangnan literally means "south of the Yellow River." This tiny prefecture, with a population of 180,319 people spread over an area of 190,000 square kilometers (76,000 sq. mi.) of mostly high-altitude mountainous land, is tucked away in the far southeastern corner of the province of Qinghai. It is 180 kilometers (about 119 mi.) from Xining, the provincial capital, and is only

311

accessible by road—a drive through spectacularly beautiful mountainous country.

The best time for the traveler to visit is from April to September; the rest of the year the land is covered with snow, and it is bitterly cold. The high altitude can make breathing difficult. Although 4,917 meters (about 14,750 ft.) above sea level is the highest altitude and more than half the prefecture is around 3,800 meters (about 12,540 ft.) above sea level, the prefecture township is only 2,800 meters high (about 9,240 ft.), which is moderately comfortable.

Tibetans comprise 66 percent of the prefecture population; Mongolians, 13 percent; Hui (Moslems), 7.6 percent; Sala, 0.6 percent; Tu, 3.8 percent; Han Chinese, 7.8 percent; and the remaining 1.2 percent includes other minorities such as the Baoan people. Tibetans and Mongolians, many of whom are nomads, speak Tibetan. They and the Tu people follow Tibetan Buddhism. Mandarin Chinese is, of course, the official language, and among ethnic minorities, only those who have an excellent command of both spoken and written Chinese can ever become government officials. Most of the Tibetan officials have been educated in Chinese schools or universities and are quite Sinicized. The Han Chinese do not excel in learning other people's languages; thus, those who have been sent to work in these parts can rarely speak the local language even after ten or twenty years of living there.

Although the Tibetan written language is uniform, there are many different dialects, and Tibetans in Qinghai speak with a very different accent from those in Lhasa. In Huangnan, there is much traditional Tibetan culture. It was here in the fifteenth century that the Buddhist religious Tankga paintings originated, and the tradition remains today despite having been banned from about 1958 to the mid-1980s. Another local tradition subjected to radical communist censure was what the Chinese called June Meeting Dances, or in Tibetan, Leru (Spirit Dances). These were also banned for some thirty years, but since the opening up of China in the eighties, these dances have returned even more strongly, in all their pageantry and color.

The Spirit Dances take place in the sixth month of the lunar calendar, which is around the end of July in our modern calendar. The festivities involve the participation of the entire village—men, women, young people, and children; even those who have been hospitalized try to return to the village for the event. The dances are a form of prayer to the spirits for a good

Girls on their way to the village temple

harvest, prosperity, and an auspicious year for each family. It is also a time for harmony and goodwill among the people. Each village has its spirit medium who, while in a trance, leads the dances. It is believed that some of the village spirits are brothers and that they must meet once a year in peace, friendship, and harmony; thus, the people of the villages concerned must also meet together in peace, friendship, and harmony. There is always great ceremony with drums and cymbals, firecrackers, and warrior-like cries from the men when the spirit medium from another village arrives at his spirit brother's village and, together with the dancers and the villagers, they all go to the village temple where the dances take place.

There is also a maidens' dance, which is extremely graceful and peaceful. All the girls wear dark red robes with deep indigo blue cuffs and have their sleek, black hair combed smoothly back under a long headdress of silver cymbals hanging down to the waist. The gentleness of the dance contrasts greatly with the drum dances of the young men and other dances performed on stilts.

The Spirit Dances provide a good opportunity for the villagers to dress up in their festive clothing. Normally the nomads and ordinary Tibetans wear their traditional clothing, while officials and students wear the Han Chinese attire consisting of Western trousers and jackets. But for the Spirit Dances, most people don their best thick woolen robes trimmed with otter fur and their silk brocade blouses. Those who do not have robes may borrow from their neighbors, friends, or relatives; young people will often stop in the homes of the older villagers to be shown how to dress.

The dances last for a week. They begin with a ceremony where the village spirit medium goes from house to house with a blessing and receives, in turn, the good wishes of the villagers. Then each day the villagers go to the temple to watch the dances being performed in the courtyard. All families make offerings to the gods and spirits and to Buddha, while prayers are chanted. Incense and small pine branches are burned day and night. The dances are not only celebrated by the Tibetans, but also by the Mongolians and the Tu people. Perhaps these dances are also partly remnants from the Bon religion, which was largely shamanistic and traditionally practiced for centuries in Tibet prior to the introduction of Buddhism in the seventh century. Among the men, rites are performed in which the village medium will go into a trance and have young men stick needles

The maidens' dance

On her way to the temple

into his cheeks or cut his forehead. Yet these wounds will heal quickly without leaving a scar.

Consumerism has not yet found its way to these parts as it has in China proper, so the people remain as yet unspoiled by the greed, extreme individualism, selfishness, and self-indulgence of consumer societies. Even crime is not a problem as there are only about three criminal cases a year in some of the counties of the prefecture, and these do not necessarily involve nomads, but generally officials or other townspeople. There is almost no industry and therefore no pollution; the air is pure and clean, and the land still in its natural beauty. Maybe you should go before it changes.

Here people have time for each other; they are warm and hospitable to each other and to any stranger who may pass their way. It is the custom to give food and rest to anyone who comes to the house. First, guests are given tea, then water is brought for them to wash their hands and faces after a dusty journey, and finally food is offered. There is always bread with a crispy brown crust, as well as vegetable and meat dishes. In the extended family, where grandparents, parents, sons, and daughters-in-law live in the same household, it is the mother who does most of the cooking with the help of the daughters-in-law, who do the heavy work and the cleaning up. Grandchildren are also cared for by the mother, while the sons and daughters-in-law work in the fields or care for the animals.

The scenery is magnificent, the land remains as yet unpolluted, and the people are kind. Their philosophy is to live in harmony with nature and all sentient beings, as dictated by Tibetan Buddhism. Many of the Han Chinese are also followers of this religion, yet some people consider it "backward." There are many valuable minerals in these mountains, including gold, and according to Chinese government officials, the area has great potential of being transformed and exploited. And they are doing their best to find the capital to change it all.

WOMEN FARMERS
IN QINGHAI PROVINCE

Pamela Tan

China, the third largest country in the world, was in ancient times comprised of seven kingdoms, each of which
had its own written and spoken language, customs, government, and army. In 221 B.C. China was unified by the first
emperor, Qin Shi Huangdi, who subjugated the six other kingdoms and unified the language, currency, weights, measures,
and roads, thus making possible the China that we know today.
Nonetheless, traveling through China in the late twentieth century, be it in the north, east, south, or west, one is struck by the
tremendous diversity of the land and the people. The landscape
and the flora and fauna vary; the spoken dialects differ considerably; and even the the physical features of the people are as
different as are their many customs, attitudes, and lifestyles.

Agriculture has always been important in China, and until
recently China was primarily an agricultural country. Today,
however, agriculture accounts for only 30 percent of the gross
domestic product, although it is still the source of over 80 percent of employment. Life in small towns and villages in the remote Chinese countryside is so different from the cities. Here,
the drive to modernization and industrialization is largely
thwarted by the lack of capital and technical skills as well as inaccessibility due to long distances, poor roads, high mountains,
and high altitudes. So rural folk live between a traditional subsistence economy and growing market forces that are slowly
challenging and changing their outlook, values, lifestyles, and
family structure.

In the mountainous northwest province of Qinghai, peasants work on small-scale farms. There is no population density
problem here as some four million people live in an area of
737,000 square kilometers (294,800 sq. mi). Houses are made

A mother and her two daughters weeding the winter wheat. "It hasn't rained for eight months—what will we do if the crop fails? There'll be nothing to eat."

Some women make extra money weaving carpets at home. "My shoulders and back ache," she said, "but it makes me happy dyeing the wools in the colors I like and making up the patterns."

of packed earth. They are brown like the earth around them. Most houses are built in the traditional style with a high wall, a large wooden gate, an outer courtyard for the animals, and an inner courtyard for the family. Some of the houses have beautifully carved wooden eaves and beams inside. Tibetans particularly like such houses. Trees and flowers grow in the courtyards, which are cool in the summer and sheltered from the icy winds of the winter. These parts are high above sea level, some three thousand meters (9,900 ft.) and more. The temperature goes down to a freezing minus twenty or even thirty degrees Celsius (–4° to –22°F) in the winter but is a pleasant twenty-five to thirty degrees Celsius (77° to 86°F) in the summer.

In ancient times Qinghai was part of Tibet and is referred to as Amdo in Tibetan. It is home to many ethnic minorities, mainly Tibetan, Hui (Moslem), Tu, Sala, Mongolian, and Kazak. Today the Han Chinese are gradually increasing in numbers. Yet despite the diverse ethnic mixture in one province, the people can live peacefully. The Hui tend to live together in their own villages, sometimes with the Sala who share their Moslem religion. The Tibetans, Mongolians, and Tu—who all follow Tibetan Buddhism—often live in the same villages, together with some Han Chinese, while a large number of Tibetans, Mongolians, and Kazaks are nomads.

For those who live in villages, the wheat or corn they grow feeds their families and livestock for the coming year. In 1994, rain was scarce for the first eight months and the drought choked the winter wheat as it struggled through the parched earth. One of the biggest problems in these parts is water. There are few reservoirs and no pipes, only small water cellars belonging to each household, which collect the snow and the little rainfall there may have been during the year. What is to be done if the crop fails? There is no welfare system. To relieve the situation, the local government might organize for a few months a group of men to build roads, do mining, or even dig for gold, which is plentiful in the high altitudes of Qinghai. This means the men must leave home to earn some money, and the burden of the children and the household falls on the women.

Women in Qinghai are strong and capable. In this part of China where there is very little industry and people are still in tune with nature, life is simple, hard, and revolves around the basics. From the time they are young, girls help their mothers to weed the wheat (everything is done by hand for there are few machines), feed the animals, and fetch firewood. Grain is stored, and ground when needed; in most villages there is usually one electric grinding machine. Cooking oil is also processed as the family needs it. By the time a girl is married, she knows how to run a household and understands family life. She is brought up to learn how to be a good and wise housewife. In these parts, a girl's physical appearance is not the only criterion for marriage; people look for character, the ability to manage a household, knowledge about animals, and so on. The Han Chinese and the Hui have arranged or semiarranged marriages, in which the prospective bride and groom are introduced by a go-between, and if they feel they can get along together, they agree to marry. However, it is often the family, particularly the mother, who approves or disapproves of a son or daughter's marriage plans; the young couple generally go along with what their parents want. The Tibetans, on the other hand, have mainly love matches, and once married it is a lifelong commitment. People in these parts do not take lightly to divorce.

Be they Han Chinese, Tibetan, Mongolian, Hui, Sala, or Tu, women in Qinghai have a difficult life. For some women life is harder than most. Take Ma Saigao, a Moslem woman of thirty-eight, for example. When we entered her well-swept courtyard, she was feeding the chicks. She looked up, smiled, and greeted us as one would old friends. Her head was covered with the black georgette head cover Moslem women wear, her olive skin was smooth, her eyes bright, her jacket and trousers were simple and clean. She led us into the main room of her house, which was large and sunny. The bedding quilts were neatly folded on the large *kang*—a large earthen bed that takes up half the room and is heated from beneath. Aside from serving as a bed, the kang is large enough to carry a small, low table around which a number of people can sit, drink tea, and eat. There was very little furniture, so we sat on the side of the *kang* and chatted, while Ma, as is the custom, busied herself making tea.

Ma is the mainstay of her household. Ten years ago, her husband contracted an illness and, not having enough money for proper treatment, he was left blind. Some time after, their son became ill with meningitis, which left him deaf and mute. Their eight-year-old daughter cannot go to school because she has to stay home to help her mother take care of her father, who cannot walk far without her. For in these high mountainous villages, there are many steep cliffs and places that spell danger to a blind man. The deaf and mute son also cannot do much on his own, and there are no special schools here for such children.

Pamela Tan

Returning to the village with grain.

Yet, to look at Ma Saigao, one would hardly dream that her life was full of such difficulties. Fully confident, she cares for the sheep and raises chicks. She was sure that if she could obtain a loan, she could buy some cattle, fatten them, and sell them for a profit. Unfortunately the bank, like banks all over the world, does not consider a rural woman entrepreneur a good risk.

Life is centered around the family. The extended family is there, not always under the same roof, but often in the same village. In these parts people respect women who are capable, who can run the household efficiently, and whose families live in harmony because the women know how to sort out problems. Daughters who do well at school and can pass exams are given help by their families, for everyone knows that if they can get into a tertiary institution, it will mean a better-paying job in the future. So a family may have a semiliterate daughter at home, who helps her parents with the farm, and another daughter in college.

In my travels I came across a Tibetan man baking bread, while his wife had gone to the fields to weed. I had lunch in a Hui Moslem household, where the husband set the table, put the chairs in place, and fetched water and towels for the guests to wash their hands. He said of his wife, "She is so busy, she has too much to do" and one could see he loved and respected his wife, who was a quiet, gentle woman. They were both in their early forties, with two teenage sons at school. In another household, the Chinese host carried the food in from the kitchen, poured the tea, and then carried the dirty bowls back to the kitchen. He said laughingly, "You see, we men have made some progress. In our parents' day this would never have happened; in those days men never went near the kitchen."

The women of these parts are not meek, shy, nor do they appear oppressed by the men. On the contrary, they give the impression that they are men's partners. And women know how to give "face" to their men. In a conversation, when I asked a Tibetan woman who kept the family money, she looked at her husband and smiled, saying, "He does!" However, one got the impression from the other things she said that she actually held the purse strings. And decisions? He made them of course. Wise women understand diplomacy, especially at home. In some villages, 50 percent of the women controlled the purse strings. The overwhelming majority of women I met told me that they discussed family matters with their husbands, and any big decision taken was made in agreement.

In order to make some extra money, women weave carpets as well as grow Chinese spice pepper trees and rhubarb (for Chinese medicine). Others raise chickens, pigs, mohair goats, sheep, and cattle. Their workload is extremely heavy. The men plough and sow the fields, but it is mainly the women who weed. The men take the manure to the fields and spread it, but the women have to cook, wash, clean, and tend to the extra jobs they may have. In many areas, water has to be fetched in buckets, and although it is generally the women and children who do this, some men are often seen waiting in line for water when the springs are slow.

Traders travel to these villages to buy the carpets, pepper, rhubarb, pigs, sheep, cattle, or whatever the farmers have to sell. For their part, traders bring wools, dyes (women who weave carpets dye them to the colors they want), embroidery silks and cottons, fabrics, pots and pans, and anything the women farmers want to buy. The distances are so great, and the women do not have time to walk twenty kilometers (about 12 mi.) or more to the nearest township. One woman told me that in all her fifty-two years, she had only been to the township twice. If people fall ill or need to go to the township or to the county town (which is bigger), they generally have to ride a tractor or a truck. There are simply no buses into the mountains.

UIGURS AND KAZAKS IN XINJIANG

Pamela Tan

If you look at the map of China, you will see the largest province in the far northwest stretching up toward the interior of Central Asia. It is called Xinjiang, which literally means "new frontiers." It has an area of more than 1.6 million square kilometers (640,000 sq. mi.)—one-sixth the size of China—and only a population of some 13 million. Twenty-two percent of the people live in the cities, while 78 percent live in rural areas and are farmers or herders, some of whom are nomadic. This was the land through which the ancient silk route passed.

The principal ethnic minority of Xinjiang are the Uigurs; the whole area is called the Xinjiang Uigur Autonomous Region. Uigurs number about 5.3 million people. They are of Turkish origin and migrated to the Tarim Basin and the oases of Turfan in Xinjiang in the ninth century. Their language is similar to modern-day Turkish, thus, there is no language barrier between Turks and Uigurs. In fact, since the opening up of China in the 1980s, many young Uigur women have married Turks and gone to live in Turkey. The Uigurs are Sunni Moslems. Those who live in the cities often have small businesses, while a number of Uigurs work in government and the professions. The majority, however, live in small villages and tend to their farms. They grow fruit (melons, grapes, apricots, and pears), wheat, and cotton. Xinjiang is famous throughout China for its delicious Hami melons (like the honeydew), while the grapes of Turfan, some of which grow overhanging the main streets and every household, are sweet and delectable.

The Uigurs are an outgoing, friendly, and hospitable people. They love to dance, sing, and play the *rewapu*, a plucked stringed instrument like the balalaika. Women wear brightly

323

printed silk dresses. They also love dresses of chiffon and chiffon velvet, which they wear every day. The Uigurs of north Xinjiang are more influenced by Central Asian and Russian cultural ideas, and although they are of the Moslem faith, very few wear a head covering. The Uigurs of south Xinjiang come more under Afghan influence; women wear head coverings and often the entire burka. Professional women and those who work in government organizations are directly influenced by the Han Chinese; they wear Western-style clothing.

The Uigurs are a romantic people. In the cities they choose their own marriage partners, with the approval of the parents, of course. The family is still an important part of Uigur society. If a Han Chinese man wants to marry a Uigur woman, he must become a Moslem. A Uigur wedding takes almost two days, with the good friends and sisters of the bride spending all day and a night with her, then helping her dress in the morning, while chatting and laughing. In the afternoon the bridegroom and his friends come to take the bride to the groom's home. Nowadays they will often go to a restaurant where they will feast, sing, and dance for hours on end.

Uigur men like to have a strong, masculine image, but perhaps not all men retain this at home. A friend told me how every week her father used to lock the front door, do the washing for her mother, and help her clean the house, but he would never allow his friends to know about it. Only until recently have washing machines come on the market; previously all washing was done in a wooden tub with a scrubbing board.

The Chinese have built unsightly concrete apartment blocks in Xinjiang as all over China. However, inside a Uigur home is an entirely different culture. There are beautiful hand-woven carpets on the walls and on the floors, and draped hangings in front of the door, giving the impression of a tent. Typically there is one large sofa in the main room with chairs placed along the wall at either side. Guest sit on the sofa, with the host, hostess, and other family members on the sides. There is always a table laden with sweetmeats, which include not only cakes but different kinds of fruits—some dried, some preserved in honey, and some cooked. Tea, usually served with milk, is offered with the sweets. After the sweets are eaten, the meal is served. The Uigurs eat pilaf, flat unleavened bread, and mutton.

Ürümqi is the capital of Xinjiang and is situated on the northern foothills of the Tianshan Mountains. It was formerly known as Dihua and renamed Ürümqi, Mongolian for "fine

Pamela Tan

Cooking

pastureland," in 1953. Today it is a sprawling metropolis with heavy traffic and pollution, spewing from its newly established industries.

Han Chinese are now the second largest group in Xinjiang, also around the 5.3 million mark. Since the 1950s, the Chinese government has had a steady policy of relocating Han Chinese to Xinjiang. Many were sent as youths in the 1950s to set up and work on large state farms. Their children were born and grew up in the region and know only Xinjiang as their home. Today it is customary for newly married Chinese couples to make a honeymoon trip to the eastern interior of China to visit relatives and friends of their parents. However, for centuries Xinjiang was one of those faraway places where the emperor sent disgraced officials or relatives he did not want killed, and for most Han Chinese it remains remote and quite foreign in language, custom, and environment.

In ancient times this land belonged to various small kingdoms, which were subjugated by powerful Chinese armies in the first century A.D. There remain many ethnic minorities such as the Kazaks, Mongolians, Hui (Moslem), Kirgize, Tajik, Russians, Manchus, Tartars, and Uzbeks in Xinjiang today.

The landscape here is very different from the scenery of China proper, and offers great variety within the region. Some

325

of the mountains rise as high as 8,611 meters (some 28,416 ft. or 9,472 yd.) above sea level, and even in the scorching heat of summer one can always see snow-capped mountains in the distance. The surface of Aydingkol Lake, however, is in the Turfan Depression and is 154.43 meters (about 510 ft. or 170 yd.) below sea level. China's largest desert, the Taklimakan, covers 129,600 square miles (335,664 sq. km.) in southern Xinjiang. In the Tianshan Mountains, which divide north and south Xinjiang, the scenery is majestic and awesome; its glacial features are similar to that of Switzerland or New Zealand. One of the most exquisite places in the Tianshan Mountains is the Lake of Heaven, set against snow-capped mountains and renowned for its peaceful beauty.

In the mountain regions live the Kazaks who are herders. The majority are nomadic, but gradually the Chinese government has been establishing settlements to provide them with permanent housing. This spells a change of lifestyle for the Kazaks: they will cease to be nomads. Yet for the older men and women, children, widows, and those whose health is poor, a permanent home means warm shelter during the bitter winters when the temperature goes down to around minus thirty degrees Celsius (−22° F). It means the animals, too, have a shelter for the winter; when the summer comes, the eldest son and his wife can take the sheep and goats to the summer pastures, while their parents remain in the permanent settlement and care for the grandchildren. The children can go to school and in the evenings there is entertainment for the family in the form of television and radio. In Xinjiang, radio and television are broadcast in Uigur, Kazak, and Chinese.

On an ordinary day, the Kazak herder woman is the first up and the last to retire in her family. She begins by milking the animals, then starts the fire and cooks breakfast. She has to boil the milk, make butter, do the washing and cleaning, and, when she has the time, she will make felt from lambs' wool, dye it in the colors she chooses, then sew clothing from it. Her house may not have running water, but her husband or her son will fetch the water from the well, as the men generally help the women do heavy jobs. You would be surprised at how much clout these herder women have; their husbands respect them, for in these societies women have their place and their dignity. What counts is the ability of a woman to be a good partner and a wise mother.

Each year from February to April, during the lambing period, women work day and night with the men, caring for each newly born lamb. The families have a special room for the pregnant ewes, which is heated by coal fires—there is coal almost everywhere in Xinjiang. As soon as the lamb is born, the women cut the birth cord and tie it with catgut, then swab the lamb's navel with iodine, and pop a tablet of oxytetracycline down its throat to prevent it from contracting dysentery or rheumatism. According to some herdswomen, it takes two weeks for the fine-wool lambs to be able to find their mother, and during this time the women make sure each lamb finds the right mother. The coarse-wool lambs are more clever, they say; they can find their mother's nipple right from the beginning.

Festival time is particularly busy as there are many preparations. The house has to be cleaned, food prepared, as well as new clothes made for the children. Each Kazak house is decorated with handmade carpets on the walls, brightly colored mosaic felt rugs on the large platform beds, and embroidered covers for the sofas, the television, and the sewing machine. These are made by the women in their spare time, and they reveal the artistic abilities and sense of color of their creators. Some families have single or double four-poster beds with red velvet hangings, which are piled high with folded quilts under brightly embroidered covers. Kazak women love color and take great pride in their appearance. They, too, like to wear dresses of chiffon and silk and will wear these to work in the shearing sheds, with colored scarves on their heads. In the winter they wear thick woolen skirts and stockings.

Kazaks always pay great attention to relations with their neighbors. Neighbors help and care for each other as though they were of the same family. Families that have no grandparents to care for the children when the parents go to the pastures with the sheep will often leave the children with neighbors, who care for them as their own. When a misfortune such as death strikes a family, the whole village will come to help, to comfort, and to pay respects. When an occasion of joy arises, everybody comes to congratulate the family. In celebration, the family will kill a sheep and serve it with pilaf to the guests. It was on such an occasion that I visited a herder household when they were celebrating a good turn in the family's fortune. While the sheep was being slaughtered and cooked, relatives and close family friends sat and chatted in the main room with the family. Women guests sat together drinking tea and talking in one room, while male guests were in another. Kazak women sing beautifully and the custom is to improvise words to ancient tunes. One woman, a widow named Zaieenashi, sang to me in her lovely deep and melodious voice:

You have come from afar,
We welcome you and invite you to partake
Of our food, our kindness and protection,
Before you fly again with the birds to
Distant mountains.

Do men beat their wives? It happens, I was told, because life has changed and there are young men who cannot find jobs, so they get drunk and when they come home they may beat their wives. But neighbors and other family members will intervene to try and calm things. Consumerism and unfullfilled ambitions, as well as lack of suitable jobs, skills, and schools are causing changes in ideas, attitudes, and lifestyles

Eating Bitterness, Eating Fragrance: The Cultural Context of Food

Lida Junghans

In China the language of food and eating is used to express far more than the mere fact of a meal. "Have you eaten?" (*Ni chi guole ma?*) was in recent times, and in some parts of the country still is, a common way of asking about a person's well-being, harkening back to times when famine was a very real threat and when having a full stomach was the greatest contentment imaginable.

To eat from an "iron rice bowl" (*tiefanwan*) means to have a permanent job in the state sector of the economy. The idea is that such jobs have the guarantee of security, unlike temporary jobs, or jobs under the more rickety auspices of the collective. (Collectives are usually based on geographic association, at the level of the street, neighborhood, village, or township.) Nowadays people say that everyone's rice bowl has turned to mud, excepting of course the lucky few who have secured "golden rice bowls" (working in banking or any highly lucrative field) or "porcelain rice bowls" (nice to look at, but easily shattered—used to refer to employment in joint ventures with overseas investors).

To eat bitterness (*chi ku*) is to suffer and endure hardship, an ability with which, it is said, Chinese people are well endowed. To eat vinegar (*chi cu*) is to be jealous, as of a rival in romance, while to eat fragrance (*chi xiang*) is to be well-liked and sought after.

To eat at all is to eat cooked grain, usually assumed to be rice (*chi fan*), for it is not a meal unless there is the *fan*. Generally, the grain of choice for southerners is rice, while northerners and westerners eat milled grains in the form of noodles and buns. These differences have everything to do with the ecological conditions of agriculture, because the infrastruc-

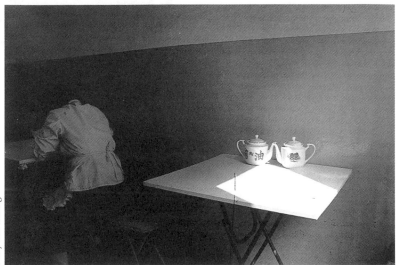

Nelly Rau-Häring

Nelly Rau-Häring

ture of the country cannot support the large-scale transport of staple foodstuffs.

The fact that food is consumed close to where it is grown makes for profound differences in regional cuisines. The regional differences in cuisine are imagined to affect the tastes of individuals. "You're from Sichuan? You must like hot peppers in all of your dishes!" Anecdotes about regional tastes in food as well as regional pronunciations of standard Mandarin are common conversational currency on board trains and in other places, where people who are unfamiliar to each other find themselves together temporarily. Because the mass transport of foodstuffs has never been widespread, indigenous travelers often bring back local delicacies (known as *te chan*, or specialty products) as gifts and souvenirs from their journeys. Tea, from the hills of Anhui and Zhejiang, where the clouds are known to hang low, providing the optimum growing conditions; vinegar from Zhenjiang; melons from Xinjiang; tree ears from Jiangxi; pineapples from Guangxi. Following this logic, fresh fruits are generally considered a great luxury in all but the southernmost provinces where they grow in abundance. A bulging sack of choice fruits is a far more common gift to take to someone's home than a bouquet of flowers would be.

The logic of Chinese medicine and of Chinese cuisine each grow out of philosophical and aesthetic notions of harmony and complementarity. Traditional Chinese cosmology orients the things of the universe according to intricate theories of correspondence. The principles of *yin* and *yang* organize the natural world into interdependent complementarities. The five essential elements (metal, wood, water, fire, and earth) also have their correspondences in the vital organs of the body (heart, liver, lungs, kidneys, and stomach) and in the five tastes: bitter, sweet, salt, sour, and hot.

In cooking, yin and yang relate to foods that promote hot and cold principles in the body. But the particular foods associated with hot and cold are difficult to grasp intuitively. Fish with eggs in the belly are hot, while egg-less fish are not. Crustaceans and mung bean soup are good cooling antidotes to the hotness that can be aggravated in summertime. This knowledge forms part of every Chinese cook's common sense about how to combine foods harmoniously. Ideally every dish should be composed in a way that is pleasing to see, to taste, and to smell.

Banqueting is an extremely important social ritual in contemporary China. Business deals are clinched over toasts at the banquet table. Powerful sorghum- or maize-based liquors are served in thimble-sized cups and are ceremoniously downed before the commencement of any eating. Many who can afford it prefer to entertain distinguished guests at banquets in restaurants rather than in their own humble quarters, and the measure of a wedding is the number of tables of guests the groom's family invited to the celebratory meal.

While banquet tables are not segregated, it is nevertheless striking to note the small numbers of women participating in the burgeoning restaurant-banquet culture. The male domination of ritualized banqueting corresponds with the gender imbalance in the upper echelons of power within the party organization as well as in the newly emerging business and entrepreneurial classes. Mixing business with the pleasures of food and drink at the table seems to follow the model of Japanese *sarariiman* practice, where drinking, smoking, and singing along with the karaoke machine are all used to signify alliance and close collegial relationships. Rarely do women participate in these events, which generally grow out of work-place obligations. Women who do take part and enjoy it, however, are thought of as either an unfeminine breed apart, or as extremely self-sacrificing, since it is assumed that women are more comfortable in familiar and domestic settings than they are out in the social world.

To be invited for a meal in a private home is a great honor, and often promises far more satisfaction than any meal that money might buy. It is impossible to generalize about the household division of labor, especially regarding food purchase and preparation. It is quite common for both members of a couple to share in the marketing and cooking.

Even though refrigerators are becoming common in the home, it is still thought necessary to shop every day for perishable foods. While there is a trend toward the use of bottled gas for cooking, many households still rely on coal bricks in the kitchen. Because stir-frying—a common technique in the preparation of many popular dishes—produces a great deal of smoke, there is an unusually high incidence of lung disease among Chinese women (cigarette smoking among women is rare).

Sturdy, large-capacity thermoses are a standard kitchen item. Boiled water for drinking, cooking, and cleaning is kept in them because tap water is never safe to drink. Drinking cold beverages is uncommon. Notions of the effects of cold liquid on the internal organs along with knowledge of the dangers of drinking unpurified water combine to make the present generation who drink cold, carbonated beverages pioneers.

Soda pop is not the only newcomer to the mainland Chinese diet. There is a growing awareness about the benefits of milk products for children and pregnant women. Snackfoods, sweets, and instant soups that are recognized throughout much of the world are gaining a presence in Chinese markets. And fast-food chains are becoming noticeable in prominent places on the streets of large cities. Most adults, however, are not tempted to forego the tastes, flavors, and lifestyles they have grown up with. According to the sensibilities of many, the art of food and the rituals of eating are vital aspects of their Chinese identity.

DOS AND DON'TS FOR TRAVELERS

Margit Miosga

Dos

1. At least once, get up very early in the morning—6:00 to 7:00—and go to the closest public park to watch people doing *taijiquan*. No one will mind should you join in!

2. Do go to a Chinese film, if the opportunity arises. Even if you do not understand a single word, the experience will be fun and interesting as well.

3. Visit the many "night-markets" in China, where clothing and food are sold. Do enjoy the sights and do not hesitate to try the tasty, fresh-fried little dishes available for pennies.

4. Dare to try local restaurants. If no menu is available in your language, look at what others are eating and point to the dishes you want, or go into the kitchen and choose from what is there.

5. Always have your own chopsticks with you. You will need them in local restaurants in the large cities, and even more so in small towns and villages. Try practicing at home with chopsticks: if you can manage raw cucumber pieces or oily peanuts, you are doing well. If you prefer, of course, you can carry your own fork!

6. In China, you order as many dishes as there are persons at your table—plus one. Rice comes separately. Soup is always the last course. If there are three people eating, you might order one meat dish, one fish dish, one vegetable dish, and one tofu dish plus rice. Of course, the custom is to share all food around the table.

7. Always have toilet paper with you.

8. When you plan a long stay in a city, the best way to move around is on bicycles. Follow the mainstream of riders! You can hire bikes everywhere.

9. If you plan to travel by train, you must get your ticket at least one or two days in advance. To travel to smaller towns, perhaps even three days in advance. There is no computer network linking the cities, so you cannot book for a long journey with many stops all in advance. And yes, this will slow your journey somewhat.

10. If you want to meet, or even to observe, ordinary Chinese travelers, take the "hard sleeper" or the "hard seater" (i.e., the cheapest class of ticket). If you do so, you must not be fussy about noise, odors, or perhaps even hygiene. If you take the "soft sleeper" or the "soft seater," you will be more comfortable, and you will be traveling with Communist Party cadres or a more financially comfortable group of Chinese citizens.

11. Do prepare yourself for some level of discomfort or some surprising sights. While spitting on floors does not occur often in large cities, you may see some of that. Similarly, you may experience overcrowded buses, delayed planes, curt or uninterested salespersons—but, of course, you may find these at home as well!

Don'ts

1. If you must argue with a member of a hotel's or restaurant's staff, or some bureaucratic personnel, don't shout, scream, or insult a Chinese person, even if you are certain you are right. Such behavior will not help you. Search for a way to settle the problem courteously, with an agreement. Loud attacks or confrontations make people feel as though they have "lost face." If there seems to be no way out of the situation, ask to see the supervisor or "boss."

2. Don't be careless about your belongings. Pickpockets are new in China, and especially active at tourist spots and in overcrowded places.

3. Don't trust traffic rules. There are none! The winner is always the strongest or largest or fastest.

4. Don't buy antiques at the markets, since they will not have the red seal of governmental approval necessary for export. If you buy in government stores, you will not only get the official seal but will also be assured of legitimacy; imitations are plentiful.

5. Even if the heat is sizzling, don't drink tap water or any other liquid that does not come out of a bottle you open yourself. Never accept ice cubes in a drink.

6. Don't eat ice cream or other milk products (except yogurt). Never eat fresh fruit that you cannot peel, and never eat fresh salad.

7. If you are lucky enough to be invited to a private home for dinner, don't stay long after the dinner itself has ended, no matter how many times your host urges you to do so. In "bohemian" or Westernized circles, this rule is not valid.

SUGGESTED READING

Susan Hawthorne

Increasing numbers of the many books and articles about China focus on women's achievements and on women's lives. The following is a small selection of books available in English that highlight women's lives. These books represent a range of perspectives, from Western women's views and analyses of China and its culture to works of autobiography, fiction, and poetry that delve deeply into the psyche of Chinese women. They also represent a range of views, from work that celebrates Chinese politics and culture to work that is highly critical.

Nonfiction

Gilmartin, Christina K., Gail Hershatter, Lisa Rofel, and Tyrene White, eds. 1994. *Engendering China: Women, Culture, and the State.* Cambridge, MA, and London: Harvard University Press. Pb. 454 pp.

A diverse collection of articles that offers a new look at historical representations of women, the role of learned women in the eighteenth century, and *nüshu*, women's writing. Contemporary Chinese medicine, prostitution, birth planning policies, work economics, and feminism are also considered.

Jung Chang. 1992. *Wild Swans.* New York and London: HarperCollins. Pb. 696 pp. Index, photographs.

In this powerful and astonishing book, Jung Chang creates a vivid portrait of three generations of women, in particular of her mother, Bao Qin. The book documents the travails of what appears to be the very model of the perfect Maoist family. The author's father, a cadre member before the Communist Party came to power, becomes the governor of a province; her mother is highly placed in the education system and had assisted in the downfall of the Guomindang. The children are bright and become peasants and members of the Red Guard. Even so, they are disgraced and made the objects of shame in a system that is too prone to the excesses of jealousy and fabricated crimes. But there are some lighter moments, such as the story told at family dinner to encourage Chinese children to eat: "Think of all the starving children in the West."

Kristeva, Julia. 1975. *About Chinese Women.* Translated by Anita Barrows. New York and London: Marion Boyars. Pb. 206 pp. Bibliography, photographs.

An interesting, if rather idiosyncratic and controversial, book about China and its women. Kristeva examines the social structures and the impact they have on women's lives. She looks at the historical shifts including a brief consideration of matrilinearity and a lengthy chapter on Confucianism, as well as at feminism, women's role in the Communist Party, and marriage laws and the difficulty of divorce. It includes portraits of mothers, artists, and intellectuals.

Min, Anchee. 1993. *Red Azalea.* New York and London: Pantheon. Pb. 252 pp.

Most of this story takes place on Red Fire Farm where Anchee Min meets Yan, the company leader. Her first impressions of Yan as powerful and forbidding are followed by a deepening respect and love for her. Anchee Min begins to emulate Yan by trying to work as quickly as the leader does, and Yan begins to reward her. As Anchee Min's awareness of her sexuality grows, she falls more and more deeply in love with Yan, and it is not long before they are sharing the same bed. Then, Anchee Min's life changes when she is chosen to audition for the role of Red Azalea in the fledgling Chinese film industry.

This is an unusual book—autobiography that reads as fiction, with a lesbian relationship during the Cultural Revolution, and a journey from Red Guard and peasant to film star. All of these are extraordinary stories in themselves. As an extra plus, the book is well written and carries an emotional truth that's hard to achieve. The author's real strength is her ability to make a political point, to show the way that ideology creeps into every act, by conveying how life under the Cultural Revolution feels in her bones.

Morgan, Robin. 1992. "The Word of a Woman" in *The Word of a Woman: Selected Prose, 1968-1992.* New York: W. W. Norton. Pb. 304 pp. Index.

The work of Robin Morgan, a poet and theorist, is sheer pleasure to read and full of new ways of seeing—even the things we think we already know about. Her final essay, which gives the book its title, is an inspiring piece which draws on an ancient Chinese language spoken and written only by women. *Nushi* (women's writing)—also called *nüshu* in some texts—is believed to have been developed because women were forbidden to learn the standard script. (See the essay by Silber in Part 1 of this volume.)

Raymond, Janice. 1986. "More Loose Women: The Chinese Marriage Resisters" in *A Passion for Friends: Toward a Philosophy of Female Affection.* Boston: Beacon Press; London: The Women's Press. Pb. 320 pp.

This excellent chapter details the resistance of Chinese women to marriage, focusing on the silk industry workers of the Guangdong region. Raymond provides a feminist analysis of the reasons for the sisterhoods of the *Bu Luojia,* women forced to marry who never consummated their marriages, and the *Zishu nü* or "self combers," women who comb or arrange their own hair. The *Zishu nü* could not be engaged to or marry a man. Instead they formed partnerships with women and often lived collectively with other women. (See also *Women of the Silk,* fiction, below, and "Silk Workers" by Agnes Smedley in Part 1 of this volume.)

Smedley, Agnes. 1976. *Portraits of Chinese Women in Revolution.* Edited by Jan MacKinnon and Steve MacKinnon. Afterword by Florence Howe. New York: The Feminist Press at CUNY. Pb. 203 pp. Photographs.

This volume collects writings from the late thirties and forties, when Smedley spent many years behind the battle lines, often accompanying the Red Army, and working to support the revolution. Her portraits show a diversity of women's lives: the young and the old, rural workers, silk workers, miners, widows, and refugees. Three essays from this book are included in *China for Women.*

Yu Luojin. 1986. *A Chinese Winter's Tale: An Autobiographical Fragment.* Translated by Rachel May and Yu Luojin. Hong Kong: Renditions Paperbacks, The Research Centre for Translation, The Chinese University of Hong Kong. Pb. 210 pp.

An account of the Cultural Revolution that is both personal—the author describes the horrors of her marriage—and a compelling political tale. Yu writes vividly of the violence and paranoia of the Red Guard and of her brother's arrest and execution. Because of the controversy this book generated in China, the author sought political asylum in West Germany in 1986. The volume also contains a very useful "Glossary of Maospeak," which gives an insight into the abuses of language during the Cultural Revolution.

Fiction

Ding Ling. 1985. *Miss Sophie's Diary.* Translated by W. J. Jenner. San Francisco: China Books; Beijing: Panda Books. Pb. 271 pp.

A collection of short stories by China's foremost twentieth-century writer. The title story, first published in 1928, portrays the frustrations and emotions of a young woman. Controversial at the time of publication, this novella deals frankly with the sexual feelings of its narrator. Other stories in the collection center on Shanghai in the 1930s, rural life, death, and the war against Japan.

Li Ang. 1990. *The Butcher's Wife.* Translated from Chinese by Howard Goldblatt and Ellen Yeung. Boston: Beacon Press. Pb. 142 pp.

A most disturbing book, *The Butcher's Wife,* described as pornographic when it was first published in Taiwan in 1983, chillingly portrays the range of brutalities perpetrated against the butcher's wife. Lin Shi is raped, beaten, starved, and publicly humiliated and degraded. Li Ang, in passages that resolutely resist a pornographic reading, describes how the husband, Chen Jiangshui, a pig slaughterer by trade, experiences pleasure. Eventually, Lin Shi kills her husband, and although all in the village know what he has done to her, it is Lin Shi who is punished.

Li Fu-ching. 1975. *Island Militia Women.* Beijing: Foreign Languages Press. Pb. 296 pp. Illustrations.

If you want to get a sense of what kind of fiction was being pushed during the Cultural Revolution, this is a useful work to look at. Highly ideological, complete with militia chants, it also tells a good story. The novel centers on the leader of a women's militia unit on a small island off the coast of China. The unit works to defend China from the United States and Taiwan while developing skills of leadership. This is very much a period piece and should be read for the insights it gives into the power of ideology.

Nieh, Hualing. 1981. *Two Women of China: Mulberry and Peach.* Translated by Jane Parish Yang and Linda Lappin. Beijing: New World Press. Pb. 257 pp. Also available under the title *Mulberry and Peach.* London: The Women's Press. Hb. 201 pp.

Mulberry's life begins in Nanjing in 1929. She runs away during the war with Japan and later watches the fall of Beijing and the disintegration of the old order. By 1958, while Mulberry is hiding for two years in Taiwan, Peach comes into being. It is Peach who deals with the U.S. Immigration Department, while Mulberry tries to hold onto her memories. An extraordinary novel about psychic disintegration and the emotional impact political events have on individuals.

Tao Yang. 1986. *Borrowed Tongue.* Hong Kong: Renditions Paperbacks, The Research Centre for Translation, The Chinese University of Hong Kong. Pb. 216pp.

Tao Yang, exiled at age seven from mainland China to Taiwan and separated from her mother and sister, feels forced to speak in a borrowed tongue. When she returns to China to see her family as her mother is dying, she must confront at last the betrayal she has felt, the fear that perhaps her mother never wanted her. Caught in the contradiction of an obsession with her absent mother, and the down-to-earth truths of her own children, who reassuringly tell her, "You're weird, Mum, weird," the narrator is able to finally settle the fear. But she is still speaking in a borrowed tongue.

Tsukiyama, Gail. 1993. *Women of the Silk.* New York: St. Martin's Press. Pb. 304 pp.

Set in the early years of the twentieth century, Tsukiyama's novel describes the lives of girls who are sold or given away to

work in the silk factories of China. Nine-year-old Pei is left at
the Girls' House by her father, a peasant who cannot afford to
keep two daughters at home. The Girls' House becomes home
for Pei, in a world much bigger than her parents' plot and the
village nearby. Pei is taken under the wing of Lin, an older girl
from a privileged background who is at the house to earn
money and to escape the restrictions and hypocrisies of the
Chinese meritocracy. Although the girls in the house work hard
there is a great deal of goodwill and some choose to spend their
lives in the trade. The women who do so go through a hair-
dressing ceremony, in which an older woman styles the hair of
one or two younger women. Instead of the single plait worn by
younger women, the women now have a bun and they commit
themselves to not marrying. They also commit themselves to
one another, and a sexual commitment is often part of that.

Wang Anyi. 1990. *Baotown*. Translated by Martha Avery.
London: Penguin Books. Pb. 143 pp.

Baotown is about a small, ailing rural community in northern
China, and the carving out of an identity for a place and its people. The novel's central character, a boy named Dregs, was not
expected to be born, because his parents are old. Even as a very
small child, he is filled with a kind of saintly virtue. Unlike
most children, he gives away things that are important to him;
he cares about those who are uncared for; and he tries to save
someone from drowning. But Dregs remains an unsung hero
until the village writer, who has never had any success with his
stories, finds a publisher for his work, and Dregs is raised to the
status of national hero. Life in Baotown has been a kind of exile,
but after Dregs's canonization the village becomes a tourist destination. The book is painful in its raw clarity, inspiring, and
beautifully written, and captures quite precisely the lives led by
the rural poor in China.

Also by Wang Anyi are: *Love in a Small Town* (1990) and *Love on
a Barren Mountain* (1991). Both translated by Eva Hung. Hong
Kong: Renditions Paperbacks, The Research Centre for Translation, The Chinese University of Hong Kong.

Wang Ying. 1989. *The Child Bride*. San Francisco: China Books
Inc.; Beijing: Foreign Language Press. Pb. 424 pp. Line drawings, photographs.

An autobiographical novel that follows the extraordinary early years of Wang Ying's life, in the first two decades of the twentieth century. The novel focuses on the time leading up to and following the event that gives the novel its title: the author was sold as a child bride at the age of twelve. The book ends just as the revolution is gearing up. The introduction and photographs help to put Wang Ying's life into focus. She died in prison in 1974 during the Cultural Revolution.

Poetry

Barnstone, Aliki, and Willis Barnstone (eds.). 1987. *A Book of Women Poets from Antiquity to Now.* New York: Schocken Books. Pb. 612 pp. Index.

Some of the same poets as in *Women Poets of China* (below), but also many others including poetry that extends back to the seventh century BCE from *The Book of Songs.* Yü Hsüan-chi, the eighth-century poet, courtesan, concubine, and Taoist nun who was executed as a criminal, has an intense and poignant voice. The translations of Li Ch'ing-chao's work (tenth century) seem to preempt the work of modern Western poets.

Lin, Julia C. 1992. *Women of the Red Plain: An Anthology of Contemporary Women's Poetry.* London: Penguin Books. Pb. 162 pp.

A collection of over one hundred poems by twentieth-century poets from all over China. The title poem by Jia Jia (b. 1954) describes the lonely life of nomad women. "The Clay Pot" by Li Xiaoyu (b. 1951) refers to the discovery of the Banpo Ruins of the Yanshao Culture in Shaanxi Province (see Sternfeld's essay in Part 1 of this volume). Xiao Min (b. 1955) describes the daily toil of women in her poem "They, the Women."

Rexroth, Kenneth, and Ling Chung. 1982. *Women Poets of China.* New York: New Directions. Pb. 160 pp.

A classic collection of poetry that covers the range of poets active over the last two thousand years. Particularly notable are Chao Luan-luan (eighth century), a courtesan, Huang O (fifteenth century), a poet who grew up at the Ming court, and Wu Tsao (nineteenth century), China's best-known lesbian poet.

A CHRONOLOGY OF CHINESE HISTORY

B.C.

1766   Shang Dynasty
1122   Zhou Dynasty
221   Qin Dynasty
206   Han Dynasty

A.D.

220   Period of the Six Dynasties
589   Sui Dynasty
618   Tang Dynasty (685–705: Reign of Empress Wu)
907   Five Dynasties Period
960   Song Dynasty
1279   Yuan Dynasty
1368   Ming Dynasty
1644   Qing Dynasty
1911   Republic of China
1949   People's Republic of China

NOTES ON CONTRIBUTORS

Authors

Dagmar BORCHARD, born in 1961, studied sinology and law in Bonn, Berlin, and at Nanjing University in the People's Republic of China. She wrote her master's thesis on the law of inheritance and family organization in China and has lived and worked in China.

Iris BUBENIK-BAUER, born in 1947, has studied sociology, psychology, ergonomics/politics, geography, and education and social sciences. Her dissertation is titled "Problems of Women's Emancipation in the People's Republic of China." She teaches in an interdisciplinary women's studies program at Bremen University.

Award-winning journalist DAI Qing was formerly a reporter for the *Guang Ming Daily* in China. She is the author of numerous collections of short stories and essays as well as several books on contemporary Chinese issues. A 1992 Nieman fellow at Harvard University, she was a research fellow at The Freedom Forum Media Studies Center at Columbia University, New York, in 1993 and 1994. Dai Qing

DING Ling, born in Jiang Bingzhi in 1904, is known today as one of China's most important twentieth-century writers. She achieved fame as a fiction writer in the 1920s, and by the 1930s, as an avid revolutionary, was imprisoned by the Nationalists. Her feminist views caused problems for her within the Communist Party, but not until the Cultural Revolution

(1966–76) did she suffer for those views. She did not appear publicly again until 1978, at which time she made a number of trips to the West. She died in 1985, still uncomplaining about her silencing.

Anna GERSTLACHER was born in the Year of the Tiger in Bavaria, southern Germany. She studied sinology and German studies in Berlin. For the last fifteen years, she has been organizing tours especially to Asian countries.

Susanne GÜNTHNER was born in 1957 in a small village in the Black Forest in southwest Germany. She studied linguistics and literature, with a focus on feminist linguistics, in Constance, southern Germany, and in the United States. She worked as a language instructor in China from 1983 to 1986 for DAAD (German Academic Exchange Service). Her dissertation is titled "Intercultural Communication between Chinese and Germans."

Susan HAWTHORNE is a writer, publisher, and festival organizer. She was the major force behind the sixth International Feminist Book Fair (Melbourne, Australia, 1994) and is chair of the board of *Australian Women's Book Review*. She is the author of *The Spinifex Quiz Book: A Book of Women's Answers* and a novel, *The Falling Women*. Her collection of poetry, *The Language in My Tongue,* was published in the volume *Four New Poets.* She is the editor of five anthologies and coeditor, with Renate Klein, of *Australia for Women: Travel and Culture.*

Bret HINSCH holds a doctorate in history and East Asian languages from Harvard University. He is associate professor of history at National Chung Cheng University, Chiayi, Taiwan, and the author of *Passions of the Cut Sleeve: The Male Homosexual Tradition in China.*

JIEHU Asha, a member of the Yi ethnic group in China, was born in 1964 in Sichuan Province. She studied at the Central Institute for Minorities in Beijing and in France.

Lida JUNGHANS has lived in China for three of the last eight years. She is a student in the anthropology department of

Harvard University and is currently writing a dissertation that explores the ways that political and economic transformations at the national level in the PRC have shaped the experiences of "ordinary" urban workers.

LI Xiaojiang was born in Jiujiang City, Jiangxi Province. She studied for her M.A. at Henan University, Kaifeng, Henan Province, where she was a European literature major. Currently, she is president of the Women's College of Zhengzhou University, PRC, where she also teaches. In addition, Li Xiaojiang is director of the Preparatory Committee of the Women's Museum, editor-in-chief of the Women's Studies Series (now 17 volumes), and the organizer of the "20th Century of [Chinese] Women's Oral History."

LIANG Jun was born in Yiyang County, Henan Province, and graduated from the History Department of Beijing Normal University in 1968. She now works as a senior professor at the Henan Women's Cadre School.

Jutta LIETSCH, a political economist, studied in the People's Republic of China for two years and was a research assistant for nine years in the Department of Political Science at the Freie Universität Berlin. Her dissertation is on women in the process of modernization in the People's Republic of China.

LU Danni was born in 1959 in Hefei, central China. She graduated from Beijing University with a major in history, then taught at the Shanghai Foreign Languages Institute from 1982 to 1986, and later took her master's degree in American history at Beijing University.

Renée MARK was born in 1958 in Berlin, Germany. After extensive travels abroad, she studied sinology, Romance languages and literature, and American studies in Berlin. After studying Chinese language in Beijing for two years, she has worked on various China-related projects and currently lives in Berlin.

Born in 1946 in Munich, **Margit MIOSGA** attended a Waldorf school and is a dressmaker, mother, gal Friday, half-educated sinologist, and radio journalist—for the love of it. Since 1972, she has been pitching her tent in Berlin when not traveling.

Julia MOLLÉE, born in 1950, is a bookseller and sinologist. She spent a year studying in the People's Republic of China and in Taiwan. Currently teaching language in Berlin, she has lectured and published on China.

Barbara NIEDERER was born in 1959 in Basel, Switzerland. She studied Romance languages and literature in Rome, Bologna, Paris, and Basel, and sinology in Paris. She was a student at Beijing University from 1986 to 1989. She is now in Paris working on a dissertation in Chinese linguistics.

NING Lao, a Chinese peasant woman born in 1867, grew up in the port city of Penglai in Shandong Province. As the second girl and youngest of three children in a once well-off family, Ning Lao experienced poverty, suffering, and oppression by the Japanese during her lifetime. Living in Beijing in the 1930s, she recounted her story to Ida Pruitt (see below).

Ida PRUITT, the daughter of American missionaries, was born in China in 1888, where she spent the first twelve years of her life in a village in the province of Shandong. Educated in the United States as a medical social worker, she returned to China as the head of the Social Service Department of Peking Union Medical College Hospital from 1918 until 1938. As a writer, Ida Pruitt illustrated intimate knowledge of Chinese women's lives; *A Daughter of Han* captures the way of life of a working-class Chinese woman, while *Old Madam Yin* reflects the experiences of a wealthy Chinese woman.

Melinda Tankard REIST is an Australian freelance writer and researcher with a special interest in coercive population programs and their ramifications on women. For the past six years, she has been documenting the abuses committed on women in family-planning programs worldwide. Her work has been published and broadcast in Australia and other countries, most recently in the radio documentary "Bullets or Babies" for the Australian Broadcasting Corporation and in the chapter

"Whose Consensus Is It: The Feminist Challenge to Cairo" in *The New Imperialism: World Population and the Cairo Conference.*

Monika SCHÄDLER, born in 1953, is a sinologist and economist. She spent over two years studying at Beijing University and has worked on rural development, population policy, and economic problems in the People's Republic of China. Self-employed, she works in Hamburg teaching and doing research and translations.

Cathy SILBER is writing her Ph.D. dissertation on *nüshu* at the University of Michigan. Her writings on *nüshu* include "From Daughter to Daughter-in-Law in the Women's Script of Southern Hunan," which appeared in *Engendering China: Women, Culture, and the State,* edited by Christina K. Gilmartin et al., Harvard University Press, 1994. She recently translated *Maidenhome,* a volume of contemporary short stories by Ding Xiaoqi, Aunt Lute Press, 1994.

Born in Berlin, **Ina SIMSON** studied sinology and German language and literature, finishing her master's degree in 1987. She has gone on several study trips to the People's Republic of China, Taiwan, and other Asian countries. She currently works at the Museum for East Asian Art in Berlin.

Agnes SMEDLEY lived from 1892 to 1950, and was a novelist, journalist, political activist, and feminist. Born into the rural poverty of northern Missouri, she devoted her life to advancing the cause of human justice. The author of five books about China, Smedley also wrote *Daughter of Earth* (The Feminist Press), an autobiographical novel first published in 1929. She worked in and wrote about China from 1928 to 1941, and is buried in Beijing, beneath a tombstone inscribed "Friend of China."

Eva STERNFELD (zodiac sign: Pisces) is a sinologist trained in Berlin. She went to Beijing University in 1986, where she studied the Beijing water shortage, reported on Chinese television programming, and co-founded the Institute for Unorthodox Sinology in 1987. Because of the events of 1989, she returned to Berlin earlier than planned.

Pamela TAN was born in Australia. She went to China in 1951, studied French at the Beijing Foreign Languages Institute, and has worked as an interpreter and translator in English, Chinese, and French. She experienced all the big political purges, and during the Cultural Revolution was sent to the countryside to do three years of manual labor in Henan Province. Tan now lives in Australia and is a consultant on community development and gender for aid programs in China and India. She is also a freelance writer and has published a book of short stories, *The Friend in Shanghai*, and *Women in Society: China*, a general introduction to women in China. Her most recent trip to China was in 1994.

Elke WANDEL, born in 1951, studied English language and literature, political science, and theology; she worked as a teacher in Berlin. Since her stay in Taiwan (1978–81), she has been studying China and the role of Chinese women. From 1987 until June 1989, she taught at the Beijing Language Institute.

WANG Jian was born in 1953 in Beijing. During the Cultural Revolution, she spent five and a half years as a factory worker in Beijing. She studied German language and literature and worked at the Chinese Academy of Social Sciences before pursuing her Ph.D. at Freiburg University in Germany.

Born 1957 in Tianjin, China, WANG Xiaohui trained in engineering, but became an architect. She has taught at Tongji University in Shanghai and the University for Applied Science in Munich. She has published numerous works on art and architecture in China and Germany.

WEI Hong, born in 1962, studied mechanical engineering. She was a lecturer at Tongji University in Shanghai. Since 1989, she has been a housewife in Germany.

YA Lu was born in 1953 in Beijing. She studied biology and is now a housewife and mother.

Mavis YEN was born in Perth, Western Australia, and has spent her life intermittently between Australia and China. She was educated in both countries and has held jobs ranging from office worker to teacher and editor. She now lives in Canberra, Australia, and is currently interested in the history of the early Chinese in Australia.

Born in 1937 in Beijing, **ZHANG Jie** studied production engineering and worked as a specialist at the First Ministry of Mechanical Engineering for twenty years. She wrote her first stories in 1978. Her first novel, *Heavy Wings*, appeared in 1981. *The Ark*, published in 1982, is considered to be China's first feminist novel after 1949.

Xiaodan ZHANG worked as an editor in the Chinese Social Science Publishing House in Beijing before receiving a master's degree in women's studies from the Graduate Center at the City University of New York. She is currently a doctoral student in sociology at Columbia University

Photographers

Kosima LIU-WEBER, born in 1958, studied sinology in Bonn and was a scholarship student at the Central College of Art in Beijing. She has been living in Beijing with her family since 1980 and works as a freelance photographer there.

Born in 1947 in Basel, Switzerland, **Nelly RAU-HÄRING** has known all about biking since 1952 and all about photography since studying at the Lette-Schule. In 1988 and 1989, she spent four and a half months as a scholarship student in Beijing and Shanghai.

Eva SIAO was born in Breslau, Poland. A photographer by profession, she has lived in Beijing for forty years.

Pamela TAN: See Authors, above.

Translators

Ulrike BODE was born in Germany in 1951 and raised in India. Her sojourns in foreign countries include about a year in Turkey, Iran, and Afghanistan, and three and a half years in Haiti. Living in New York City since the mid-1980s, she works as a freelance translator in diverse fields (finance, travel, development, law, social sciences). She co-translated *Anarchism: Left, Right, and Green* (1994), by Ulrike Heider, into English. She has also begun working on nationalism and gender in South and Inner Asia and is researching a book on women in Inner Asia.

Ilze MUELLER is Latvian , and lived in Germany and Australia before making her home in the United States. She is a member of the German and Russian Department of Macalester College in Saint Paul, Minnesota, and translates German and Latvian prose and poetry into English.

PERMISSION ACKNOWLEDGMENTS

Dai Qing's "How I Experienced the Cultural Revolution" is published here through the courtesy of the editorial staff of the series "History of Our Time" (*Zeitgeschichte*) of the German television network ZDF (Zweites Deutsches Fernsehen).

Ding Ling's "Thoughts on March 8" is reprinted by permission of Beacon Press from *I Myself Am a Woman: Selected Writings of Ding Ling*, edited by Tani E. Barlow with Gary J. Bjorge (Boston: Beacon Press, 1989), 316–21. "Daughter of the Chinese People" was originally an address to the International Writing Program at the University of Iowa, in which Ding Ling participated in 1981. The address is published by permission.

Bret Hinsch's "Views of the Feminine in Early Neo-Confucian Thought" is an abridged version of "Metaphysics and Reality of the Feminine in Early Neo-Confucian Thought." It is reprinted with permission from *Women's Studies International Forum* 11, no. 6 (1988): 591–98, Elsevier Science Ltd., Pergamon Imprint, Oxford, England.

Jiehu Asha's "Facing the Yangzi Rapids in a Rubber Boat" is excerpted from an essay published in *Zhongguo Qingnian Bao* (Chinese Youth Newspaper) in thirteen installments, 17 July to 18 August 1987.

Li Xiaojiang's "My Path to Womanhood" appeared originally in *Women's Studies, Women's Lives: Theory and Practice in South and Southeast Asia,* edited by the Committee on Women's Studies in

Asia (New Delhi: Kali for Women and Melbourne: Spinifex Press, 1994); the volume is also published with the title *Changing Lives: Life Stories of Pioneers in Asian Women's Studies* (New York: The Feminist Press at CUNY, 1995). It is reprinted by permission.

Li Xiaojiang and Zhang Xiaodan's "Creating a Space for Women: Women's Studies in China" was first published in *Signs: Journal of Women in Culture and Society* 20 (Autumn 1994): 137–51. © 1994 by The University of Chicago. All rights reserved. Reprinted with permission. The authors are especially grateful to Roslyn Bologh (Graduate Center at The City University of New York), Yuanxi Ma (China Institute in America), Laura O'Keefe (New York Public Library), Annette Rubinstein (Science and Society), Mary Ruggie (Columbia University), and Shen Tan (Chinese Social Science Academy).

Liang Jun's "A Serious Mission" appeared originally in *Women's Studies, Women's Lives* (see Li Xiaojiang, above). It is reprinted here by permission.

Liu Qian's "Beijing Snacks" is reprinted from *Women of China* 4 (April 1994): 12, 13–14, with permission.

Ning Lao's "Childhood and Growing Up: 1867–1881" was originally published in *A Daughter of Han: The Autobiography of a Chinese Working Woman* by Ida Pruitt, from the story told her by Ning Lao. © 1945 by Yale University Press. Reprinted with permission.

Cathy Silber's "Women's Writing from Hunan" is reprinted by permission of *Ms. Magazine*, © 1992. This is a slightly revised version of the essay that appeared in *Ms.*

Agnes Smedley's "Silk Workers," "The Women Take a Hand," and "Shan-fei, Communist" are reprinted with permission from *Portraits of Chinese Women* by Agnes Smedley, edited by Jan MacKinnon and Steve MacKinnon, afterword by Florence Howe (New York: The Feminist Press at CUNY, 1976), 103–10, 120–27, and 153–61. "Silk Workers" originally appeared in *Battle Hymn of China*. For an earlier, more abbreviated version

$14.95 paper, $35.00 cloth.

The Slate of Life: More Contemporary Stories by Women Writers of India, edited by Kali for Women. Introduction by Chandra Talpade Mohanty and Satya P. Mohanty. $12.95 paper, $35.00 cloth.

Solution Three, by Naomi Mitchison. Afterword by Susan Squier. $10.95 paper, $29.95 cloth.

Songs My Mother Taught Me: Stories, Plays, and Memoir, by Wakako Yamauchi. Edited and with an introduction by Garrett Hongo. Afterword by Valerie Miner. $14.95 paper, $35.00 cloth.

Streets: A Memoir of the Lower East Side. By Bella Spewack. Introduction by Ruth Limmer. Afterword by Lois Elias. $19.95, cloth.

Women of Color and the Multicultural Curriculum: Transforming the College Classroom, edited by Liza Fiol-Matta and Mariam K. Chamberlain. $18.95 paper, $35.00 cloth.

Prices subject to change. Individuals: Send check or money order (in U.S. dollars drawn on a U.S. bank) to The Feminist Press at The City University of New York, 311 East 94th Street, New York, NY 10128. Please include $4.00 postage and handling for the first book, $1.00 for each additional. For VISA/MasterCard orders call (212) 360-5790. Bookstores, libraries, wholesalers: Feminist Press titles are distributed to the trade by Consortium Book Sales and Distribution, (800) 283-3572.

The Feminist Press at The City University of New York offers alternatives in education and in literature. Founded in 1970, this nonprofit, tax-exempt educational and publishing organization works to eliminate stereotypes in books and schools and to provide literature with a broad vision of human potential. The publishing program includes reprints of important works by women, feminist biographies of women, multicultural anthologies, a cross-cultural memoir series, and nonsexist children's books. Curricular materials, bibliographies, directories, and a quarterly journal provide information and support for students and teachers of women's studies. Through publications and projects, The Feminist Press contributes to the rediscovery of the history of women and the emergence of a more humane society.

New and Forthcoming Books

Always a Sister: The Feminism of Lillian D. Wald. A biography by Doris Groshen Daniels. $12.95, paper.

The Answer/La Respuesta (Including a Selection of Poems), by Sor Juana Inés de la Cruz. Critical Edition and translation by Electa Arenal and Amanda Powell. $12.95 paper, $35.00 cloth.

Australia for Women:Travel and Culture, edited by Susan Hawthorne and Renate Klein. $17.95 paper.

Black and White Sat Down Together: The Reminiscences of an NAACP Founder, by Mary White Ovington. Edited and with a foreword by Ralph E.Luker. Afterword by Carolyn E. Wedin. $19.95 cloth.

Changing Lives: Life Stories of Asian Pioneers in Women's Studies, edited by the Committee on Women's Studies in Asia. Foreword by Florence Howe. Introduction by Malavika Karlekar and Barbara Lazarus. $10.95, paper, $29.95, cloth.

The Castle of Pictures and Other Stories: A Grandmother's Tales, Volume One, by George Sand. Edited and translated by Holly Erskine Hirko. Illustrated by Mary Warshaw. $9.95 paper, $23.95 cloth.

Challenging Racism and Sexism: Alternatives to Genetic Explanations (Genes and Gender VII). Edited by Ethel Tobach and Betty Rosoff. $14.95 paper, $35.00 cloth.

The Dragon and the Doctor, by Barbara Danish. $5.95, paper.

Japanese Women: New Feminist Perspectives on the Past, Present, and Future, edited by Kumiko Fujimura-Fanselow and Atsuko Kameda. $15.95 paper, $35.00 cloth.

Music and Women, by Sophie Drinker. Afterword by Ruth A. Solie. $16.95, paper, $37.50, cloth.

No Sweetness Here, by Ama Ata Aidoo. Afterword by Ketu Katrak. $10.95, paper, $29.00, cloth.

Seeds 2: Supporting Women's Work around the World, edited by Ann Leonard. Introduction by Martha Chen. Afterwords by Mayra Buvinic, Misrak Elias, Rounaq Jahan, Caroline Moser, and Kathleen Staudt. $12.95, paper, $35.00, cloth.

Shedding and Literally Dreaming, by Verena Stefan. Afterword by Tobe Levin.

of this story, see *Chinese Destinies: Sketches of Present-Day China* (New York: The Vanguard Press, 1933) pp. 116–19. Also from *Battle Hymn of China*, "The Women Take a Hand" draws on Smedley's experiences among the Chinese Communist guerrillas in southern China in late 1938. An earlier version appeared as "No Sacrifice . . . No Victory" in *Vogue*, 15 April 1942, 48–49, 87. "Shan-fei, Communist" is also included in *Chinese Destinies*, pp. 35–42, and first appeared in the *New Masses*, May 1931, pp. 3–5.

The excerpt from Zhang Jie's "The Ark" is from *Love Must Not Be Forgotten* by Zhang Jie (San Francisco: China Books and Periodicals, Inc., 2929 24th Street, 94110, 1986), pp. 151–59.